mudlarking

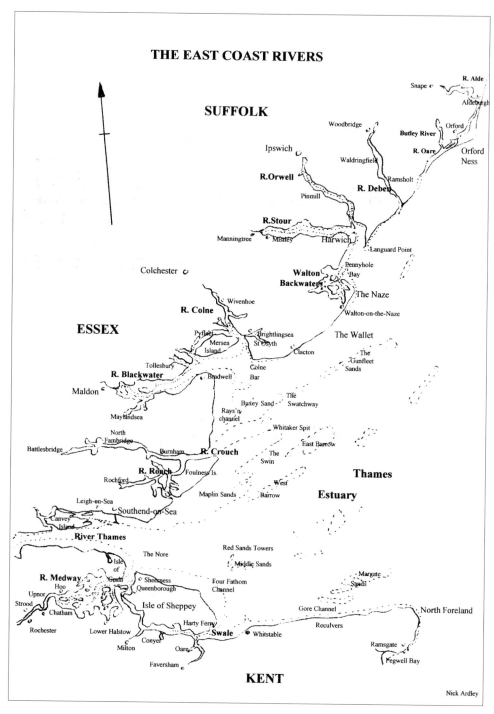

Whimbrel's Thames Estuary cruising ground.

mudlarking

Thames Estuary Cruising Yarns

Nick Ardley

By the same author: *The May Flower: A Barging Childhood*. Tempus;
Salt Marsh & Mud: A Year's Sailing on the Thames Estuary.
Amberley Publishing.

AMBERLEY

For Alexander and all the other crews who, in the mists of time, have sailed with or put up with the skipper: this is for you all.

First published 2010

Amberley Publishing Plc
Cirencester Road, Chalford,
Stroud, Gloucestershire, GL6 8PE

www.amberley-books.com

Copyright © Nick Ardley 2010

The right of Nick Ardley to be identified as the Author of this work has been asserted in accordance with the Copyrights, Designs and Patents Act 1988.

ISBN 978 1 84868 492 8

British Library Cataloguing in Publication Data.

A catalogue record for this book is available from the British Library.

Typeset in 10pt on 12pt Sabon.
Typesetting by FonthillMedia.
Printed in the UK.

Contents

Illustrations: unless attributed, illustrations are from the author's own collection.

Acknowledgements

Acknowledgements are accorded to all those who have written East Anglian sailing and coastal books before me. For all sources that I may have borrowed from, I offer my sincere gratitude. Inspiration was fortified. Quotations have, inevitably, been used and some well-known facts spoken about, but it is hoped a new freshness has been added, too, to our delightful sailing grounds.

My heartfelt thanks must again be accorded to my wife, Christobel, for her unstinting reading of drafts and practical comment; my mother, Gwendoline Ardley, for her accompanying artwork; to all those sailors who have allowed themselves to be characterised again; to my publisher, editor and all the back-up team, especially Nicki Giles, at Amberley Publishing for their superb attention and support, and finally, to those who have allowed me to use various photographs to illustrate the text.

Introduction

This is a quiet and gentle meander by a skipper and a mate sailing in their wooden, clinker sloop, around the coastline of East Anglia.

As they weave through the marshland environment that pervades this idyllic watery world, from North Kent to Suffolk, they take time to look around them as they sail. They observe the topography and history of places visited and passed by: even relatively recent history often appears buried and unseen. Yet, it lurks, enticingly, close to the surface, or on it, if one cares to look.

Within the Thames archipelago, numerous rivers and creeks indent the land. They creep up shallow sunken valleys, passing huge modern ports and bustling towns – some still conscious of their maritime heritage. Little waterside hamlets, old farm wharves and vibrant, modern marinas mingle sleepily, it sometimes seems, in a continuation of our mating with the environment. There, they explore. What history has gone before them? Who truly knows? A little of that history is brought to life, just a small part, reminiscing as they go.

And too, from those modern marinas, filled, on the whole, with shining fibreglass craft, people spill out at the weekends, to go in search, perhaps, for a little quiet and solitude. Others gather in small groups for convivial enjoyment: to mess about in boats, Swallows and Amazons style, is their intent. Then, perhaps, like the skipper and his mate, they would enjoy the quiet of the evening – *far from the madding crowd*.

The stories encapsulate simple sailing. There are no dashes or mad adventures across 'the channel' to foreign parts; nor even deep-sea wanderings, against ferocious winds and gigantic seas; just contemplative sailing in and out of the East Coast's rivers and muddy creeks. The pleasures of an arrival in a creek fringed with saline plants, with their heady scents of summer, are enough for this sailor and his mate. The sight of traditional craft, smacks, old wooden yachts, classics or otherwise, or the ubiquitous, evocative spritsail barge adds immensely to the aura: to fetch up with any of these, in the same anchorage, adds timelessness. A going where others have gone before and will continue to do so, it is hoped. 'Ah!' and, of course, 'never to be forgotten!'

Nick Ardley

I

Daydreaming ...

The skipper had had a bad start to his sailing year, with just a few days afloat during the short days of January and February. Although those early weeks had been unseasonably warm, amongst them, there'd only been a meagre sprinkling of pleasant days. It was most unusual. Those days, though, had been a gift: gratefully received, they were grabbed with glee on the part of the skipper.

The skipper, though, began to miss the glory of the open marshes in those late winter weeks with a hint of the coming spring. When seen from the water, up Benfleet Creek, amongst the tranquillity of the salt marsh maze, 'it was' he always said, 'an absolute treasure.'

Sometime during January, whilst sailing up towards Benfleet, on a cold, yet bright day, the skipper was hailed by two acquaintances walking along the sea wall. The walkers had stopped to stare at the lonely sailor carving a zigzag course upon the sparkling waters, while tacking up the creek.

'You seemed to be feeling the way from bank to bank,' one said later.

'It was a beautiful sight,' said the other. 'Just you on the water, cutting serenely along, amongst all that abundant wildlife ... It looked enchanting.'

'Thanks,' the skipper quietly, almost reverentially replied, 'Yes, I remember it well. It had been a gorgeous day to be out on the water. Enchanting? It was indeed.' The skipper and the mate often walked that path too, and he added, 'And for a walk along the wall too.'

Many of the walkers, seen by the skipper on his forays up his local creek, were prone to stop and stare for a while, to take in the wonderful environment they were privileged to enjoy. And too, it was assumed, to watch the tan-sailed yacht make its way along the often-lonely waterway.

One afternoon, late for the time of year, the skipper's attention was drawn to camera flashes. Even though it had been clear, the sun was nearing the horizon; it was heading fast towards dusk and the coming night. The flashes, from near some hides which sat towards the western end of Two Tree Island, were from an unknown admirer. 'They'll make a fantastic picture,' the skipper thought, 'with the sun behind the boat.' The skipper wanted to call out, 'Send me a copy,' but the distance precluded that. That evening, he'd slipped back into his berth after the sun had dipped beyond the mixed skyline of tinkling masts and misty-looking houses.

Bird-watchers rarely waved; why, the skipper had never figured out: a yacht sailing quietly by created little disturbance. Birds may fly up from their roosting or feeding positions and re-alight, after the yacht passes by, to continue with their preoccupations. 'Those short flights gave another aspect,' the skipper thought, 'for the watchers to gaze at.'

March had been torrid, full of winds and dirty days. There'd been a fine spell; typically it occurred during neap tides at the darker end of those winter days. Days that in the skipper's part of England often meant cold northerlies and, if conditions were right elsewhere, easterlies that blew in from the near continent of Europe, bringing snow. Snow had been rather scarce though. It would have provided a distraction, at least; so the skipper continued to mope.

'Never mind the seven-year itch; he's passed the seven-day itch and has become quite tetchy even ...' the mate was overheard relating to a friend on the telephone.

Looking up from the novel he'd been reading during one of those dismal days in early March, whilst sitting in the warmth of his conservatory, he watched the wind-lashed trees thrashing to and fro in some nearby woods, and wondered, 'When, oh when will this stop.'

His mind wandered to an event in his sailing life that occurred the previous year, 'During the last spring, in fact ...' he said, with more than a little grimace at his reflection in the glass of the conservatory surround. He shuddered: the event was certainly worth remembering ...

The day was one of those days that sounded, from the start, quite promising and it had been. The forecast – showers at first, dry later, thirteen degrees with a north-westerly two to three increasing four in the afternoon – announced to the skipper's subconscious that he could have a decent sail on the tide.

'As Jerome K. Jerome had succinctly put it in his brilliant yarn of boating on the Thames a hundred years before, "There is no more thrilling sensation I know than sailing," and it is still as true today as it was then,' the skipper was oft heard to state: no more needed to be said!

The skipper left his place of work at eleven thirty prompt. Upon reaching the creek, and boarding *Whimbrel*, he quickly made ready, before lastly hoisting the burgee. It flapped in eagerness – in unison with the skipper's thoughts. He looked aloft, as he often did, as the engine pulled the boat clear of the berth. Then, the skipper's heart quietened appreciably: he'd been rushing. 'I'll set the sails immediately,' he said, with his characteristic chuckle, to no one in particular.

'Phew,' he gasped – it's only a half hour since I left work.

An old wag at his sailing club often said, 'You know, not even a millionaire could lead the life you do.'

The skipper grinned, smirked even, making some remark about 'work-life balance ...' It was something that in this supersonic age (well, it was supersonic before Concorde was grounded) had been pushed aside in the name of progress.

The sail was simply gorgeous. The afternoon sun shone brightly from a deep blue with a scattering of high, fluffy clouds that passed slowly over. It felt warmer than forecasted. The engine was quickly silenced: peace!

Stemming the eager flood tide, the skipper, in his boat, ran serenely and silently out of the creek, except for a gentle gurgle from the forefoot. He breathed the saline air luxuriantly. He revelled in it. The wind proved to be of admirable strength and the boat left a mesmerising curving wash over the protected waters, rippling amongst the piles of the club's moorings. Brent geese paddled in amongst the rivulets that ran deeply into the marsh fringes. It was captivating.

Grinning widely, the skipper nipped below to fill his mug from the kettle, which soon began to whistle its joyful tune, quickly reappearing, mug in hand. 'Ah,' he said, sniffing at his mug, 'tea!' And then he shouted, exultantly, 'Yes ... Yes!'

The skipper noticed, upon leaving, that the tide seemed somewhat more advanced than was normal, with about an hour to go: the thought, though, immediately slipped his mind, overridden by the spell ...

Clearing the creek, the skipper headed up Hadleigh Ray sailing nonchalantly past numerous lonely boats. Some, though, had people lazing in their cockpits, enjoying the spring sunshine, tacking casually round the stern of a yacht with two reclining figures;

Whimbrel creeping out of Smallgains Creek against a sluggish flood.

he wanted to call out, 'Drop that mooring ... Set those sails ... Get out sailing ...' but hadn't. The skipper merely returned their acknowledgements and sailed on. He was known locally to sail, if humanly possible, up any creek, or gut, wherever there was a dusting of water, as if on the high seas.

Clearing the moorings towards the western end of Two Tree Island, the skipper blithely tacked. The boat and the skipper 'were as if welded' his mate always said, 'like the mind meld – as seen in that classic Sci-Fi space series, Star Trek,' if it were possible; one was never sure who was in control. They sailed this stretch of water (the skipper and the boat) so many times, it was as if the boat knew its own way. The skipper had two sounders, one electrical (switched off most of the time) and the reliable centre plate.

Passing a buoy, conveniently laid by 'The Benfleet', the skipper's mind registered the fact that another tack was soon necessary. He promptly forgot. His mind went off on a tangent, thinking of smooth water, reflections and colours. The tide was well over the saltings. Stalks of vegetation poked suggestively above the placid surface; their short reflections wobbled in the slight swell caused by ships out on the London River. It had a magical feel – mesmerising even – idyllic. The skipper, it seemed, hadn't a care in the world.

Gazing towards the opening behind Two Tree Island and the sweet little waterway that ran back into Leigh Creek, the skipper whispered, 'I must go and get those pictures ...' The remnants of a barge, the *Diligent*, sat in the middle of the secret water. It was an island of marsh, but in recent times an increased water flow had caused a scouring around the 'island' and one side had collapsed – the whole starboard side of the vessel. The skipper had visited during a walk – without his camera ...

The skipper's reverie was broken by the realisation that he was looking down at tufts of grass poking above the water. 'Bloody Hell,' he exclaimed as he pushed the tiller over to tack. In that same instant the centre plate jumped with a loud 'thwack' forcefully reminding the skipper that he'd run out of water. 'We're on the marshes – stupid boy!'

The skipper went mudlarking to find the remains of the spritsail barge *Diligent*. She slumbers quietly in the mud behind Two Tree Island.

The marsh, Marks Marsh Island, was a patch of salt marsh that sat in the lower reaches of Benfleet Creek, to the south of the western end of Two Tree Island. It had lower fringes with a higher central ridge that may have been part of a more substantial marsh in the past. The marshes had changed hugely in position over the previous one hundred years, and the run of the creek had changed its priority too: it used to run to the south of the marshy island.

The saltings were etched with shallow gutways and rivulets from high-tide run-offs. The skipper's boat was, it first appeared, marooned amongst a mass of cord grass and sea purslane that waved back and forth from the action of little wavelets. The nodding vegetation tops seemed to quiver with laughter!

The slack plate wire was rapidly wound in: it was no more than fifteen minutes to high water. Time was of the essence. As a rule, the boat's engine was little used. His mate, as has oft been related, believed it needed a secret pin number. It was running in an instant. Full astern was no good. Thinking quickly, the skipper looped a line over the tiller, before going forward to reduce the draft aft. Nothing initially happened. Then, some movement – a little was felt. Then more consistently – with gentle bumps.

The heart palpitations the skipper had felt since the beginning of the incident, only moments earlier, had eased slightly. Looking beneath the bow, the skipper saw that the boat was moving towards deeper water away to the port side. The skipper rapidly strode aft and watched his boat's slow passage past stalk after stalk of cord grass. Progress seemed painfully slow.

Astern, a plume of water spewed marsh plants, torn from their moorings, scattering them in the prop wash. Gulls, always quick off the mark, frolicked and chased each other as tasty morsels came to the surface. The gulls, increasing in numbers, screamed and hawked at one another, as if laughing at the 'silly man' beneath them. Terns appeared too, to hover and drop, dart-like, rising with tiny silvery fish ... The skipper took all of this in, in the blink of an eye: there was now no time to daydream.

The boat had begun to turn. The forward's bumping motion was increasing too. A surge of relief began to course through his veins – a little. The breeze on the backed jib was at work too. He knew that the tides were falling ... And that days tide was an abnormally high one ... A myriad of thoughts still raced through his mind.

'What if ... ?' It didn't bare thinking about: for to be stuck up on those marshes would be a tragedy of great proportions. 'Least of all, I'll be a laughing stock – for a very long time ...' Pursing his lips tightly and grimacing, he said, 'The mate will be livid ...' adding, '... I've got to get off,' quietly and firmly to himself. He was maintaining control!

Then, all of a sudden, the boat shot forward, the skipper leapt for the tiller. In a trice, he'd flicked off the tiller line to take control.

Glancing overboard, the top of the rudder still showed, 'I shouldn't be afloat,' he muttered, but the boat had kept moving. Beaming with exultation, he shouted, 'Go girl!'

By then, both of the sails were helping, forcing the boat onto a heel. The heel reduced her draft a little more. Then, good girl as she always was, she was free of the marsh, afloat and sailing again – but still trapped.

'We're off!' the skipper gasped, '... but not free.'

The boat was in a rill: vegetation showed to both sides. The skipper slackened the sheets, eased the engine to a tick over and carefully studied the water ahead. He cast a covetous gaze towards the deep water of the main channel – 'There ... there must be a way out ...' he stammered, his heart starting to pound again.

Then: the Gods had answered his prayers. The water got deeper on the creek side of the boat: the tops of tall strands of cord grass, which stood a good half a metre tall,

'The mate will be livid ...' (Drawn by Gwendoline D. Ardley)

had gone beneath the surface. The skipper saw his escape: the boat only drew barely three quarters of a metre.

A snap decision: he'd judged it deep enough … The engine, that earlier slowed to idle, was gunned to near maximum power. Letting the speed of the boat build before pushing the tiller over, the boat was turned towards the underwater ridge of marsh. The skipper had a momentary heart-stopping flutter as he felt the bow of the boat rise up, then like a rocking horse, the boat, with its forward momentum, hopped out into the deep water of Benfleet Creek.

The skipper then breathed a huge sigh of relief, 'Thank you!' he called skywards.

Feeling somewhat embarrassed, sheepish and greatly chastened, the skipper continued sailing up to the Benfleet Yacht Club, before turning for home. The event, though, was recorded, dutifully, in the boat's logbook. It would be a reminder, if nothing else. 'It was a case of, "mind in neutral, finger up bum" as old seafarers are apt to say …' he said to the mate later.

Back at his moorings, the skipper bashfully recounted his adventure to several people he met around the club moorings; it's always best to own up: you never know who may have seen you. It was just as well: little did he know, he'd provided a great deal of interest to another sailor watching the world go by during that fateful day!

Three days later, the skipper returned to the creek for another sail. A voice, with a chuckle within it, had cut sharply through the air. The skipper shuddered, and an icy chill traversed his spine; then he felt a hot bolt run through him: a watcher would have seen the colour rise above his ruddy neckline and spread across his cheeks – leaving them very flushed. The skipper glowed with acute embarrassment, barely hearing the words that attacked him.

The voice, for it piped up again, had called: 'Bit of … !' Then the skipper saw the culprit. The voice had emanated from the cockpit of a boat sitting on the hard standing – her owner climbing out of some deep, dark recess grinned broadly. The owner had seen the spectacle of a few days earlier. He lived by the sea wall, in a house that overlooked the panorama of salt marsh and creeks beneath Hadleigh Downs.

The words remain firmly embedded. The skipper had repeated them to his mate later, when talking about their respective days, 'Walking towards the moorings I heard a voice, I felt an icy chill …'

'What … ?' asked the mate impatiently, grinning widely at the skipper's embarrassment!

'I heard, "Bit of bother the other day." I was mortified.' The skipper had not forgotten. And never would.

However, he was still in his conservatory and after remembering his brush with the marshes, the skipper said, 'Aha!' Then thought, 'I'd rather be out there than cooped up reminiscing – although many an old sage will tell you that "it's best to be in harbour than out at sea wishing you were in harbour." Well … yes, indeed.' So, nodding to his own reflection, he stayed put, reading a novel by Conrad. It required careful attention.

And … the wait continued …

The island of marsh that the skipper had briefly gone aground on had sat, more or less, in the same place for centuries, but the main channel running past it, Hadleigh Ray, had over the last century effectively changed sides. The Ray truly ran to the south of Marks Marsh Island, but that channel had become badly silted. The deep water now ran immediately to the north of the island with a mud horse on its other side. A wide but shallow swatch ran between the horse and the marshes along the edge of Two Tree Island. The skipper came across an interesting map of the area showing the water courses as mapped in 1898, in an excellent book, *Hadleigh Salvation Army Farm – A Vision Reborn*. (A book that tells the tale of the Salvation Army lands here

Whimbrel captured on a glorious day for sailing off the western end of Two Tree Island. (Courtesy of I. Kemp)

about, along the shores of the creek, and on Hadleigh Downs.) At the time of the 1898 map, Tewkes Creek, a creek that ran into Hadleigh Ray was deeper, wider and ran much further into the island of Canvey. Damming and resultant ongoing silting had caused a gradual change to the tide runs. Now, to the south of Marks Marsh, a sea of cord grass and other marsh plants had crept inexorably southwards year by year.

Thinking about the marshes led the skipper's mind to a tale he'd been told. It happened many years beforehand. It was related to him by an uncle. The skipper's father had had a brush with the marshes round Benfleet Creek too. The mate said something along the lines of, 'Like father, like son ...'

'Yes, well!'

The skipper's father and his crew were attempting a circumnavigation of Canvey Island aboard the family yacht, *Lynette*. (S. Platt mentioned *Lynette* in his book, *My Three Grey Mistresses*. A friend of his, Michael Beaumont, owned her before the Ardley family.) In those enlightened days, it was possible to take a yacht round the island: the bridge at Benfleet was an opening affair. A lift and roller mechanism allowed the span to be moved clear for river traffic – that was no longer the case: unlike our Continental cousins, we, in the British Isle, have, it seems, done our very utmost to obstruct minor, but historically navigable waterways, one by one, and it should be said, continue to do so.

The skipper's father had cut across a bend in the creek. The tide, a spring, was well over the marshes, 'but the edge had been visible,' the skipper was told. It sounded just like the skipper's day!

'All of a sudden,' the relater said, 'we came to a stop. Nothing we did made any difference – we were well and truly stuck. We were round in East Haven Creek, west of Benfleet Bridge. When the tide dropped, and it went in a great rush, we had a mile hike across the marshes and along the sea wall back to the bridge, then a long walk to Leigh. Your Grandfather was extremely furious. He'd said, "You can jolly well get the damned boat off." We had to dig a channel over the mud. I was not best pleased,

My grandfather's yacht *Lynnette* (later my father's) perched in the marshes in East Haven Creek in 1949. The cotton sails are being aired. (Courtesy of G. D. Ardley)

but felt duty-bound to help ...' Shaking his head, he'd added, 'It was a damned dirty job too.'

A long pause had then ensued ... He grimaced deeply, 'We were at it for a week, between tides. Then we had to wait for the next high tide before we were able to get the bloody boat off!'

'Well I never ...' the skipper had said at the time, thinking, 'yes, that would have been my father to a tee ...' But he felt, for some reason, that the tale had been watered down somewhat. It had been a long time ago, but none the less, something was missing!

The skipper, at a later date, tackled his mother about the incident: it hadn't been discussed during his childhood – well, not that he could remember.

'Oh yes,' his mother said, in a serious tone, 'my brother was one of the crew. The whole saga and the digging of the channel all but created a rift between the two of them ... It lasted quite some time.'

'Ah!' Perhaps that's what was missing ... Later a picture turned up in the post. It showed a yacht perched high up in the marshes.

Meanwhile, almost a whole month had passed by. The skipper helped around his club. He'd not been too firmly attached to the land though: he'd learnt how to operate a twin-engine workboat. It wasn't sailing but it was a distraction, providing little fun.

One weekend, during the month of his enforced period of landlubberlyness, the skipper helped to launch the boat of a very old boy, distantly related to the skipper's family. The old boy had been sailing since the early 1930s, starting out as a cadet at one of the sailing clubs in Leigh-on-Sea. He'd had a yacht from around 1938. His last boat had just been sold, having owned her for some forty years. The launching was its farewell.

The old boy and his wife, a real lady, of the old school, still striking, and a renowned beauty of her day, were visibly moved by the impending departure of their old boat. Tears were close to the surface. The skipper had seen one or the other surreptitiously wipe the corner of a dampened eye. Both were from a time that many modern sailors would find hard to envisage. Their early years were much more akin to the Corinthian age of sailing, at the start of pleasure for the masses.

The old boy related to the skipper a couple of stories about sailing during the 1940s and 1950s. The first happened around 1948. The old boy, then a relatively young man, had been crewing on an old timer, a yacht built in the early part of the twentieth century, or before; she was gaff rigged, with running backstays and deadeyes on the shrouds – nothing unusual for the age, and still seen.

The yacht and her crew were participating in a race to Ramsgate from Leigh-on-Sea. Coming in towards the harbour entrance at Ramsgate, on an opposite tack, but with the right of way to another yacht, it became apparent that the other boat was refusing to give way.

Relating this to his mate, the skipper said, 'The old boy said, "We were coming round, onto a new tack," to take them out of the way,' the skipper added.

'Then the old boy said, "Mind you, in those days, you had to sail a yacht round through a tack. Things took time. Yachts didn't turn on a sixpence like modern things do. Things started to go wrong. Maybe our skipper was annoyed at being forced to tack, and we got caught in stays. There was a lot of shouting. The other boat's skipper was notorious for that sort of thing. He liked to make others feel guilty! That damned boat just came straight onto us, then luffed past and carried on." He'd paused then,' the skipper said. 'Grinning, he'd carried on, "Anyway, I'd realised our forestay was broken and leapt forward to grab hold of the stay – shouting back aft. I just hung on, leaning my weight on the foresail – hoping that the bloody mast would stay up! Our skipper quickly unhooked a backstay and flicked it round the mast spreader and got it lashed forward as a temporary forestay. It held the heavy old mast and gear up though." He then shivered a little,' the skipper added.

'He hadn't finished though, he said, "We then had to get all the sails off of her quickly. It was only then we'd appreciated our good fortune. The whole lot could've come crashing down around our heads! Fortunately, another yacht with an engine appeared and towed us into the harbour." He'd paused there briefly, adding, "Later some harsh words were exchanged with the perpetrator!"'

The skipper grinned at his mate and said, 'At that point he'd laughed, murmuring, "That's how it was in those days. No screaming about insurance claims and the like." Even though,' the skipper added, 'some rudimentary repairs were needed.'

The mate smiled benignly: she knew that the next story would follow quickly, hard on its tail ...

'The other story related to my old sailing home, the spritsail barge *May Flower*. The old boy said, "We were racing into Queenborough, fighting the ebb with very little wind," I'd chuckled at that.'

The mate nodded sagely: they themselves often patiently stemmed the tide – their engine remaining silent.

The skipper continued, 'he said, "Our course was inshore along the edge out of the worst of the ebb. Ahead of us was this great lump of a barge – your dad's barge. I'd said, 'Lord, we'll never slip past the inside' to my sailing partner. Then, to our amazement, we saw a body amble forward and begin to wind the windlass. The rhythmic clink clank of the pawls drifting down was a pure delight. Slowly, bit by bit, the old barge moved, right out of our path. Passing, as we offered our thanks, the chain was being thrown over the windlass barrel to run overboard. Your father lifted an arm and grinned! I've never forgotten that." That was it,' the skipper concluded.

Coming in from school on a pleasant evening, the mate said, 'Have you been out today then?'

'No, there wasn't any water in the creek – neaps – I did some stuff with the boys.'

'Oh yes ... well ... never mind.'

His wait was becoming somewhat frustrating.

The creek where the skipper moored his boat had once been a hive of waterborne industry. Farm barges came and went. A building supply company operated their own barges from a creek-side wharf it owned. The company in question was still operating locally. Much of the building supplies for the Canvey's early-twentieth-century development came in by spritsail barge: barges were the lorry of the age.

Once the first bridge was built at Benfleet in the 1930s, new road infrastructure made lorry movements much easier: both coincided with larger, technically more reliable motor lorries and the gradual demise of sail, or water transport around our coasts, rivers and creeks. The last barge visited Smallgains 'some sixty years ago' according to an old sage sailing out of the skipper's creek.

The old boy, now well on in years, crusted with age and as deaf as a door-knob, had recently remarked to the skipper that he and others of a similar age, then typical, young, gangling youths who wished for nothing more than the excitement of the waterfront, would go aboard the barges trading into the creek. 'We were invited aboard to help,' he said. 'We helped to pole or row the barges with long sweeps up to the wharves – poked them out too.' The skipper nodded.

'Those sweeps were long, thick-shafted oars – well, you know that,' he said, grinning broadly. 'There used to be a lot of trade into the creek in them days,' he said, looking about.

The old boy had retained his 'youth': he still sailed, and, the skipper thought, 'put many of the younger sailors to shame.'

The skipper knew a thing or two about getting a spritsail barge into a berth or safely to anchor. Ah, kedging. He knew that too. The art of kedging, rowing a lightweight anchor forward, laying it and then returning to wind in the light wire kedge line, thus moving the barge, gradually, towards its goal was hard graft. He had helped to row his old sailing home with long sweeps too: their barge hadn't an engine.

Sometimes the trading barge sailormen had to punt their barges up lengthy, twisting creeks, perhaps to reach a little farm wharf, and apart from their own brawn, they had only tide to help. Often, the exercise was repeated to extricate themselves. Maybe, if they were lucky, a breeze would be friendly enough to set a topsail … All those things were in the past now.

In the skipper's home creek were the remains of a spritsail barge. It lay at the head of the creek and which of the many thousands she was, the skipper hadn't known. It rested, under marsh and rubble, at the base of high, steel-piled, concrete-clad sea wall. The skipper clearly remembered the piles being driven through the remains of her bottom when the new wall was constructed in 1979. The piles had bent and gone askew: the construction engineers hadn't recognised the toughness of a barge's elm bottom. Ha!

Over in the marshes on the north side of the creek, an old barge rudder had been dumped in a rill. Surprisingly, it remained semi-buoyant and often moved about on spring tides until it disappeared under infill for a car park. Now, no visible sign of the creek's maritime trading past existed: an old barge wharf had long gone beneath land infill too. That wharf had had a crane. A narrow gauge tramline with flatbed trucks for transferring cargoes ran over the top of the then relatively low embankment.

After the war of 1939-46, the Island Yacht Club bought an old spritsail barge, the *Louise,* and a club member's family had a house barge, reputedly the *Black Duck* of Rochester and renamed the *Old Upton*. Both were berthed towards the top of the shallow mud creek's silted head. The *Old Upton*, poor thing, was burnt after stranding up on the marshes during the 1953 floods, and the club barge was broken up shortly afterwards too. Another old barge bottom still rested on the creek bank amongst the club's moorings, but was thought to be an old lighter.

Another old sailorman, the *Shannon*, ended her days here too. By all accounts, she was buried in the inland section of the creek that was cut off from the sea, along with numerous other vessels, a motley selection of old lifeboats, landing craft and many other types, following damming after the 1953 floods. Little historical record remained of their presence, other than photographs in 'Canvey' books. A schooner, which was moored high up the creek, lay buried too. The old bed of the creek could still be traced across a stretch of flat, open, featureless ground – a little-used area that purported to be a playing field.

1953 East Coast flood sea-wall realignment was seen as the 'be all' in flood prevention. Now though, low land was being given back to the marshes: they were superb tidal sponges. The dam had destroyed a once-proud and useful tidal creek. The more recent piled and concreted wall had made that cut-off much more permanent. Shame!

The *Mary Miller*, a schooner thought to have been built during the 1880s and cut down to a motorised coaster by the 1940s, appeared in the creek during the early 1960s. She was, it had been said, bought by a local ship-breaker. The vessel had been a houseboat on the River Mersey before her arrival and was known locally as the *Merry Miller*. She was eventually abandoned, becoming derelict by 1970. The old ship was broken up by 1978 by the skipper's sailing club to clear her remains from new moorings. Recently, a section of one of her frames had come to light during some work around the creek. A treenail the skipper looked at was as good as the day a long-dead shipwright had crafted it.

Beyond the creek's entrance, rusting wreckage littered the marshy point. In recent years, it had become a hazard as marsh wastage deposited 'old ironwork' across the mud flats. Bits of wood, probably from old spritsail barges, had been seen by the skipper: part of a leeboard slept in a mud hollow near the marsh edge. All were the remnants of a breaker's yard that salvaged materials from unwanted vessels following the end of the Second World War. The family running the salvage business had departed long ago. For a time, they'd used some buildings of a redundant boatyard just above Benfleet Bridge. The yard had been used by Underwood's – a firm that built MFVs for the War Department during the Second World War who'd operated from around 1940. Those sheds were used until the area, near a derelict wharf adjacent to Benfleet train station, was cleared at the end of the 1950s. There too at Benfleet, above and below the bridge, were a motley collection of old barges and other 'tore-outs' used as houseboats. All long cleared away.

The marshes at the eastern end of the island hid a more poignant scattering of wreckage too: a United States Air Force bomber crashed onto the marshes during the Second World War conflict, sadly killing all of the crew. Parts of the plane had been found over the years. A memorial was recently instituted on the island to commemorate those long-dead, but forever-remembered brave airmen.

For many years, on the southern side of the point, a concrete lighter sat on the foreshore. It lay near the yacht club and was within its jurisdiction on a sand and shell beach that mingled with the saltings. Those barges were built in huge numbers to service the needs of the military during the Second World War, carrying fuels and water. It was said that the barge had come ashore during a storm, but over the years, the stranded hull had attracted the attention of vandals – the more so in recent times. Finally, it was considered a danger and was removed. It was not, as had been said in a recent publication about Canvey Island, a vessel in need of protection: hundreds still litter numerous creeks. Many were still in use too!

Before the 1939 world conflict, bawleys congregated off the long spit that then ran eastwards from the eastern end of the island. The mate had a much-loved painting encapsulating the view. There, bawleys were able to remain afloat, unlike at Leigh-on-Sea where the cockle boats and shrimpers sat 'lusted' over on the bed of the creek after the tide had gone. Fishing boats had continued to use the anchorage.

... bawleys congregated off the long spit ... (Drawn by Gwendoline D. Ardley)

Across the marsh from the skipper's moorings was Oyster Creek. Here, the marshes were once used as an oyster-laying ground. Pits were dug into the marshes for fattening and spawning. Some had been said to still exist but there was scant evidence, even on a recent aerial photograph.

It had been a dreamy sort of time, but, finally, the skipper had his long-awaited sail – after what seemed an infernal age! Being a fastidious keeper of records, he found it had been twenty-seven days ... It was a time lapse not experienced since finishing with his career at sea, on large, noisy, ocean-going motor ships that reeked of oil.

From the start, the day dawned promisingly, the forecast was for light to moderate winds ... He beamed at the radio, letting rip a shout of joy, as he blew it a kiss. Later, readying the boat for his tidal sail, the skipper luxuriated for a moment with a mug of tea and reflected on how lucky he was: many could not enjoy the advantages that it was his good fortune to enjoy.

The sun shone from an almost cloudless sky. It was cold, but ideal sailing conditions. 'It was like this some weeks ago,' he thought. 'A mid-range tide would allow a comfortable three hours too,' he added. The tide making up the creek seemed to take its time but was soon round the boat; finally, it lifted from the clasping mud. Worm-holes popped and bubbled as the tide crept over the mud bank and around the clinker hull; a reflection grew as it did so.

The wind was acutely on the starboard bow. The skipper set the mainsail and then the foresail, leaving the sheets slack, the sails slating in the breeze. Finally, with a burst from the engine, sternwards, he was away. Clearing his mooring, the foresail picked up the breeze, and with a slackened mainsheet, the boat fetched across the tide. As the mainsheet was gathered, the breeze flicked at the sheets and the boat had a purposeful momentum of its own. The engine, by then, had been silenced. Bliss!

Brent geese milled about in the creek and along the edges of the marsh. Birds, a myriad of species, swooped and dipped around the marshy eastern end of the island marshes that had been used by the Romans for the extraction of salt. 'Which way?'

Brent geese milled about in the creek along the marsh edges ... (Drawn by Gwendoline D. Ardley)

thought the skipper, but the boat knew. The hardening breeze, clear of the creek, had pressed onto the sails: the skipper, in his reverie, hadn't slackened the main sheet and the boat had decided for him. She'd shaped up, south, for the North Kent shore.

It had been exhilarating. No other sails were in evidence. A fishing boat or two were busily engaged in the hunt for fish. A few ships passed by, bound up the London River, as he approached the deep-water channel. For one ship, the skipper luffed up to slow his boat's speed before proceeding southwards.

The North Kent shore had never been developed ... nor had the hidden Hoo villages beyond the skyline, except for a sprawling caravan park that tumbled down the sloping hillside from the ancient village of Allhallows. All had remained, largely, a farming community. In the distant past, the military had had a presence on the hillside, at Slough Fort. Other forts or batteries had been established on the curving coast round towards the entrance to the River Medway, and at Sheerness too. Now, the dominant building was a water tower. It sat atop the spine of the high ground, partially hiding a distant chimney of a polluting, coal-fired power station along the banks of the River Medway. They were the only signs of modern life, until one's eye, moving eastwards, took in the tall cranes of Thames Port, also on the River Medway, and the huge, oil-fired power station, on the Isle of Grain that, on misty days, did eerily seem to float, suspended in space. It was a shore so unlike its sister to the north, on the southern shores of Essex, which was a conglomeration of housing. Of it, Norman Shrapnel, writing about the Thames and this southern shore in particular, said, 'How long, I wonder, could this oddly appealing family of villages, St Mary Hoo and all the Hoos, hope to survive?' Survive they had, and largely unspoilt by housing developments: those were constrained to Hoo St Werberg, over the ridge beside the River Medway.

Numerous bird reserves existed along the northern shore of Kent. One was located at Northward Hill, east of Allhallows. Its woodlands fell via scrub into the marshes beneath the hills. Some freshwater marshland to the east, beyond the dammed Yantlet creek, used by the military to blow up unwanted ordinance, was also a magical, safe haven for birdlife. To the west, on a butt of land that stuck out into the east/west course of the Thames forcing it to take a sharp ninety degree turn to the south, was an extensive area of freshwater lakes, marsh and gravel pits – now a reserve run by the Royal Society for the Protection of Birds. The whole area, including the creeks around the skipper's home waters, were a magnet for wintering birds, and for many species, the fresh and saline waters were a paradise, a lifeline to their survival.

Leaving the shores of his boyhood county astern, the skipper set a course towards the Chapman Sands Bell buoy, west of his earlier southern outward track. It was a broad reach. The boat revelled in it. She picked up her skirts. Looking astern the skipper had seen a froth of spume scudding before the breeze, like petticoat lace, as it was whipped across the boat's wake.

In that manner, the little clinker yacht had surged across the tideway. At the 'Chapman', the skipper turned to a run, close under the austere, concrete sea wall that ringed Canvey Island. Beyond that wall, house roofs floated a whisker above the parapet. From the river, the skipper thought, it felt uncanny; it was almost as if it, the island, were a goldfish bowl. The bell buoy had soon disappeared astern. The Chapman buoy, whose mournful clang had rung since the demise of a lighthouse, could be discerned on quiet, fog-bound days for miles around.

'The wash of ships sends that bell's reverberations far. It permeates the island's streets, and those of Hadleigh, away to the north beyond the crest of the distant, dark-looking Downs,' the skipper murmured, having heard them on quiet, misty mornings.

The Chapman lighthouse had been instituted nearly 200 years before and was named after the shoal of sands, shell and shingle that ran ominously out from the eastern corner of the island – the Chapman Sands. The lighthouse was one of many to make navigation of the London River easier: many of the shoals were more pronounced then; now the buoyed and dredged deep-water channel had taken away those dangers. Dangers too that the modern cargo vessel would know nothing of: their sisters of yesteryear had to sail, or wait for a suitable slant, before the advent of tugs.

In 1951, the centenary of the last Chapman lighthouse, members of the Island Yacht Club delivered Christmas fare to the keepers in a flotilla of sailing yachts, mainly little clinker cruisers (Dauntless class – built locally up by Benfleet bridge) and motorboats. The lighthouse was in place for only another few short years, turned off during 1956 and dismantled soon after, leaving no trace.

Before heading back to his mooring, the skipper sailed round the end of the sea wall, at the eastern end of the island, towards his club house perched up on reclaimed ground beyond the edge of the saltings. Then he followed the shoreline round the marsh edge, marvelling at the huge numbers of birds. Knot, they hadn't gone then, red shank and dunlin amongst others, which had swooped up in thick, dark, curling clouds. Suddenly, they'd dive down to the shoreline to settle briefly before attending another aerial dance: ballerinas of the sky. They were awaiting the fall of the tide and a spot to alight to begin a fresh feeding frenzy.

'Ah!' he said, sighing deeply with relish and a huge dollop of satisfaction. 'That was a sight to behold … evocative, it's what makes sailing in these waters so precious.'

Later, at his mooring, the skipper, cocking his head sideways, had grinned. His look, as if wanting to say something, as he gazed lovingly across the salt marshes around him, would have said it all. He pinched himself: had it really happened? Flinching from that pinch, the skipper knew his daydreaming was over: it had been real.

Then another grin, no, a broad smile, spread from ear to ear. Chuckling at an unseen audience, he said, 'I'm damned lucky, so damned lucky …!'

2

'With Stately Ladies' over a Weekend in May

The mate had been sitting quietly outside in her pretty suburban garden. It was a gorgeous day, full of sunshine and spring warmth. A taste of times to come, perhaps, but the mate, for some hours, days even, had been cooped up inside ... 'It feels great to be out,' she murmured to herself, looking around.

Earlier, her head had been abuzz with the school reports she'd been slaving over. After a short period of reflection, she settled down to relax with a novel. Some of her reflections drifted. Reports had, year by year, required more care in their writing. Their intricacies, she thought, were not dissimilar to those of the sands and shoals of the Thames Estuary: a passage read wrongly could cause great angst! She had, however briefly, been at peace, deep in the world of her book.

Some time later, deeply engrossed in her book, a shadow fell over her. The shadow drifted back and forth for a short while, traversing her book like the movements of a swinging cabin lamp. Her consciousness was aware, for no more than a trifle. She initially ignored it, but ignoring the intrusion, because that's what it felt like, was soon out of the question. The hovering, swaying, intrusive shadow persisted. Ignoring it was impossible. Looking up, she saw what her innermost thoughts had surmised. It was her skipper. She smiled. She wanted to say, 'Go Away! Leave me alone!' but released a slow, drawn-out 'Yes ...' with strong tones of her recent thought of 'you're interfering with my space ...' leaking through. It was something the skipper had, after many years, come to recognise.

'Yes, I know ... but ...' ventured the skipper, tentatively, as he placed a mug of hot chocolate down beside her, as an act, he thought, of mollification.

'Err ... yes,' the mate mumbled, patiently waiting!

'At the end of your half-term week ...' he paused, briefly, 'we could pop over to the Medway for a few nights ... you said this morning that you're nearly finished...'

'Perhaps even ... spend a night up river at Upnor ... Stangate too ... along the edge of Greenborough Marsh.' The skipper knew the mate loved those places: they often sat and watched egrets and avocet feeding on the mud flats along the water's edge – it was a place at peace with itself and that aura enveloped all that anchored there too.

'Perhaps ...' he stammered, '... Queenborough for a night? And the Medway match is on Saturday ...'

'Ah,' she thought to herself, 'so that's what's been troubling him.' Her skipper had been on tenterhooks, but she'd been too busy to deal with the matter. 'He's been good. He's kept me fed and watered during these damned reports ...'

The skipper had planned a trip down memory lane to watch an evocative fleet of stately, tan-sailed beauties battle it out: that year was the one hundredth barge match on the River Medway. He'd taken part, as a youngster, in the barge matches on the River Medway back in the 1960s. The skipper's memories of racing went back to 1961. The participation of a true sailing home was unheard of now though: most barges were working charter vessels.

The hovering, swaying, intrusive shadow persisted. (Drawn by Gwendoline D. Ardley)

'Okay. But listen ...' pausing, to let her point sink in, 'I'm not promising we'll get three nights away though ...'

The skipper then, after planting a warm 'thank you' peck on his wife's lips, disappeared, engrossed in plans.

The skipper, also on a break, had, for the period his mate was busy, kept clear, enabling her to get on. He spent time working around his sailing club enjoying some manly bonhomie, graft and tea with other retired or semi-retired members. Some 'pleasurable' hours were spent titivating varnish and paintwork around their yacht as well as enjoying some sailing out on the tide. He'd not idled!

The mate, between times, began to quietly plan for the trip too. A stack of reading matter, more important than a collection of old sailormen, was assembled with other items, such as bedding and sensible clothing. The day before their trip, the skipper gaily loaded a huge pile into their car, grinning as he'd driven away, boat-wards.

Departure day dawned fine. The skipper ushered the mate out, clasping their bedding and perishable stores between them, breathing a sigh of relief.

The sail over to the Medway was mundane to the extreme. A decent westerly breeze allowed them to negotiate the Medway entrance before the turn of the tide. Then on, it was going to be a beat up river, but the tides were lazy.

While entering the Medway, they heard the sailing barge *Gladys* hail the port authority, on the open channel, '... bound for Gillingham.' A number of spritsail barges were seen across the marshes, beyond Deadmans Island, anchored in Stangate Creek. It was a sight, unfortunately, all too rare on this river: historically, the Medway area was at the heart of spritsail barge development – truly a barge river. Only a couple of active craft remained on the river. Most preferred the glamour of London, berthed in Saint Katharine Dock, or Maldon, 'The Barge River' – it was said!

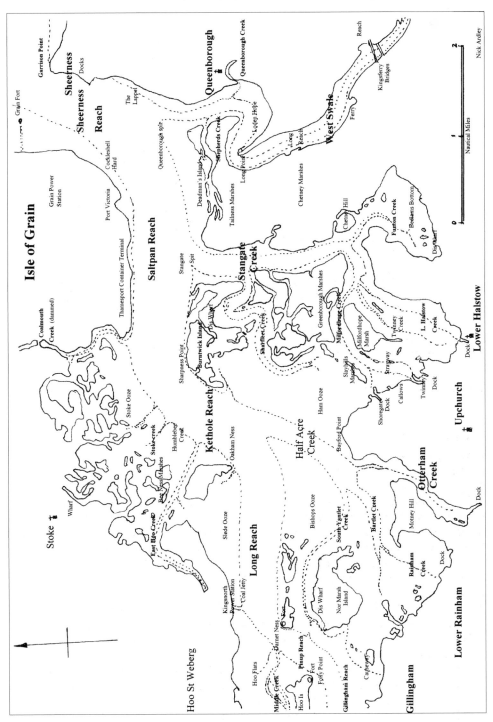

Chartlet of the River Medway from Sheerness to Hoo.

'Faversham has remained a barge port. Good craftsmen are based there too, all carrying out responsible repairs and reconstructions ...' the skipper started to say, his voice trailing away as he saw the look on his mate's face. 'I'll leave it ...' he thought to himself.

A barge was seen to get underway, across the marshes. She'd shot out of Stangate in fine fashion, then crept to windward over the last of the ebb. Soon, only her sails were visible beyond the bulk of Burntwick Island. Along Saltpan Reach, the skipper started to feel the ebb too – it stalled their progress.

Some time later, when rounding into Kethole Reach, close in under the hard, bluff clay nose of Burntwick Island, it became obvious to the skipper that they were catching the barge ahead of them. She seemed to be toiling up Long Reach towards the power station. It was about then that the skipper's ears pricked up as the radio again crackled, his attention grabbed by the name of the calling vessel. The *EDME*, was about to leave Stangate, bound for Gillingham.

'This'll be interesting,' the skipper said, looking at his mate.

'Why?' she enquired.

'Well, when, or where, do you reckon that fleet-footed barge will overtake us?'

'Haven't a clue – except she's pretty fast – you keep telling me that ... you're the expert! Maybe ... oh, off Gillingham, perhaps? ... I don't know!' She shook her head and looked wryly across the cockpit and added, 'Anyway, why's she called *EDME*?'

The skipper scratched his chin, glanced astern at the *EDME* as she hardened up for a reach across Saltpan, then looked ahead. 'I think she'll have us in Pinup, between the two forts,' he confidently predicted, settling down to concentrate on sailing. 'Her name,' he said, after a short period, 'has something to do with her original owners ... I heard that the last two letters were for, Malt Extract.' He paused to tighten the jib in, then said, 'There's much debate about the first two – even the present company in Mistley, now the Anglia Maltings Group, aren't sure!' He grinned and added, 'Her registered name were the initials of a product.'

It was a grand sail, the reaches were taken in long and short tacks, but lessening wind as they approached the hills above old Gillingham slowed them appreciably. The barge astern had eaten up the water between them, her topsail catching the higher velocity streams well above the little yacht. Rounding into Pinup, the skipper briefly lost sight of the barge behind the bulk of Darnet Ness Fort. He grinned: they'd done better than he expected. Ahead, the other barge had still not rounded into Gillingham Reach and seemed to be toiling – who would reach Short Reach first?

By the time the skipper had tacked round Folly Point, the *EDME* was close up to them, on the opposite tack. The skipper tacked inshore to give the barge room; the barge's crew watched them from the lee shrouds, at the ready for a tack: she was the give-way vessel. (The skipper had had no intention of enforcing such rules though.) He said, 'The old barge won't come in here, it's too shallow – even for her. She needs a bit of leeboard down.' The mate nodded. 'We'll tack down the moorings' pointing ahead, 'and keep out of her way.' There, along Hoo Island, the ebb ran less strongly too – a good enough reason for the manoeuvre.

The mate watched the spectacle of the *EDME* overhaul the other barge. Smiling, she said, 'Don't you wish it were you,' knowing full well that the skipper had 'done with barges'.

He shuddered – at the thought!

Watching though was a pleasant diversion as they tacked gamely in *EDME*'s wake watching the spectacle ahead. 'Overhaul' was too understated: the graceful *EDME* slipped beautifully past the *Gladys*, tacking beneath her, close in by Gillingham Marina, to fetch up into Short Reach. It was a wonderful piece of sailing, live art, a joy to witness.

Spritsail barge *EDME* sailing serenely through Gillingham Reach in 2008.

By the time the skipper and mate had rounded into Short Reach the engineless *EDME* had reduced sail and was bringing up to her anchor in amongst a fleet of spritsail barges.

The sight reminded the skipper of forty-five years before, when he himself had sat on the aftercabin top of their sailing home as Father had marshalled the crew in readiness for the finale of the trading matches in 1963. 'Only the *Henry* and *Marjorie* were still sailing,' murmured the skipper, 'most have suffered the fate that awaits old sailormen – the indignity of the breakers or a slow death along a marsh-fringed bank.' He grinned, thinking of another that had escaped, 'The *Edith May* should be sailing again soon!'

On the approach to Upnor, the mate took the helm whilst the skipper had dealt with the genoa, then the mainsail, getting both stowed as their intended berth, for that night, got closer. The skipper readied the mooring line then attached the buoy hook to the boat hook – the mate's favourite toy ... but it was the mate's turn to pilot them in! A trusty buoy, belonging to the Medway Yacht Club, soon hove in sight, one the skipper 'was sure was not in use,' he said: it had no mooring line attached.

Sitting relaxing, after clearing up and putting things shipshape, the skipper said, 'Look, there's more housing going up on Saint Mary's Island.'

The mate looked at her skipper: she had remarked on that earlier ... the skipper, looking at mooring buoys, had taken no notice! So, she repeated her comments, 'Looks like infilling, but they're another different style.' The whole waterfront had been built with a number of styles – 'I suppose they're reminiscent of old dock buildings,' adding, 'some of the others are in a more modern.'

'Yes, it's a strange mix.' It was not to the liking of everyone the skipper knew: he grinned, remembering a recent conversation about the area.

After a welcome mug of tea, the skipper had rowed ashore to check if the mooring was free. That done he set the tan lug sail on the dinghy and pottered up river, tacking along the shore towards the castle at Upnor. With a dying breeze, he reluctantly turned for home. The breeze though was from behind. The little dinghy moved gently, in a very sedate manner, over the fresh flood. It was a pleasant, beguiling way to wile away the half hour it took the fickle breeze to waft him back. It had become noticeably busier on the water around the club. The club's watermen (he used that term loosely: both men and women manned the boats), in two separate launches, had begun to run a continuous service to and from yachts moored along the trot. 'Pity our club isn't as committed to getting out onto the water,' the skipper muttered to himself: they'd been one of only a few boats to leave their creek that glorious morning – a decent breeze – sunshine – a good weekend weather forecast ... 'What more is needed?'

That evening, they tidied themselves up, a little more than usual, and rowed ashore. A call was made at the yacht club. The cost of a glass of ale was little enough for a safe mooring and supped while enjoying the view from the club's vantage high above the river was grand too. A convivial welcome was always experienced. Later, they wandered along to a waterside hostelry for dinner. (But, good food can be had at that club!)

The skipper and mate quenched their thirst – it was a pleasantly warm evening – before glancing over the menu. They remembered, as they chatted, an incident of a time long before. Well, there were two, in fact, that came specifically to mind. The first was when they'd lost a set of oars. 'Well,' said the skipper, 'they weren't actually lost.'

'No!' exclaimed the mate, 'they were taken – stolen!' At the time it was something that surprised them both greatly, for having left their dinghy moored in many a lonely place over the years, they'd suffered from little interference.

The other incident had been the saga of the rowlocks. It was back in the days when they towed two dinghies around the estuary, trailing them in a line astern: ducklings following in Mother's wake. While gamely mooring his dinghy, their son had placed his rowlocks, very carefully, on the pontoon. Getting up from belaying his good ship's painter, he'd accidentally kicked the rowlocks. Sploosh! Gone! The angst was immediate, prolonged and torrid. Fortunately, the little hamlet still had a chandler. The shop had been on the waterfront for many, many years, back to the skipper's childhood, and the day was saved. Now though, like so many waterfront shops, it had closed.

At the time the oars were pinched, the chandler at Upnor had gone. The oars had to be replaced: a dinghy without oars is of little use. Fortunately, a chandler had then still conveniently been sited at the top of the old hard at Queenborough, but that too had closed now. 'It's sad,' the skipper thought gravely: he'd heard a recent tale about a chap who'd had to sail many miles to obtain spares, for a sick sea toilet ... a failure would have forced a return to the old days of – bucket and chuck it!

'Oars and rowlocks are such an essential part of a yacht's tender – even if an outboard is carried,' remarked the skipper. 'Tenders are often seen without oars – a danger – surely?'

'Drink up,' said the mate, 'it's time we were off.'

Early morning brought a clear sky, allowing the sun to brighten the day immediately. There was little or no breeze. 'It's a fine day for the beach ... not for moving heavy, ponderous, spritsail barges,' the skipper called below as he fitted the ensign into its socket on the pushpit.

While bacon spluttered and spat under the grill and eggs cooked gently atop the stove, the skipper kept a look out from his vantage point, by the companion-way steps. Barge after barge came out of Chatham marina and motored down towards Gillingham, setting sails that drooped full of wrinkles in the calm conditions. A steamer appeared. She was an old puffer, *VIC 56*, a ship from a different era. She was built in 1945 by James Pollock & Son & Co., at their Faversham shipyard.

The steamer *VIC 56* and, astern, the pretty spritsail barge *Whippet* provide an evocative throwback against the backdrop of Upnor Castle.

Dimensionally, she was little different from large coasting spritsail barges. She was, in fact, mixing with her peers: little steamers, like her, replaced her sailing forbears. A large number were built to service the British naval fleet's anchorages. The skipper got so engrossed that the mate eventually took over the cooking ... Ha!

The food was soon ready and was passed out into the warmth of the sun-drenched cockpit. The mate ignoring the skipper's frequent hopping up and down: he was a boy again ... and she said, 'boys will be boys...'

Later, as the mate finished clearing the debris of their breakfast, she heard the telltale signs. She sighed – they were on the move. The mainsail dropped onto the cabin top moments before she heard it rattling aloft. Looking out, she said, 'We on the move?' The skipper grinned avidly before nodding. The mate skipped back below, quickly reappearing with their life jackets. 'Here,' she said, passing the skipper his jacket – 'at least put this on!'

Leaving their jib on deck, the skipper motored down the mooring trot. Along the edge of the Hoo mud flats they found a little breeze, so the engine was slowed as the boat gathered way under sail. The river was full of stately old ladies getting underway, jostling and preparing their lightweight sails. They'd the appearance of yachts rather than the humble working craft they really were. The skipper thought back, many years, to the patched-up, home-made sails that had hung from the spars of his sailing home, 'It's a different world now.' he murmured reflectively.

Sailing past the committee boat, the skipper called, 'Much like it was in 1965 ...' There was a flourish of conversation, then a wave of recognition. Finally, a grin came from another too, after the skipper had removed his sun hat. The chap had, for some time, been rebuilding an old spritsail barge, the *Edith May*, in the old dock at Lower Halstow.

The older man had the look of a proper mariner, of the old school too: he'd a ruddy complexion. A polka dot kerchief was tied nonchalantly around his neck and his wave had displayed hands, the size of hams. He'd been a working bargeman, used to the toil pulling on thick ropes and heaving on heavy flax canvass ...

The little farm barge, *Cygnet*, off the
entrance to Gillingham Docks.

The pretty little *Cygnet*, a little farm barge of a little over forty feet, built in 1881
by Curel of Frindsbury, with one hold, was jostling with two other small barges. They
were the *Dinah*, a barge yacht, but built to carry a tiny cargo back in the 1880s it was
said, and there was the *Whippet*, fashioned from a steel lighter, of around sixty-five
feet, and as pretty as any sailing barge could be.

A hail from the shore caused the skipper to shiver. A blast from his childhood – especially
when he'd done something wrong. It was the voice of his Mother, 'Nic … ho … las …' it
was unmistakable! He glanced quickly at the mate, before looking shoreward. A distant
person was waving wildly on the edge of a throng of watchers on the shore. Turning
towards the shore, an old, brick-built quay by Gillingham slipway, they soon realised that
the hail was indeed from 'Mother' standing precariously at the top of a flight of steps.

Whilst the mate gilled around, the skipper went off in the dinghy to pick up his
mother, who was handed down, by a kindly gentleman, as the skipper came alongside
the weed-infested steps. His mother had waved a cheery goodbye to her noble friend
and called out, 'probably see you tonight at the dinner then,' as the skipper rowed
back out to the slowly circling yacht. Mother soon climbed aboard and was very
quickly at home.

As soon as the skipper had himself climbed aboard, clutching the dinghy painter,
the mate abandoned the tiller to disappear below. The kettle was soon on the stove
– coffee! Mother, meanwhile, quickly found a good vantage point and was busy
snapping the barges manoeuvring around the start-line. A grin, as wide as could be,
had spread across her face. She loved it. Her day was made!

Dropping down river … with the barges, with what little breeze there was, the
skipper's mother was in raptures: it had been a good few years since she'd seen a
match from a position out on the water. The last had been with an old friend, one of
the skipper's godparents. The gentleman had had a little barge, the *Dipper*, converted
to a yacht before the Second World War, sailing her until sold during the early 1950s.
After that, he crewed on occasions on the skipper's childhood home until moving to
the West Country. Many years later, the chap met up again with his old buddy, the

The *Kingswear Castle*, a river-class paddle steamer.

skipper's mother, for a once-a-year trip down memory lane, aboard the paddle steamer *Kingswear Castle*, which, as it happened, silently ghosted past with a barely heard 'shushing' of her paddle-wheels.

Later, a picnic lunch was enjoyed in the cockpit, watching the slowly moving craft drift down on the tide, manoeuvring, so very slowly, with what little steerage they had. The mate's pile of books was a godsend and she ignored her twittering companions and read deeply. Lovely as it was sitting under the lee of Oakham Ness, the skipper was very conscious of the time.

'It's going to be a slow old race,' the skipper chortled. 'I don't expect they'll get very far.'

His mother concurred, saying, 'I'd be surprised if the course wasn't shortened to a buoy off Sheerness, somewhere inside the river at least.'

'Though,' she added, 'they seem to do some funny things these days ...'

'Yes,' the skipper added, 'they rely on their engines to get them home ...'

'You remember, don't you?' his mother said, 'They used to remove the propellers before matches,' adding, 'once, we were becalmed and left short of the finish. Got there eventually. No tow ... crew missed their supper!'

The skipper merely nodded: few believed it – knew – or even cared.

Later, after dropping Mother off at Gillingham Marina, the skipper and mate motored back down river with no obvious breeze in the air. Rounding Sharpness, there was a breeze – from the east. They'd tried to sail – faltered – drifted – and in the company of a few other yachts, completed a few pirouettes with the tidal current swirls, before they'd given in.

Away down river, many barges still appeared to be endeavouring to sail out – against the fresh flood. 'Madness,' thought the skipper, aloud. From amongst the fleet though, two barges were seen to be ploughing a steady furrow inbound, sails billowing to the light breeze that wafted them along. They'd soon come by. It was a sedate, but glorious sight.

The two craft, the *Repertor*, chased closely by the *EDME*, their sails poled out

How it used to be: the Medway fleet tramping down Long Reach in 1963. The barge sixth from the right is the *May Flower*. (From an original print by Leslie G. Arnold, courtesy of Keith and Marian Patten)

'goose-winged' to harvest every little drop of the light easterly air. Slowly, as the skipper and mate made their way towards their chosen anchorage for the night, the skipper watched the much smaller, pretty-looking *EDME* first draw level, and then sweetly pass the *Repertor* as the two majestic craft slid round the distant point of Sharpness.

A few other barges were, by then, running in past the entrance to Stangate Creek, but the breeze that carried the front two had waned ... the radio crackled ... a voice was heard, 'One's still trying to reach the outer mark ... she'll be an hour yet ...' Then, 'Collect them all up for a return home ... positions as they are...'

Looking at the mate, the skipper had commented, 'We didn't have a radio in my day – well, some of the barges probably did. It's not like it was. With their propellers off – you might have heard Mother say so earlier – there'd be no motoring home!'

Leaving the main river behind them, the thoughts of the yacht's crew turned towards their anchorage. The sails were stowed and tidied by then and the yacht glided easily, under low throttle, with the tide under her into Sharfleet Creek. There, a number of craft had already come to rest, lying to their anchors. Recumbent figures were seen lazing in cockpits reading, drinking tea, perhaps, and gazing about. The skipper, by then up forward readying the anchor, looked up, occasionally, to wave nonchalantly as they passed by, eyes firmly fixed on his spot. The mate, looking ahead too, checked the depth as they approached, before coming astern as the anchor ran. She watched the skipper snub the cable and indicate, in their coded manner, neutral, and finally stop.

'Tea,' the mate called out ... 'I'm off for a nap – kettle's on!'

Making his own tea, he dug out a wedge of cake too, taking his repast out into the cockpit.

The skipper dozed; waking later, it was just after the turn of the tide. He noticed, looking up from his book, from time to time, little zephyrs of a wandering air ruffling the languid surface of the water; he murmured, 'A breeze is coming ...' and grinned,

The spritsail barges *EDME* and *Repertor* (different classes) running towards Sharpness Point in 2008.

'I'll get a sail later – in the dinghy.'

Scattered here and there on the flat water, circular ripples appeared as if a stone were thrown into a pond. They were caused by a myriad of small fry jumping and plopping through the mirror-like surface. The little fish were relatively safe this time: the many terns that had all afternoon been on a continuous and frenzied hunt for food for their young, who waited noisily in their nests up in the marshes that surrounded the backwater, had ceased their frantic search. That was apart from a few, who now enjoyed a period of happy hunting. The skipper watched, entranced, as the little birds, from a seemingly great height, dropped dart-like into the still waters, seeing what he, the skipper, could not, and rose with a bill full of food. A bird flying low over the water, with a glistening fish in its bill, reared up in a turn sharper than any man-made machine could do, then it dived into the water, disappearing briefly from sight. The skipper marvelled at the sight of that perfectly proportioned bird adding another fish to its bill and watched it fly back shoreward to feed its vociferous young.

Later, after dinner, succulent pork in cider (the meat, well insulated, had remained bilge-chilled after thawing from frozen), the skipper had slipped away for a lazy evening sail, leaving the mate to clear up: he'd cooked! He sailed, or more truly – drifted away. He luxuriated in the warm evening sunshine, lazily propping a leg up on a gunnel. Little zephyrs moved the dinghy gently along. The burgee, a length of blue ribbon that streamed gallantly at the little boat's masthead in anything other than a near calm, fluttered falteringly.

Suddenly, the skipper felt an intrusion. He was aware of being watched. It was one of those creepy moments, a sixth sense perhaps. Close by, on the bathing platform of a swish modern motor yacht, stood a man using his mobile phone to take pictures ... while talking loudly to the world as he did so. Above him lolled a svelte, un-yacht-like blonde, not taking any notice of her man: she continued to leaf through a glossy magazine. The skipper looked away – !

A breeze slowly built up, the clouds too. An ominous-looking sky was moving

… the little birds had … dropped dart-like into the still waters …
(Drawn by Gwendoline D. Ardley)

towards the pretty little anchorage. By and by, the breeze lifted even further to a point which was about as much as was comfortable. It was an exhilarating finale to the sail though …

Heading back to the mother ship, the skipper skittered past an anchored yacht upon which two young children were looking eagerly and excitedly at the sight of the little dinghy working up to windward. An adult appeared. Then the children, two girls, having got the attention they'd craved, were seen to gesticulate towards the skipper. The skipper had briefly thought of calling out 'Swallows for Ever': the three on the yacht could have been Nancy and Peggy, the Amazons, with their Uncle – all characters from a series of tales told by Arthur Ransome about a group of sailing children, that never seemed to grow up. 'Two budding sailors dying to have a go,' thought the skipper. 'I hope their parents get them into a dinghy,' he remarked dryly, looking at the inflated rubber bag, tugging at its painter, close under their stern. Sailing away, the skipper grinned broadly. It seemed he'd made their day!

Later, back aboard, with the evening setting in, the mate and skipper sat chatting: it was too dark for the mate to read.

'You know, this environment, it looks so natural, doesn't it?' the skipper said quietly. 'It is, in fact, largely sculpted by man … as you know,' the skipper paused.

The skipper was reflecting about the work of man and nature. Earlier that afternoon, while the mate slept, buried in the forecabin (well deserved after all those school reports!) his mind had wandered to times past within the delightful wilderness.

On a chart of 1802 in a recent book, *Sea Charts of the British Isles: A Voyage of Discovery Around Britain and Ireland's Coastline*, by John Blake, a house was shown on Burntwick Island. The island was then known as 'Sharpfleet' Island, as was the creek. The house sat on the high ground that still remained above the spring high water contour near a derelict wharf. Westwards, Sharfleet was blocked by a delta of marsh. The 1802 chart had shown a creek running south through an area, now known as Slayhills Marsh, then east, probably along what was now Milfordhope Creek, one of three creeks leading westwards from the southern foot of Stangate. Sharpfleet was also marked as an oyster fishery, a worthwhile and productive industry in those days too. Oysters had gone by the mid-1900s. Other old maps seen showed the same features. The sea of tidal marshland which existed to the west, between Sharfleet and Half Acre Creeks, was now open mud flats.

Man, though, had greatly influenced, interfered and shaped this environment. Many channels were blocked off to create the extensive offshore grazing marshes. Time and rising sea levels soon caught up with that grazing paradise, destroying the good sheep-fattening land. Sea walls were punctured, once too often, returning the land back to salt marsh. Of course, the Romans had used the area for salt panning and pottery making. It was thought possible that Samian Ware had been made here: items and shards had been found. On a later visit, the skipper was given a section of a bowl rim by a local Medway sailor he met in the creek. The chap, the owner of a converted Leigh Bawley, had spent years searching the mud flats around and about.

On a subsequent visit to the British Museum, the skipper found that Samian Ware was mass-produced in Gaul. The ware is a red glass pottery and was produced on a north-east south-west line from the Moselle valley region down to Toulouse during the first and second centuries after Christ. The ware was later produced in North Africa, and briefly, for local distribution, at Colchester. If it hadn't been made local to these marshes, then why the quantities found? No record of this was seen at the museum!

In Sharfleet, when the skipper was musing over how things were, he watched a fisherman scraping and painting the bottom of his vessel. The boat was on a beach close by, across a stretch of wet-looking, popping mud, only recently uncovered by the receding tide. The beach sat to the west of an old wharf on Burntwick Island. Later, the boat had come off on the rising tide to putter away round the marshes to the west, bound up river perhaps?

The skipper had watched the man bird-watching too, or it could have been the reverse: the birds seemed to mob the fishing boat at times! The man had wandered along the beach and shoreline looking: this beach contained a mass of shattered Victorian and Edwardian crockery from household rubbish, probably dumped as backfill for the wharf when it was constructed. Many years before, the skipper, mate and their son had explored this eerie, abandoned place too. Now, though, the skipper was content with its status as a no man's land, a haunt for birds. Beside the wharf were the remains of a wooden lighter, of unknown origin, and a boiler drum. The drum was a red of several shades, rusted and wasted, full of jagged holes, from which tendrils of weed hung.

The wharf was used by mud barges as well as, probably, the military to supply stores for the men who'd operated and manned a defence boom that was placed across the River Medway during the 1939-45 European conflict. Along the Medway shore of the island, the attachment points and run to the winch house can still be seen when sailing close in. One source, read by the skipper, says that the boom dated to the Victorian era, but the remains were typical twentieth-century constructions.

The buildings, although crumbling, still stood, or sort of – in the case of an accommodation, or barrack house, in an expanse of sea purslane, often seen flooded at high water. Others sat on or round a ridge of ground that remained above the spring tide levels. One of those buildings was the chimney and walls of a boiler and winch house. Over the past decade or so, the skipper had witnessed the gradual collapse of the disused gun emplacements and blockhouses, as the frontage to the River Medway

Wartime relics on Burntwick Island showing, left to right, barrack building, defence boom anchoring point and boiler-house chimney.

had rapidly eroded. The blockhouses ran in a line along the remains of the island's sea wall. They were, without doubt, built for the protection, during the Second World War, of the refinery that was, until recent times, located on the Isle of Grain.

The marshes within the Medway basin had been heavily dug out for the valuable blue clay that lay beneath. Ordinary mud was removed too. The products were loaded into spritsail barges, operated by various brickmakers, for different types of bricks. Mud and clay was also used in the cement-manufacturing industries that abounded on the Medway and Swale. The barges were loaded by a team of 'muddies' who, between tides, could fill a 100-ton barge. The skipper shook his head when he thought about that!

Just across the island and the River Medway beyond, in comparison to 200 years ago, the marshes to the north, Stoke Marsh, had been severely denuded by the digging for blue clay. A few remaining tongues had, over the years, been eroded by ever-increasing tidal heights. The marsh edge had crept inland towards the land ridge of the Grain Peninsula. Stoke wharf, which sat up a creek there, now only had a veneer of marsh left protecting it. Stoke Creek had originally had the name 'Stocfleet' and was a deep channel leading up to a village wharf. To the east, a dense patch of saltings had existed between Stoke and East Hoo creeks, indented by Humblebee Creek. And the passage through to the Yantlet was then still clear, though a road bridge had blocked the way. In 1688, a through passage could still be made by vessels with fixed masts.

Robert Simper, in *River Medway and the Swale*, said about the mud and clay diggings in the Stoke Marshes, 'The barges sailed at high tide into the "clay holes" and gangs of men, who lived in houseboats on the saltings during the week, loaded with shovels day or night in one tide.'

The mate was still engrossed, leaving the skipper silent and deep in his own world ...

They'd followed in the wake of those barges during another short cruise, exploring Stoke Creek, just after low water.

Near the low-tide entrance to Stoke Creek and a deep mud hole, a tongue of

Wreckage scattered on the Stoke Flats. Beyond the remains of the barge's windlass barrel can be seen the other vessel's ribs.

marsh, nothing more than a clay ridge with a tiny, lonely patch of saltings marked by a lopsided beacon, the skipper went off in the dinghy and found the bottoms of two vessels. Little remained of them, but one was identified as a spritsail barge: it had a hard chine – the right-angle join of the bottom and the sides. The other hadn't had that feature. She'd had a rounded bottom and no chine. It intrigued the skipper immensely.

Scattered around and within the remains of those vessels were a large amount of domestic detritus. Back aboard their yacht, the skipper said, 'I wonder if those vessels were lived in … there's so much broken pottery, the remains of an old cast-iron fo'c's'le stove and loads of other stuff too.'

She grinned, not knowing what to say.

'Perhaps they were the dormitory barges referred to by Simper,' the skipper mused – but who could really say?

Later, they sailed up to the head of Stoke Creek. The skipper went off in the dinghy for a poke about, finally landing at a hard and meeting a group of wizened, old waterfront characters – joining them for a mug of tea.

'We watched you come up 'ere on the tide' one had said.

'It's just a canal between the marshes,' another added, waving his arm towards the skipper's boat by then floating a little higher, '… all silted up like now …'

The skipper grinned over his tea, 'Yes, we enjoy creeping up any creek that takes our fancy,' adding after a sip of tea, '… had a fancy to come here for years …'

Reflecting on what the chap had said, the skipper added, 'Yes, granted, it's silted up in here, but out there,' pointing well beyond the immediate banks of cord grass and purslane, 'it's wasting away rapidly, year by year …'

'Yer, we've noticed.'

They chatted about this and that. A man knew about the barge bottom – 'she was berthed in the creek,' he said, 'for a long time before being towed out and burnt on the flats.' The old boys knew nothing of the other remains though. At the time, the skipper giggled: the group could have been the boys at their own club!

To the west of Stoke Creek, a tongue of broken and scattered marshes remained, through which Humblebee Creek ran. The creek's course was nonexistent at low water, but early on the tide, the marshes could be accessed by dinghy from East Hoo Creek, past the decaying obstacle of a jetty that ran inland. Remembering that, the skipper's thoughts then ran to a glorious day the season before ...

They'd sailed up into East Hoo Creek to search for an elusive submarine. It was on a very quiet morning, before breakfast even. It was the weekend of a hair-raising 'attack' on a nearby power station by members of an anti-coal-burning alliance ... big, burley men piled out of a van and watched the antics of the boat as it tacked lazily into the creek ... was this another attack? After several boards, it finally proved too shallow to sail, so the sails were stowed. The trusty diesel made do! Searching, through binoculars, amongst the rills as they slowly motored in on the sluggish flood tide, the skipper suddenly hollered, 'There she is! Stop! Round up! We'll anchor up here,' pointing hastily to a patch of water nearby.

'It's not very deep,' the mate said tentatively.

Looking aft to his mate, the skipper grinned, gently reminding her of the rising tide, as the boat slid to a halt! The skipper let go the anchor and waited while she swung, with the tide under her stern. They were soon brought up in a metre of water. The skipper beamed excitedly towards the cockpit. The mate had other thoughts ... 'Shall we have breakfast then?' The jaunt was entirely for his benefit. 'And you're cooking' she added.

As the tide swirled round the hull of their boat and rushed, seemingly, at an ever-faster rate into the rills and gutways around them, the skipper and mate enjoyed the titillating aroma of sizzling bacon and tomatoes, grill-sweetened. It was as enjoyable in the eating, especially after their earlier two-hour sail. Quickly finishing his, the skipper had donned his life jacket.

The mate, looking up, said, 'I suppose you're off now ...' silly question really and added, 'Be careful ... watch the mud ... don't forget the tide ...'

'Yes ... yes ... yes,' the skipper said, thinking at the same time, 'All the usual stuff – but she's always right ...' as he stepped into the dinghy, grinning and saying, 'see you in an hour ... I've got my phone.' He was away nearly two hours by the time he got back ... still watched by those burley bruisers on the creek's western sea wall.

The skipper had rowed his dinghy under the dilapidated ruins of the old oil jetty. Its pipes sagged, dripping a filigree of decayed lagging that hung in long tendrils. Once-stout supports hung alone, free, separated by rust and rot, but, fortunately, enough of them remained intact to take the weight of the structure high above the skipper's head. 'But for how long ...' a momentary thought ... a few swift strokes on the oars quickly dispelled any more as clear sight above was regained.

Rowing with the run of a gutway, the skipper came close to his prey. There she sat – the rusted carcass of a German First World War U-boat. Her hull, wasted in places, was broken at each end, but very much discernable for what she was. '... at last,' the skipper said in a hushed tone.

Resting on his oars and gazing at her, from some distance, for the tide had not yet made sufficiently, the skipper saw something else beside the submarine's hull. The realisation was rapid, 'It's an old barge,' he said. Her rotting stem and windlass bitts stood erect, and her mast case sat on her deck, awash with marsh.

Eventually, the skipper floated with the rising tide up to a patch of cord grass. He secured his dinghy anchor carefully amongst some sea purslane on a hump of saltings. Wandering through the cord grass, he stumbled over her hidden rails. They were intact, out of view amongst the growth, as the mud engulfed them. Her hull too was still in evidence, remnants hanging to rusting fastenings from gnarled frames.

The German First World War U-boat with the spritsail barge *Swale* keeping her company up Humblebee Creek.

The mast case still stood on the deck, the mud level with its base. That meant, the skipper knew, that her ceiling and bottom planks lay nearly two metres below his feet. Outboard of the mast case, still attached to her rigging chocks, were the rusting iron rings that once held deadeyes for her stays.

Moving his gaze to the submarine, it struck the skipper, deeply, how surprisingly small she was. He was fascinated by the thinness of her outer hull plating, the arrangement of ballast tanks between it and the inner pressure hull. He noted the thickness of the inner hull and the smallness of the conning tower tube that had joined it. A myriad of pipe connections and valves were still in place too. The central part of the hull had, it seemed, suffered most from the ravages of time. Perhaps, crushed by a barge he knew that had sat on it. Walking to her forward end, the skipper tripped over the sternpost of the barge hidden in the cord grass. The forward end of the U-boat was in relatively good condition. A section of the hull remained clear at high tide, it was obvious. The skipper peered down the banks of her forward torpedo tubes. It felt sinister.

One could only admire the German sailors who had sailed in such craft, no matter that they were such superb hunters of shipping – what untold lives had this single boat cost? She and their souls, surely, now rest in peace – she, in this quiet, silted backwater, they, in the ocean depths. It should be remembered, we, Britain, had such craft too, and wreaked the same havoc. The skipper had quietly, reverently, said a few words for them all.

Looking back at both of those vessels as he'd finally bade farewell and set to, to row against a swiftly flowing tide, the skipper had shaken his head, saying, '... a strange experience indeed.'

The wharf, Halstow.

The spritsail barge *Plover* in Lower Halstow dock during the 1930s, sometime after her stranding and rescue. (Courtesy of Pauline Stevens)

Some time later, arriving back alongside the yacht, fairly puffed from his rowing exertions, he'd garbled excitedly at the mate.

'But how did they get there,' she enquired, after he'd slowed down.

'Well,' he said, 'the barge was the *Swale*.' (She was built in 1864.) 'On a big spring tide, another barge, the *Plover*, got stuck across the submarine during the early 1930s. The *Swale* was owned by the same firm; she'd been stripped of her gear some years previously and laid up. She was towed down river, from Hoo, and placed under the *Plover* hoping to lift her off. It worked, but the *Swale* was hulked after that last job.' He paused.

'The *Plover* … ?'

'She ended up as a hulk in Whitewall Creek.' The skipper remembered.

'Seeing the barge and the submarine, lying side by side, in the ooze, was an eerie experience.'

'I bet,' the mate murmured.

But, all of that had been late during their previous season.

In Sharfleet too, during the dark days of the Second World War, the anchorage was used by coastal patrol and mine clearance craft. Deep inside some of the tributaries close by, around the foot of Stangate Creek, lighters with valuable stores, often ammunition, were moored. Camouflaged from the air, they were difficult to spot.

Old spritsail barges were used as moveable barrage balloon bases. They were anchored in lines with the balloons tethered to a winch attached to their hulls. Close by were not only the oil installations on the Isle of Grain, but also the important naval dockyard at Sheerness. Many of those barges suffered severely, from planes crashing onto them, bomb damage and mainly a general lack of maintenance for nearly five years. Many were dumped afterwards. It was their last job. Except that it wasn't: many were put against the sea wall to offer protection and provide a base for marsh development. Some could still be seen, opposite the entrance to the pretty little creek the skipper and mate sat in, along the eastern shore of Stangate was a bed of scattered timbers protruding or interred in the mud ...

'Wake up,' said the mate, 'are we going to have that coffee?'

He'd dozed? Maybe, but it had gone beyond dusk!

'You were muttering – again...'

'Err, yes, was I?' said the skipper, '... you put the kettle on and I'll make it. And – I wasn't asleep.'

'Well, it looked it to me.'

He'd been at peace with the world in that lonely, empty anchorage.

The next morning was idyllic. A gentle breeze wafted over the tops of the marshes, gently ruffling the surface of the creek. Some cloud hung around, slowly passing over, but didn't look threatening. The forecast promised broken sunshine and light breezes. The skipper setting their ensign at the stern grinned broadly – a lazy day – a potter round to Queenborough and a bite to eat ashore were all they'd planned.

'This is the life,' he called below to the mate who was slipping into her things ... 'Breakfast?'

Later, much later, the skipper shortened in the anchor chain, a signal to the mate, happily enjoying her novel, that departure was imminent.

'I guess we're about to leave,' she called, knowing full well the answer: the tide was ebbing. Reluctantly, the mate put her book away, checked that the cabin was ready for sea, and as an afterthought, she put the kettle on – because she knew the skipper would call for it. That call came as soon as they'd got underway.

It was a peaceful sail out of that little backwater, slowly out into the wider Stangate, then the Medway itself, finally, gently into the Swale, hugging the western shallows as they crept over the ebb.

Finally, the breeze petered out completely, leaving them motionless on a smooth, oily-looking surface with not even a ripple to disturb their reflection. The mate started the diesel while the skipper stowed the sails, and they eased across the tide, towards a mooring off Queenborough.

'You know,' said the mate, looking intently at her skipper, 'I love this place. I've been to many places around our East Coast.' She paused, '... but ... I do wish something was done about the facilities though.'

'Yes, but it costs even more now!' the skipper had snapped. Their love affair with the place had waned of late.

'It's been a grand few days though ... a good break.' The mate had sat looking at her skipper before adding, 'I'll make you a pot of tea, then you'll leave me alone with my book – just for a bit more.'

Later, back aboard their boat, after a pleasant supper ashore, they sat briefly in the cockpit, reflecting on the tranquillity of the past few days. Sighing, as she polished off the last of her coffee, the mate said, fondly, 'Come on you, we've an early start in the morning ...'

'Tomorrow –' the skipper said, yawning, long and loudly, and it seemed, leaving something unsaid.

The mate looked at him, expectantly.

'Oh yes, tomorrow, we're homeward bound ...'

3

Wending Their Way to Pin Mill

The great British writer, J. B. Priestley, in *English Journey*, when nearing the end of his 1930s land voyage around England and wanting to get home, had skipped a host of East Anglian towns, including Ipswich and Colchester. Of Essex, in particular, he said, 'I would not set foot in Essex. Because Essex begins somewhere among backstreets in London's eastern suburbs, some people think it has no mystery, but I know that Essex is a huge mysterious county, with God knows what going on in its remoter valleys.'

'How true that is,' the skipper commented.

Some of the Essex valleys referred to by Priestley were those that ran between the long, hilly fingers that gradually peter out, as the rolling Essex countryside falls away to gentle slopes and ultimately, the flat coastal marshlands. From the hills and valleys, streams flow into freshwater rivers that meander into intertidal salt marsh-fringed creeks and finally the tidal rivers. The geographic locations of some of Priestley's East Anglian towns sit on a tidal fringe and can be approached from the water: their rivers and estuaries indent the lush countryside and all spill into the greater Thames beyond.

Of these rivers, the Stour – in the north and for most of its length the natural border between the counties of Essex and Suffolk, terminating in the natural harbour of Harwich Haven – and the Walton Backwaters could not honestly be counted as waters that fed the Thames Estuary. On the other hand, the River Crouch and its sister the Roach, the Blackwater and Colne did. All are surrounded to a lesser or greater extent by rolling green hills, sometimes distant in their tidal reaches, with acres of marshland between.

Like Priestley, the skipper and the mate would eschew most of Essex on their journey northwards: they were Pin Mill bound, via an overnight anchorage deep in the marshes. After leaving their native sailing grounds, their Essex would largely be a smudge on the distant horizon, until the Tendring Peninsula's high ground near Clacton and further north at Walton-on-the-Naze, were passed by.

Pin Mill sat on the southern bank of the Orwell, or Ipswich River. The river fed the sea up to the port town of Ipswich, deep into Suffolk and sluiced too, for a short distance, along the banks of the River Gipping, the non-tidal waterway beyond the salt-water limit. Ipswich was still a bustling market town, port and friend to the yachtsman. On the other hand, Colchester, on the River Colne, a prosperous port in the time of Priestley's *English Journey*, had been disenfranchised by the town council. Its Hythe, once bustling with maritime life, was nothing more than a conduit of riverside housing. The waterway was choked with silt. Trading craft no longer come and go. No – the skipper and the mate would not be heading that way. They had, though, in the distant past, sailed up to Rowhedge, and since, had recently been up to Wivenhoe, on the tide, for a luncheon stop.

However, they were bound first for Pyfleet, an eerie channel of silt, salt marsh and mud, which encircled the northern posterior of Mersea Island, separating it from the mainland. It was an aspect of Essex the skipper and mate knew well and loved. It is doubtful Priestly knew such marshland jewels existed, unlike Essex's Margery Allingham: this had been her territory. The boat's crew would be in a land known deeply by Barring Gould too, a local cleric, hymn writer and author. It could be paradise. It has a supreme beauty: it was wild and lonely.

They left the River Medway during the mid-morning, running along the edge of the Grain spit: the breeze was a friendly westerly, past the gaunt, weed-infested masts of the *Richard Montgomery*, keeping well outside her ring of yellow, spherical buoys, screaming, it seemed, to those with common sense, but indicating to all, 'Do not stray inside!'

By coffee time (which could have been at any time ...), they'd crossed the main artery of the outer reaches of the London River. There, the coastline, in all directions, turned to a smudge as they frolicked into the Swin with time and tide still on their side.

'You know,' the mate spluttered, nibbling at a chocolate biscuit, crumbs dropping like a shower of snow around her feet, 'wasn't it out here that two of those ships were mentioned on that programme we watched recently?'

'What?' the skipper almost barked, his mind on those sticky chocolate crumbs, that would, if not picked up, be trodden into the cockpit floor. 'Oh yes,' he said nonchalantly, while bending to pick up the last particle and casting it to the fish.

'Well, one was a ship,' the skipper commented, 'the other was a large motor yacht commandeered by the navy to patrol these waters looking out for mines. They got her first – unfortunately. The ship was a German P Clipper, a full-rigged ship. She'd been confiscated from her owners because of her cargo of nitrates – fertiliser,' the skipper murmured, watching two of Prior's ballast barges, direct descendants of the humble spritsail barge, pass by, their black-painted bluff bows shouldering the ebb aside. 'That ship,' he continued, 'stranded on a sandbank and broke her back.'

The estuary was full of wrecks, many dating back to ancient times. The mate's wrecks lay well to the south, close to the main shipping channel. Clearances were taking place in readiness for dredging of the channel up to the site of a dismantled oil refinery at Shell Haven. Arguments had rebounded, back and forth, about the building of the port. Few knew that the haven had been a harbour – for in excess of 500 years. To those arguments, the skipper had always retorted, 'Humbug!'

Later, as they reached the outer River Crouch, off the Whitaker, the tide was still ebbing, a little. The skipper hardened the sheets to work across the sluggish flow towards the Swin Spitway. All around them, yachts converged, from the Wallet and the Colne or Blackwater. It was suddenly busy. The moment in time was, for most sailors, set by the tides, normally at the bottom of the ebb.

'Why the Swin Spitway and not the Wallet Spitway?' the mate chirped!

'Good question!' announced the skipper: he was about to be flippant. 'Well, I suppose if you're starting your passage from the other side – then you'd call it the Wallet Spitway,' he said grinning widely. The mate was none the wiser.

The Spitway was benign that day, but it could be a treacherous piece of water. On spring tides when the low tide heights were near to chart datum, with a high pressure, the swatch could have as little as one to two metres across it, and when windy, care was needed. With their relatively shallow draft, the skipper rarely worried about depths, being used to sailing, at times, in nothing more than a puddle.

Some two hours later, they ghosted with a diminishing breeze towards the eastern point of Mersea Island. The tide had, for a short time, been doing most of the work. They hadn't worried: it had been pleasant enough. Barges and Smacks were seen – motoring out against the young flood. Other yachts, with stowed sails, passed them under power, to disappear towards their intended anchorages or the delights of

The wide open Colne Valley at its seaward end. *Whimbrel* approaches Mersea Stone at the eastern end of Mersea Island. The wreck of the *Lowland* is mid-frame; to the right, the stumpy swim-head barge *Fertile* (traditional lighter-shaped); further right, the school barge *Thalatta* and the Cirdan Trust's *Xylonite* (now sold) sailing out. To the left, the curve of mud running round into Pyfleet Creek can be seen.

Brightlingsea more likely. Looking towards the entrance of the Pyefleet Channel, the skipper said, 'we'll anchor up near the island,' indicating the spot on the chart for good measure. The island, Pewit Island, was named after the pewit. Other islands share the name around the estuary's rivers and creeks and were sometimes spelt, 'Pewet'. All take their name from the lapwing, a wading bird, sometimes called a pewit.

Entering Pyefleet, on a hard reach, they passed an anchored spritsail barge. She was the lithe and sweet-lined *Mirosa*, a barge known to the skipper for some forty years. She'd been berthed, up Lower Halstow Creek, near his own childhood sailing home in Kent. A man on deck lifted an arm, as if in salute, in recognition: they'd met here earlier in the season. 'He's the owner of the *Orinoco*,' the skipper commented, 'berthed at Faversham.' The mate nodded. She knew that.

Clearing the entrance into Pyefleet, they tacked lazily, with their tender turning in the yacht's wake obediently behind them. They sailed from bank to bank, turning in the shallows, in something less than two metres, moving confidently through the permanent moorings, back and forth. Then, past bunches of anchored yachts until, as expected, the numbers thinned out near the marshy island.

'We'll anchor just here,' said the skipper, checking the depth as he spoke. 'On the next tack, I'll stow the main. Bring the boat back, slowly, over the tide – OK?'

The mate merely nodded, as she took the helm: it was standard routine and needed no long, lengthy discussion. As they came round through the breeze, the mainsail fluttered to the deck and was quickly stowed on the boom. The boat swung her way through 180 degrees and the mate let the big genoa feather to just keep steerage way on and make slowly back, over the flood. Meanwhile, the skipper smartly readied their anchor.

The mate called, softly, for they were being observed, 'You ready?' receiving an imperceptibly nod. She let fly the jib sheet. As way had come off the boat, the anchor touched the bottom and as the boat fell back, with the young flood under her, the skipper snubbed the cable a couple of times and paid more out, until satisfied. Looking up, he gazed about with a sense of sublime satisfaction: he, and the mate for that matter, loved this quiet anchorage. His reverie was broken only by the fore hatch lifting and a quiet voice saying, '... kettle's on.' He chivvied himself into action again, smiling with pleasure at the thought of a pot of tea and a hunk of cake. Releasing the jib halyard, the sail was soon gathered in and neatly stowed along the stanchion safety lines.

No sooner had the skipper set the little cockpit table in place and settled back on a cushion, a teapot had appeared through the companion-way. The table was made some years previously. The tea was soon joined by cake! After a glance, the mate came out with a knife, clutching the mugs too.

Drinking his tea, the skipper had watched as another spritsail barge was seen arriving under power, to be followed by a further that had luffed up, reduced sail and under a half gathered mains'l and tops'l had turned into Brightlingsea – 'that'll be the *EDME*,' the skipper had thought, saying nothing, and saying instead, 'There were barges here last month when I came back from the Orwell, alone.' The mate nodded gravely: she didn't like him doing passages alone ...

Some while later, after a shallow doze, the skipper had looked up from his book, fumbled for the bookmark and remembered the last time that he'd been in this anchorage ...

He'd been alone ... well, not entirely: other craft were in the anchorage. The skipper had had a tiring and pretty hectic beat down the Wallet from Harwich Harbour. It had been lumpy against a fresh south-westerly, but the skipper still made excellent time. A reef was needed and prudently, it was dealt with whilst still in the confines of Harwich Harbour. He'd been attending a meet of the East Coast branch of the Royal Naval Sailing Association. The skipper had sailed up from Canvey Island with a different crew, his youngest brother – an able and amiable crew mate. The mate, who'd had other responsibilities, had met them at The Royal Harwich Yacht Club, coming by car.

After a delicious supper, the skipper had set his boat's riding light and settled back in the cockpit with a coffee. It had something nice in it. He felt comfortably replete. Looking up, he gazed at the stars, twinkling above. It brought back memories of other times, far across oceans and distant continents, when he'd done the self same thing: he was hoping that his mate was watching them too.

It was dusk, not quite night, nor dark. From the gloaming, the skipper saw the timeless sight of a bawley coming into anchor. Her sails appeared as if black. Barely a rustle was heard as she sailed by. The sight enthralled him. 'Pity I can't sketch quickly ...' he murmured. But, 'Ah, the memory will live on,' he murmured aloud. So it had. As night had swallowed the day, a golden glow from a distant West Mersea, to the west, and Brightlingsea to the east, lightened the sky with halos. He'd not stayed up, but made his lonely way below ...

The following morning, the skipper awoke early. While waiting for the kettle to boil, the skipper watched the departure of two spritsail barges he'd seen the previous day. Their sails, dark red ochre, looked black against the morning sun. All details of their rigs were undetectable in silhouette. It was iconic – something that touched an East Coaster's heart – it was a proud sight. Then another, which must have fetched up late the previous evening, departed too.

Looking around, enjoying his early cup of coffee, the skipper mused. Then mouthed, 'This environment has always enchanted me.' He grinned thinking of his mate, adding,

... the skipper watched the departure of two spritsail barges ... sails black against the morning sun. Then another ... (Drawn by Gwendoline D. Ardley)

'She loves this too.'

Gazing around, the skipper saw that the creek was marked with fresh withies. He hadn't noticed the previous evening. The withies marked oyster beds and were to be avoided at all costs: expensive damages could result. Those beds had crept down below the island.

Along the mud banks were rows of groynes and catchments that ran up into the saltings. The marsh edges were etched with tide damage. The relatively rapid increase in tidal heights was having a devastating effect. The groynes helped to alleviate the problem by trapping silt, but the marsh had wasted away, reaching the base of the sea wall in places. The wall was faced with square, concrete blocks set in with bitumen. The skipper murmured, 'It wouldn't be long before a retreat inland was likely,' though only to himself. Something about the groynes caught his attention – their ends weren't marked!

To the west, high ground rose above the marsh and sea wall, but closer, on the island, was a hut with the look of its inventor, Nissen. The hut was streaked with rust and guano. The hut and other rusting and rotting remnants, that included an old lighter, had been part of a more productive period of the local trade: oysters. Nissen had been an extraordinary fellow. He was brought up in America. He'd a Norwegian father and after moving to Britain, he joined the Royal Engineers for the duration of the First World War. While with the engineers, he'd invented his hut, shaped to protect troops from shrapnel.

Beyond the island, towards the north, bright red flags were seen fluttering in the breeze. The flags ran for miles round the wall protecting low marshy land out of sight beyond. The colour of the flags was heightened by the sun's rays. In the quiet of that early part of the day, the skipper suddenly heard the unmistakeable crackle of distant gunfire. Infantry, based at Colchester, must have been out on early training. It was a wonder, the skipper absently mused, for there couldn't be many troops left on 'our home shores': so many were abroad fighting for and defending freedoms.

Running his eyes across the landscape, westward, above the shooting gallery, the land was speckled with differing-coloured patches. Deep greens of woodlands, honey-coloured fields of barley or wheat and varying browns of early-tilled ground. This, of course, was the backdrop to Old Hall marshes near Tollesbury.

Closer to the boat, the skipper looked south, beyond the long, straggly, grass-covered sea wall. The land, then still out of sight, sat well below the wall's parapet. The wall had probably been in that position for at least a hundred years, the land beyond forever shrinking, lower and lower. Its outlook was bleak what with the rising tides. A red roof, seen earlier; had undergone a metamorphosis. It was a dwelling: before it could have been any form of building. The dwelling, a bungalow, sat beneath a stand of trees. What, earlier, he'd thought were treetops, a spinney perhaps, became a straggling hedge running up the rising land beyond the spine of the Mersea Island. That spine, to the east, ran out into a shingle point which formed the hard nose of the island. Marsh lay inside the point. It was a place of frequent inundation and a precarious path ran across the tidal vegetation, a sea of colour throughout the year …

Waking from his reverie, the skipper remembered that they often saw vessels, of all types, ashore on that shingle nose. It was a place regularly used for mid-season scrub-offs, picnics and beach BBQs.

'My tea!' the skipper exclaimed.

'Yes, it has remained hot,' the mate said grinning at him: he'd been lost in time!

Later that evening, after a tasty dish of chicken poached in a little wine, onions and herbs, served on a bed of rice with a bowl of vegetables, neither had the urge to stay up late. Divine as the food and surroundings were, it had been a long passage, so after clearing away their supper things, they turned in.

The following day, the boat was laying head to wind, as the skipper and the mate prepared to leave. After setting the mainsail, the slack anchor cable was shortened to 'up and down' and as the mains'l filled on their desired tack, the skipper broke out the anchor and they were away. The anchor was soon aboard and the genoa was set. While the skipper had cleared the cable and sluiced the decks, the mate worked the boat, skilfully between the lines of moored craft feeling keenly the bevy of admirers were gazing her way!

On the south bank of Pyefleet, with the sun shinning on its windows, sat the building of the local Oyster Company. They'd landed there many years before and been told off! There'd been some fairly recent 'argy bargy' over access and now it seemed that the company had had its way. It was loudly marked in huge signs saying 'NO LANDING' – 'they could keep it' thought the skipper.

Clearing the creek, they passed the remains of the schooner *Lowland* marked by its buoy. She'd lain there for a long time, abandoned and then sunk and was now barely visible. Recently, the skipper had heard, a spritsail barge got atop the wreck whilst getting underway. Her anchor became entangled, while sailing clear of the anchorage ('… they'd usually used an engine' was the remark made!), and she had to let it go: efforts to pull the anchor out had driven the windlass pawls, the heavy, solid bars that yachtsmen hear 'clinking and clanking' when a barge weighs anchor, down through her rotten decks. The mate had grinned widely when the skipper had told her: the skipper was always going on about the use of engines by barges …

The skipper remembered too when as boy on the family's barge his father had wanted to get underway. They'd been surrounded by yachts the previous evening … that unmistakable clink clank of the windlass pawls awoke the anchorage in a jiffy. Soon those clinging yachts had scattered as the tops'l was released and sheeted out … a sailing barge needed space. Even now, years later, the skipper could almost hear the yachtsmen's blasphemous remarks!

It always seemed a long way down the outer reach of the River Colne, out to the point, and even longer to the Bar Buoy. The skipper rarely went round the Bar though:

if the tide was up, he cut across close under the shingle point. It saved time. And providing the water was deep enough – why not? Why go two miles south and have to work back again?

Nearing the point, the skipper, with time on his hands, pointed back away, and looked at the mate, 'For a good many years, shingle and gravels were shipped away from that beach. An elevator was built too. It ran from the gravel beds out over the shingle. Barges beached on the shore as the tide receded to be loaded.'

'Interesting!' the mate sniffed, getting on with her steering, then, realising they'd reached the point, said, 'Here you take over, I've done my hour.'

'No,' the skipper retorted, you carry on, until we're round. I'll set the genoa out on the pole – we'll be on a run soon. Should hold it most of the way too.' With that he'd gone forward, while the mate brought their heading eastwards. Then, as the mate had always said, he 'played' with his pole. Once set, an immediate increase in the rustling and chuckling beneath the boat's forefoot was heard.

The varnished pole was the skipper's patent-setting boom made from a length of Sitka spruce and an old boom from his Mirror Dinghy, dating from 1962. The two parts worked in the same fashion as a lowering topmast, with a locking pin. It worked well and had served many years. It was not a toy!

The skipper took the helm as they crossed the bar. There was little disturbance, some weak swirls of the tidal over falls only. The depth had been plentiful. Their course was around the coast, was well clear of the beach, enough, too, to clear the odd buoys that were sprinkled at the outer ends of outfalls, along the way to Walton.

It always struck the mate how strange it was that so many Martello Towers existed along the short stretch of coast between Seawick, Jaywick and Clacton-on-Sea. 'Why?' she asked the skipper.

The skipper thought that it had probably been something to do with the fact that the coastline was greatly different when they'd been built. The shore was a mass of little islands and muddy, marshy inlets or drains. 'Perhaps we should find out,' he muttered to the mate.

'It doesn't really matter, does it?' the mate murmured lightly, thinking, 'I've got him!'

'No, not really ...'

Later, the skipper had found out. The towers and other defences were ordered, by William Pitt, to help fight off an invasion and were finally completed around 1850. Some 105 were built in England. They ran all along the South Coast (with many around the Isle of Wight – then being a naval area, as it still is) up round the Thames Estuary and up into Suffolk. The northernmost was at Aldeburgh, just below Slaughden Quay. This one had made an entry into literature in a story, by Libby Purves, about the local summer sailing fraternity, during the annual school holidays – a fascinating mix of characters and of what they got up to – some sauce too, but a damned good read – especially when sailing. (At the time, it was aboard in the ship's library. It was on the skipper's reading list!)

The towers were built as far away as Southern Ireland where there were twenty-six along the coast either side of Dublin. One of the towers was the setting for the opening chapter of *Ulysses* by James Joyce.

Jaywick, Clacton and its pier, dating from 1871, were soon passed by. Clacton was a late-nineteenth-century resort. Paddle steamers provided the only direct route until the coming of the railway in 1882. Before long, they were abreast of Holland-on-Sea. It was an ancient haven, known as Holland Haven, from the low, hollow land that swept inland from the open sea. The marshy inlet had had problems with a bar; eventually, with little effort, man had completely closed it. Now the haven was nothing more than a name.

'It would make a grand place to anchor in,' the skipper said, wistfully, as they passed by. 'Just think of those extensive marshes, salt marshes, which have been stolen from the sea.' He shook his head. 'Surely, one day, the sea shall have it back,' the skipper quipped: he firmly believed that. Inland, a church sat on a tranquil-looking wooded slope. It overlooked the walled and dried-out environment. How pretty it looked too. 'One day,' thought the skipper, 'my descendents might anchor beneath that church ... but when? ... Centuries? ... No ... sooner, perhaps?' The skipper grinned broadly!

The low ground continued some distance inland. Only a low isthmus that ran out towards the heights of Walton and Frinton had stopped Walton being an island with a passage through to the backwaters beyond. Funny thing geography – a lot of what ifs?!

'We are going into the backwaters, aren't we?' the mate whispered, almost as reverentially as if Faversham had been mentioned ... both were loved.

'Oh yes ... I see no reason not to ... but later ...' the skipper stuttered, still thinking of the swiftly passing coast.

It was a coast devoid of anything other than 'the seaside'. It had been an area for illicit landings of contraband and, with the coming of coastal living, outside the needs of fishing and such enterprises, barges and coastal schooners had beached as the tide ebbed to unload. Harbours were not built, so beaching was the only way to ship in coal and other heavy, bulky needs of the growing communities. It was tough on the vessels, for weather changes often left them exposed to extreme danger on a lee shore. At times, some were lost. Trains then lorries reduced and then removed the need for this trade.

Frinton was a resort developed by Sir Richard Cooper around 1886. It was laid out with select detached houses and had remained much the same ... the snooty part – some say! Walton, on the other hand, was old. It had wharves and mills on its protected inland side. The place was expanded into a resort during Georgian times with development starting with the Marine Parade in 1825. The first pier came in 1830, which was rebuilt and lengthened in 1898.

'Have you seen those pots?' the skipper suddenly remarked, pointing. The mate nodded, then realised that she was looking at a different lot, 'watch out, the tide's setting you across.' Again, the mate nodded — then grinned as she remembered.

In fairly shallow waters, they cleared the outer end of Walton Pier and crept around the crumbling, red sandstone of the Naze headland. Crab pots proliferated. Many were badly marked, if at all, and were a hazard – something best avoided. The skipper always headed slightly to the west of north going across Pennyhole Bay. Its shallower water was not a concern to him. It has less tidal run just after the turn.

The Naze was a headland fighting a battle with the sea. It would, ultimately, lose, of course. 'The Fossil Coast,' the skipper said pointing towards it. A continuous stream had tumbled from the mount over the centuries. In recent times, a new, large, fairly intact fossil had appeared. 'It's being monitored, the skipper said. The Naze Tower, a navigation mark, was built in 1720 to warn shipping away from the west rocks, an area of shallows lying offshore. It was no longer in use, but still provided a fixed point, seen for many miles. Its future was threatened though, by cliff erosion, and a local preservation group had been formed to protect it.

For some while, boats, all sailing, had slowly overhauled them, offering up cheery salutes, as was the custom of the yachting fraternity. Then, others going faster had headed, it seemed, out towards the Stone Banks. The skipper, glancing below at the ship's clock, realised why: they were using their engines – they'd been late, probably, leaving for their passages up ... to catch the tidal gate into Harwich ... or be around the Deben entrance sometime after low water. One could often see late risers butting the tides – plain barmy in the skipper's view – but those modern, light yachts ...

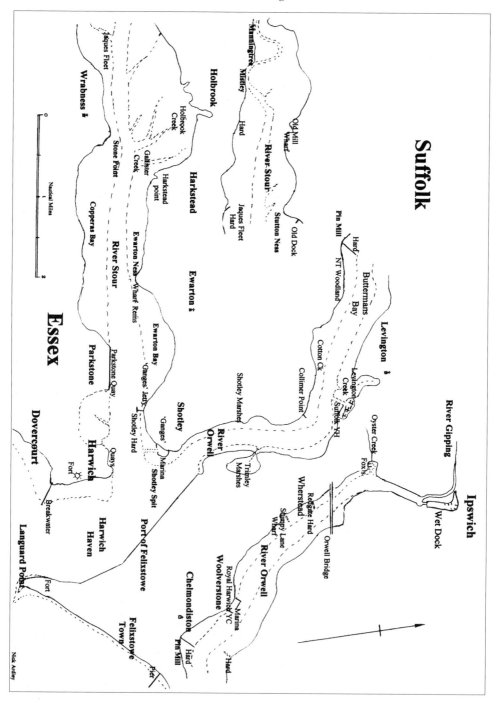

Chartlet of Harwich Haven, River Orwell and River Stour.

slipped so easily through the water.

The Stone Banks was an area of relative shallows with a bottom littered with hard nodules of boulder clay: the nodules were found both ashore and off the coast hereabout in large quantities. It was a geographical feature of the area and the material once supported a local industry.

'Lunch' the mate called, 'then I'll take over for a bit more, later, 'cos you're doing the Harwich entrance.' She was quite emphatic too!

'Okay,' the skipper affirmed, with a nod and a smile too: he knew the mate didn't like to helm into Harwich – but had done – plenty of times. The mate hadn't waited; she disappeared below to raid the ship's food locker, knowing that the skipper would have some argument. 'Good planning,' he mouthed to her bobbing body below.

Passing the 'Pennyhole', a buoy in the middle of nowhere, the skipper was reminded of a tale his grandfather told him. The family had been sailing up this very stretch of coast on a cruise to the backwaters and Pin Mill. The skipper's father insisted (why he hadn't been overruled the skipper never found out!) on cutting across the Pye Sands, on a falling tide, with disastrous results. The family's boat, although of moderate draft for its day, ground to a halt, in sight of the deep-water channel. There they sat, over at an awkward angle, for a few hours ... until the fresh flood lifted them again. His grandfather had laughed – but hadn't back in 1949 – that's for sure! The skipper always used the 'Pennyhole' when heading for the Walton Backwaters – but he never cut across the shallows on a falling tide ...

It wasn't long before the Pye End Buoy hove into sight. The genoa, boomed out since the Colne, had been set free, for the wind had gone to a more southerly, with a little east, perhaps. It had been a fine sail. A fine day too, but with the shift came the heavier wind from the sea. The breeze though, would fall away, and falter even, by the time they reached Pin Mill below her ridge of wooded hills.

In the distance, along the Dovercourt shore, they passed the two old lighthouses that had marked the way in from the sea many years before. The line incidentally wasn't so

The tall spire of Harwich church dominates the town's historic waterfront. Two of the haven's old lighthouses can be seen, to the left-hand side.

far adrift, the skipper saw, from glancing at the chart. Strange as it may have seemed, the lights had attracted a derogatory name, 'misleading lights' – shame. Another pair of lights, also disused, was situated on the edge of Harwich Town. They soon came into view too, as the boat had surged past the Cliff Foot Rocks breakwater.

Dovercourt, strung along the south-facing shore, had not always had a pretty Toyland look: the houses, hotels and guesthouses were painted in a myriad of colours. Once, long ago, a cement industry operated there. The industry used the clay boulders dredged from the sea and others dug from local seams of clay, ashore. The industry's demise was brought about by its success: dredging and digging caused a rise in coastal erosion. 'It's hard to believe it existed,' the skipper commented.

The skipper, prodding the mate and pointing across a stretch of water towards Harwich Town and its quays, said, 'There was barge yard over there ... a long time ago,' he paused. 'It was destroyed by development of the Navy Yard though.' The mate nodded.

'They built many fine craft – some are still sailing today. That old barge in Lower Halstow Dock, the *Edith May* – you know, my old school pal's barge – she's from here, built at Cann's Yard.'

'Oh yes,' the mate said, 'you've written about her in *Salt Marsh and Mud*.' The mate continued, 'Pepys was the Member of Parliament for Harwich and the Pilgrim Fathers departed from here too ... the *Mayflower*'s captain lived in the town.'

The skipper had nodded – the point was made, and he'd left the mate alone to enjoy the panorama.

The port of Harwich, or Harwich Haven, had not always been so named: Strugnell said that 'in 1338 Edward the Third granted a murage to Harwich' and referred to 'the port of Erwell (Orwell)'. It was a time of frequent strife between Harwich and Ipswich. Ipswich had looked upon itself as being of greater importance: passage through the Port of Harwich meant it had to pay dues into Harwich's coffers! Now though, Ipswich was definitely very much the lower relation to the haven ports of Felixstowe, Harwich and Parkstone – now collectively one of the largest, in cargo handling terms, in the United Kingdom.

It was the building of the Great Eastern Railway that turned Harwich into the place it became. Links to Europe had been a grand endowment. Those links to all Britain's North Sea coastal neighbours in our co-joined and peaceful Europe had benefited the country's eastern counties greatly. The town was really Harwich and Dovercourt. Dovercourt was the larger of the two and in historical terms, the senior. Strugnell, interestingly, had said, 'Harwich "a place" and belonging to its "mother" the Manor of Dovercourt' and meant (apparently) 'the enclosed place by the water.' That junior place by the water now ruled the roost.

The Royal Navy had been based in Harwich. The yard was established back in Tudor times and was the centre of 'Old Henry's Navy'. It was further developed around 1660 after a visit by Pepys, who was, at the time, Secretary to the Navy. During the 1700s and 1800s, the shipyard became privately owned under a succession of proprietors, but still built ships for the navy. A wharf known as the Navy Wharf was established in 1962 and is now operated by the Harwich Dock Co. Ltd, who deal with roll-on/roll-off vessels.

The navy later took up residence in Suffolk across the water at Shotley too, where there was a training school. The site was now a marina full of bright, white, plastic sailing and motor yachts, many of which, the skipper was sure, hardly ever moved. The training school was, initially, based on old naval ships, then as ship types changed, it moved ashore to a purpose-built complex. The mate's mother had been a nursing officer at Shotley during the Second World War, but hadn't talked about it much: it having been a torrid time for her, putting men's shattered bodies and limbs back together, following night-time torpedo-boat raids on the enemy coast, far across the North Sea. What ghastly things man had done and continued to do to one another ... it was unspeakable.

Ashore, on the green, in Harwich, was an old Treadmill Crane removed from the navy yard and preserved. It dated from 1667. The old fort, which overlooked the harbour mouth, had been turned into a place to visit too. The whole area has had such a busy military history and occupation. Even over on Languard Point, on the Suffolk shore, stood an ancient fort. All signified the haven's historic importance.

The skipper said, 'Harwich was famous for yachting.' He then talked about kings and princes who, up to the end of the 1930s, came here. 'Charles II and the Duke of York enjoyed sailing jousts against each other – their own participation in the working of the yachts must be in doubt though,' he added, grinning broadly.

'Oh yes ...' the mate murmured.

'The big J Class yachts used to meet here for a regatta too.' Then he muttered, 'I think they ended around 1936 after the dead King's *Britannia* was taken out to sea and scuttled ...' he paused. 'A barbaric act.' The last was said with venom.

'Apart from here, there were regattas on the Clyde, Southend and at Cowes on the South Coast, probably others too, I've heard, like Falmouth and Torquay. It was known as the season.'

In 1845, the Royal Harwich Yacht Club was founded. It had enjoyed royal patronage ever since. In 1946, the club moved out of Essex, up the River Orwell, to Woolverstone. The move was 'forced' by harbour developments. Telling the mate about this, the perennial question came, 'Why?'

'Well,' he said, 'the harbour authorities wanted the ground the club occupied, and more importantly, probably, a gaggle of little one designs racing round the harbour were a danger in an increasingly busy narrow channel.' He added, 'We've seen those boats up near Pin Mill – they're still being used.' He paused, then said, 'This haven is one of the finest and best-protected harbours in our country. That's why it has grown.'

'Good enough!' the mate said, emphatically.

And ...' said the skipper, getting back on his soap box, '... And it was here that the Hanover prince, who became George I, landed with his family after their journey from Saxe Coburg (now part of Germany). He was invited by Parliament to become king. They'd some claim or other.' The Stuart connection ran from Elizabeth, the sister of Charles II, who married into the Hanover family. Quite clear really – they were even part Stuart – families, eh!

'That's right,' the mate quipped. 'It was because Anne hadn't married and hadn't an heir.'

'You can see, well one reason anyway, why the royal families of Europe later ensured a healthy spread!'

Meanwhile, they crossed the harbour entrance, between the nose of Harwich, and Shotley Spit. The spit bisected the rivers Orwell and Stour in the haven and at times both areas became pretty congested.

Shortly after crossing the Stour and running sweetly along the edge of the Orwell, out of the channel, the scenery changed dramatically. It became green. Soon, the last of the mighty box boats (container ships) lined up, loading and unloading, over at Felixstowe, disappeared astern too.

The old dock at Felixstowe, situated directly east of Harwich, had gone. It was being filled in for an extension to the river-fronted wharves at that southern end of the complex. The skipper wondered what the port's founder, Colonel Tomline, would have thought, and too, the last sailing barge mate, on a loaded barge, Dick Durham. Dick had gone in there, dropping sail rapidly: it wasn't until past the heads that sail

An impressive line of container ships dominates the Felixstowe shore berthed at the Trinity Terminal.

could be reduced. Probably both would approve. Dick's barging tales had been told elsewhere. The waterside had always changed, adapted and fitted into the environment and would continue to do so. The port, known as the Trinity Container Terminal, was owned by Trinity College, Oxford. The land was bequeathed to the college by Henry VIII on his death in 1547. Tomline had been a far-sighted and industrious man, setting in motion the grand project.

The skipper grinned. They had the open Orwell before them, a sea of sail, some running in as they were, and others beating down against the tide. 'Ah ...' he said, 'this is wonderful.' He grinned widely ... the mate knew what was coming next. Grinning from ear to ear, he looked across at her, his eyes twinkling.

Her blush, for blush she had, crept, imperceptibly, up her neck and flushed her face deeply. Her face had had that special smile too, a knowing smile, but she mouthed, 'No, no! Don't say it ... I'm not listening!'

The skipper, undaunted, as ever, gesticulated widely and said, 'Ah ... those hills ... those gentle curves ... little roundels ...' they reminded him of the Three Graces. 'They're so delicious. Look!' he exhorted.

'Stop it, stop it,' the mate implored! 'I know you've seen that statue when in Edinburgh ... but ... but ... these are just hills!'

'No imagination...' he guffawed!

Soon, they swept up, into Butterman's Bay, just beyond the entrance into The Suffolk Marina, by Levington. Huge sailing grain carriers had come into this bay to lie at buoys whilst spritsail barges lightened them. Some of the grain was taken away to other milling ports too. At about half load, their displacement probably halved, the ships were towed up into Ipswich. The skipper's old sailing home, the *May Flower,* had done some of this work during her sixty-two years of trading, he'd seen from her cargo books.

At Levington, up a tortuous creek, was the remains of an old farm wharf; even by the 1930s, more or less, it had fallen into disuse. The little port was now clogged and congested with marsh and mud: like elsewhere, the marsh was gradually being obliterated by tidal rise in recent times. Cord grass, although a choking plant, may turn out to be the saviour of such marshes, but in the end, as sea levels rose, unless the marsh was allowed to move inland, it would be killed off, thus removing the natural protection given to the water's edge.

Brooke Farm, the farm of the estate of Brooke Hall, overlooked Levington Creek. The hall was originally the home of Admiral Brooke whose fame came from the capture of the USS *Chesapeake* in 1813, during the naval war between Britain and the fledgling United States of America. It was Britain's revenge: the navy sacked and burnt Washington to the ground. What a laugh! At the farm, for a time from 1935 to the end of that decade, lived Arthur Ransome, until he moved to the Lake District at the beginning of the Second World War. Ransome kept a dinghy down by the creek, near a sluice, which allowed him to get away for a potter or to reach his yacht, the *Nancy Blackett*. From his workshop, he could gaze down across the creek, southwards, down the Orwell and into Harwich Harbour. 'It must have been both an inspiration and distraction,' the skipper thought.

'Ah, the pleasures of arrival in such a picturesque anchorage ...' – it was the time-honoured saying. The skipper gazed as they dreamily approached Pin Mill.

Suddenly, a monstrosity carved needlessly towards them. It was a massive 'Oyster' and it towered above them.

Up the head of Levington Creek, the skipper found an old barge wharf, once an industrious and busy place, until the lorry became king.

'Bloody Hell …' the skipper muttered loudly, pushing their helm over.

It was soon apparent that their manoeuvre was intentional: a voice, very much upper crust, had cut crisply through the air, 'Hi, she looks so cute … and oh, the dinghy too …' from a very, non-sailor-like, scantily clad female.

'Brutes!' the mate muttered, smiling through her teeth and wanting to shake a fist at the yacht as it had gone past.

Coming up to the 'Butt', a red buoy at the eastern end of the moorings below Pin Mill, the skipper quietly said to the mate, 'I'll get the mains'l off, just potter up under jib.'

As he busied himself with the main, he added, 'We'll lose the wind shortly, start the engine and I'll stow the lot.'

The mate silently thought – 'Thank goodness – He's not going to sail onto a mooring this time – I'm tired!'

As the skipper finished tidying the sails away, the mate had spotted a buoy. They were soon at rest. It had been a grand sail. As was the custom, the skipper had busied himself about the decks, while the mate put the kettle on. The skipper, timing it to perfection, heard the comforting whistle as he came aft to tidy the mainsheet away. The cockpit table was soon set. Tea had arrived.

The skipper had had a long love affair with Pin Mill, as had the mate. It could, they'd considered on more than one occasion in recent times, be tidied up a bit. A boatyard was a boatyard, but some of what had developed along the waterfront was far and away beyond that. It was around the 1930s that house barges and old yachts were allowed to congregate under the woods either side of the working hard. The houseboats were now only on the downstream side. The hard was still working: yachts and tenders, with the odd charter barge resting up, still used it. The old barge blocks,

Pin Mill waterfront during the 1980s. Spritsail barges are, left to right, *Venture*, now hulked downstream close under the National Trust woods; *Raybel*, recently seen at Faversham being fitted with a new stem; sailing, the *May*, owned by Tate & Lyle; *Maid of Connaught*, since broken up; and the *Water Lily*, hulked downstream next to the *Venture*.

though, were rotted and broken. Mud had seeped inexorably across the shingle hard, largely from natural silting, 'but nonetheless, greater natural usage would have helped keep it clear,' the skipper muttered.

The skipper, when ever possible, went off for a sail in the tender. The present visit was not any different and he spent an hour looking at the numerous pretty traditional yachts: this area had these in abundance – since the beginning of modern yachting, back to the time of Maurice Griffiths, Arthur Ransome and others. All had done as the skipper had done, that is, 'messed about in boats.'

The old spritsail barge homes, and old yachts, which proliferated along the wooded banks, had all gone. Two barge hulks sat in their last berths. One, the *Golden Fleece*, had many years before gone in under the trees, aslant to the shore. Her bow and stern were largely intact, as were her decks, topped by an abandoned deck-house. Her slab sides had disappeared. Her decks were held up by a series of 'pit-props'. Another, the *King*, had rapidly deteriorated and was, the skipper saw, being broken up: her berth was a valuable and sought-after property. Others were no more than scattered, disjointed timbers.

Many of the large yachts of the early 1900s ended their days along the shore beneath the trees. But some were dug out and refloated: riches had returned to yachting. Men and women had found it in their hearts to rebuild them. Grand stuff!

The barges and yachts had been replaced by an eclectic mix of rusting lighters, tore-outs and other monstrosities. Though, some of the vessels, it must be said, but only a few, were kept in a good condition. Pride could be seen in some retired, Dutch-type, inland-waterways motor barges. Whether any of them were capable of moving under their own power, was open for debate. The skipper's opinion was well known: a vessel used was better maintained – in general. On the whole, he'd said to the mate, 'it's a mess.'

One pretty house barge sat against a jetty built over the hull of an old spritsail barge. The barge was the *Jess*, of Maldon, built in 1899. She was cut down in Harwich Harbour during the 1930s, when still a relatively young barge. Her bow was shattered, but her forward bulkhead had held and she stayed afloat. Repairs were eventually shelved and a Sea Scout group used her as a store for a while. Now she rested quietly beneath the walkway. The skipper sailed his dinghy over for a look. Her transom was still intact. The carving of her name and port of registry could be clearly seen. The barge was built with a small, flat 'V' transom with little tuck to the bottom. The bottom planks ran up into a rebate in the stern frame, fixed as sweetly as the day they'd been fitted.

A group of barge hulks sat on the mud flats, towards the far end of the woods, near an ancient shingle hard, where in the summer, boats collected for bottom cleaning and a weekend of open-air fireside cooking – all from a boat club up river; something they'd done for years. The skipper had often seen them. The old barges were the *Waterlily*, *Venture* and the *Mousme*. The last had only recently been dumped alongside the other two. Close by, an old fishing trawler sat lusted over, rotting away. The *Venture* had collided with the skipper's sailing home *May Flower* during the 1964 Southend Barge Match, causing huge damage to his home. That story had been told in the story of his childhood afloat.

The previous year, they'd enjoyed the powerful sight of a fleet of spritsail barges, jostling around the start-line before rushing away down-river. Later, they'd returned in a line, mostly, except for a few close tussles. It was always a sight to savour. Steam tugs and other old vessels always met here at the same time, a vibrant, colourful, floating carnival of vintage craft. It was wonderful.

After dining aboard, they went ashore. There they first walked a little, to allow the Pin Mill feeling to seep further into their pores. Afterwards, a visit to the friendly Butt

The steel spritsail barge *Melissa* shortly after her re-launch following a rebuild at Webb's yard (2004-2008). The barge looked resplendent with her lofty sprit rig, when seen during 2009.

and Oyster was made and the skipper enjoyed a pint or two, of local Adnams, the mate a Suffolk cider. The pub was beloved by all East Coast yachtsmen as it had been for a century.

The hard at Pin Mill was still home to a couple of spritsail barges, so the aura of the place had not completely evaporated: it was these elements that attracted sailors. The little *Cygnet* often rested there, between its wide-ranging voyages around the barge country. The rebuilt *Melissa*, a fine-looking steel barge, relaunched a year or two back, was re-rigging. She'd been hauled from the water by Ward's Yard a few years before on a huge trolley and had since been virtually reconstructed. 'Be nice to see her sailing,' the skipper said. The following year, the skipper saw her sail in the Pin Mill match, after only a very short trial, and win – to the consternation of the barge world!

Ashore, the quaint, rustic beauty and tranquillity, although still very much evident, had charmed the skipper and mate less over the years. The place had become more populated, especially with day-trippers. But were they themselves, not trippers? It never seemed to be quiet.

The walk up to the village though had a charm not found at other anchorages they'd been to: the voyage crossed so many boundaries. First, you had to get ashore, by dinghy, then a wade through the shallows on the hard, moor the dinghy far enough out depending upon the tides, and so onto dry land. That climb to dry land, at first, crossed the intertidal zone up an incline. It led, on the left, to the Butt and Oyster; to the right, boatyards, waterfront homes and the Pin Mill Sailing Club, and beyond, a woodland path ran to Woolverstone.

After leaving the deep, waterfront belt, ahead was an immediate sense of country. Prettily painted cottages, a delight to the eye, sat jumbled and intermixed. One, Alma

Cottage, was famed. It was immortalised by Arthur Ransome in, *We Didn't Mean to Go to Sea*. Further up the lane, banks covered in perfumed flowers ran down a valley side: gardens lovingly tended, and 'oh the smell of sweet grass after a time afloat'. Here, some of the cottages were set well back from the road. In places, too, at the height of summer, the hedgerow had a few brambles with clusters of ripe berries that would set the skipper salivating. He'd often plucked a few, enjoying flavours first found in childhood. It was, and had remained, idyllic, strangely weird even: the water, on every occasion the path up to the village of Chelmondiston was trodden, seemed so far away. A world away, once left behind. This apparent remoteness was Pin Mill's allure – a magnet.

The north side of the Orwell was laid to woodland and wooded parkland. Estates for the wealthy landed gentry and such ran from Levington up to the Orwell Bridge, below Ipswich. Some of the woodland was planted, originally, to be a future wood supply for the navy, but iron and then steel came before their need arose. The trees had been planted during the age of species discovery; many were native to continents many thousands of miles off. It made a picturesque backdrop to the river. It was one of the river's charms. 'Though …' the skipper commented to the mate, while supping a pint of ale in the Butt, '… the one thing that peeves me a little about this river is the huge number of moorings that clog the edges between the mud line and the buoyed channel.' He paused, 'Yes, people have a right to moorings, but I think it's gone over the top.'

The mate, nodding, grinned: this was manna from heaven, the skipper not liking this river just a tiny bit, and she said, 'That's why I love the Swale and the Medway …'

The skipper looked across the table, with its empty glasses, slopped ale, and soggy mats and scratched his chin … slowly, 'Yes … I know,' he replied thoughtfully. As much as they both loved this world, their hearts lay elsewhere. 'We'll be dropping into Faversham, the Swale and the Medway on the way home. And London too – don't forget!' he added. They'd a busy schedule.

Later, back aboard their little yacht, the skipper and mate sat out in the cockpit, for it remained dry and it was comfortable too. Some cheese and crackers accompanied their coffee, which the mate sweetened slightly, before adding a little something.

They sat and nattered about the day, the pleasant sail up from Pyefleet, and what they planned for the morrow. As it got dark, the skipper lit the cabin lamps. The glow of their orange-yellow flames glinted around the varnish work and seeped out into the cockpit, illuminating the floorboards, the cream paint glowing slightly. The breeze of earlier had died away too. The river's surface had an oily look as the sluggish tide flowed past them. The remaining light from the sinking sun glistened and heightened the reflections cast from the wooded slopes around the moorings.

'More coffee?' the mate asked, gathering up their mugs without waiting or expecting an answer. Settling back soon after, the mate sighed deeply – she was at peace. The skipper grinned at her, unseen in the evening's gathering gloom.

As the sun dipped, a crescent moon appeared. It glittered sparkly bright. The sun too became momentarily brighter as the cut-off approached. Its rays glistened across the rippling tide with colours of rose pink to yellow. The colours traversed the river's length, from beneath the elegant and graceful curve of the high-level road bridge, which spanned the opposite curve of the hills and river beneath it. Both found it fascinating to watch. Then the sun was gone.

Gently the panorama of colour changed, imperceptibly at first, but change it did, to a darker hue. Ultimately, the sky above became a deep blue, developing to an almost white above the horizon, which still had tinges of the sun's presence. The river changed to liquid gold during that time, changing to bronze and finally to copper,

The last Gipping Barge, the *Yare*, cocooned in her marsh mooring.

dulling with time, until it seemed to burn out.

Meanwhile, stars and planets had come out, one by one. Bright specks, hundreds, ... no thousands ... no more, twinkled and dazzled, with colours that had a tinge of blue, of deep orange and yellow. The soft, undulating tops of the Suffolk hills, clad in their trees, of a myriad of greens by day, had turned jet black.

The river was silent, except for the calls from a mixture of birds: it was neither land nor water. Calls of waders interspersed with the harsh bark of blackbirds. From beneath the canopied woods, a woodpecker called and then its tattoo beat rattled audibly across the mud flats. Moments later, a gentle hoo hoo hooo from a tawny owl, then another, floated across the dark water. As a backdrop, the soporific gurgling from the Grindle, the freshwater stream that ran down beside the hard, maintained an underlying rhythm as it met the saline river near bottom of the ebb.

With darkness came a sprinkling of lights. Their reflections danced across the river's surface, a surface that had a motion: long, rolling undulations, from the forces of the ebb. From the public house, they'd so recently departed, enjoying its bonhomie and good ale, lights poured forth across the mud flats, glistening and shining on a surface left wet by the falling tide.

It was a little mesmerising and the skipper let his coffee go cold.

'Another?' was the almost silent question.

'Why not, why not, indeed?' it was one of those nights.

The next day, they rose late, breakfasting in the cockpit, completing their ablutions afterwards. They'd decided to stay put and head up to Ipswich on the morrow.

During the morning, they walked up to the village of Chelmondiston, above Pin Mill, for stores. The village, known as 'Chelmo' to the locals, sat above Pin Mill, separate and aloof from its watery neighbour down the hill. It had, the skipper and mate knew, a fine store where fresh local produce could be acquired. It was a gem and both had, for a number of years, enjoyed its fare. Bread and bacon were their only needs though. They would restore at Ipswich. A walk through the ancient woodland owned by the National Trust, past the floating homes kept them busy for an hour too.

The wooded walk through to Woolverstone had been enjoyed during a previous visit when they walked through from The Royal Harwich Yacht Club to the 'Butt' for a jar. Along the shore was an old vessel, seemingly cocooned in the marshes: it had no natural passage to the river. The vessel, the *Yare*, was a Gipping Barge. She was built in 1891, by Orvis, at the St Clements yard in Ipswich. Gipping barges operated on the River Gipping (The Stowmarket Navigation) far inland up to flour mills and such. They'd even gone down to Harwich, and probably up the Stour too. The River Gipping, the river above Ipswich, was dredged and canalised. Work began, in earnest, in 1790. The proposal had initially hit the streets in 1719 – who says we're slow now? The navigation flourished for many decades, but the coming of the railway created a decline, even though the railway was bound, by 'an act passed in 1846' says Kearney, a navigation historian, to keep the navigation fit for use. By 1900, it ceased to be operative. The last vessels using its lower reaches had stopped by around 1920. It was the final blow. It fell into disuse, the battle with the railway lost. Now though, the skipper had heard, it was undergoing a renaissance: a faithful band of volunteers were bringing it, section by section, back into a useable state. The Gipping barges had been reduced to a fleet of one floating example. 'It should be preserved,' the skipper said during their walk ashore that day. 'The poor, old thing isn't going to last for ever,' he added, 'and her owner is well on in years.'

That evening, it was a unanimous decision; they dined ashore. The skipper would have to look out for the dinghy though: the tides were ebbing in the evening. The meal ashore, at the Butt, was rather pleasant and the ale, as always, fresh from a barrel tap, was 'lip smacking' too. The barrels rested on a trestle table, rustically, behind the bar. The mate enjoyed rather too much Suffolk cider … !

Later, on their return, the mate waited for the skipper to pull their dinghy down the

… splash! The skipper had stumbled … landing flat on his back …
(Drawn by Gwendoline D. Ardley)

Grindle. Once in the Gindle, the stream built up behind a dinghy and helped propel it seawards!

She had a happy feeling and the mate giggled, with a little mirth, 'Ah,' she said, pausing.

'What?' the skipper asked, with a knowing hint.

'... err ... do you remember ...' she giggled, '... when I batted you with a muddy oar ...' it happened many years before, at the time the mate had found she was pregnant with their son.

And yes, of course the skipper had remembered!

Then there was a loud ... splash! The skipper had stumbled over the edge of the hard; landing flat on his back in the muddy Grindle.

'I'd started to step down ... was using the wrong leg,' he later told people.

'That's a likely tale' was all he'd got in response!

When relating the event to family, the mate had giggled, almost uncontrollably, 'It was the funniest thing I've ever seen ... it was hilarious.' Her giggles then erupted into laughter. 'He's never, in my memory, fallen in the mud. There he was, on his back,' pausing, because she found it difficult to control herself, '... his arms and legs outstretched, waggling, as if a tortoise turned on its shell. Before he'd time to move, the stream rose quickly round him and muddy water washed over his head. And ...' she said, laughing more, '... the whole episode was photographed by a chap on a boat lying close into the tide edge ...' at this, it was always too much: she'd burst into a further fit of laughter, before adding, 'Sadly, we were never sent a picture though.'

The skipper had winced.

'But,' she said, more seriously, 'it took several very soapy washes to get the clothes clean the next day – even after several rinses.'

'Right, let's leave it right there ...' the skipper said firmly, still remembering, all too clearly, not only the humiliation, but the smell of dead marine life infesting the black mud in a stream that was neither fresh nor salt.

With a twinkle in her eyes, the mate continued to laugh ... uncontrollably!

'Thanks ... !' was the skipper's thought.

4
Gently around Suffolk

After leaving Pin Mill, the skipper and mate had sailed up the Orwell, to Ipswich. Well not quite: they liked the quiet backwater of Fox's Marina. They did not dawdle on the way up, and nearing the Orwell Bridge, their sails were stowed. Engine power had rustled them into the little harbour.

The marina sat inside the sweet but oddly named Ostrich Creek where the tideway was soon barred by Bourne Bridge and a flood-control dam – keeping the sea from the freshwater stream beyond. The creek, then the haunt of fishermen, was used during the 1920s by that inimitable sailor and teller of coastal tales, Maurice Griffiths. It was then the home of barge traffic too – the old wharf has long gone. Across from the marina, alongside a natural hard is the ancient Orwell Yacht Club. It was now squeezed mightily by the pontoons of the marina and the massive yachts being fitted out by Oyster Yachts, builders of large, fine vessels for the well-healed.

Domestic chores filled the first day. The laundry bag had overflowed and there'd been the skipper's muddy clothing from his dunking down stream. The skipper refuelled too and carried out a little titivating around the varnish work – clear of the washing that soon flapped colourfully from lines rigged around the shrouds. From

The quaint and homely waterfront at the Orwell Yacht Club.

ashore, their little yacht had a distinct domestic aura. It looked rather incongruous and out of place berthed amidst a number of super yachts being fitted out by Oyster, their builders. The little boat, though, collected more than a few fine comments. The mate apologised, more than once too about the draperies, and was heard telling one man, 'We've been away from a washing machine for nearly a week ... has to be done ...'

He grinned, 'No, don't worry about that ... at least you're out ... lucky to get a berth with so few away,' as he waved his arm around the marina. He was the harbour master.

'She's a lovely boat ... is she a Dauntless?' another tentatively asked, shortly afterwards.

The skipper heard the mate's gasp. He'd almost choked too, varnish brush in hand, from his position out of sight behind their bedding draped over the boom airing in the warm sunshine. There was a pause, and then the mate had succinctly and firmly said, 'NO! She's a Finesse 24,' leaving no doubt to the listener of her knowledge.

The man had wandered off ... scratching his head, awkwardly!

The next day, they went into the town, catching a bus that wound its way along the narrow hedge-lined roads from Shotley, past Pin Mill's mother village of 'Chelmo' before reaching them at Bourne Bridge, the rural edge. It led through early-1900s housing, before reaching an area that had been cleared and rebuilt with modern flats. Along the river frontage, redundant port land was being developed too. None of what

From the shore, the little yacht had a distinct domestic aura.
(Drawn by Gwendoline D. Ardley)

they saw would have been seen from the water. It gave the place realism. It was not a museum – things had to change – as it had over the centuries: archaeological digs around Ipswich, where redevelopment had taken place, showed the extent of land reclamation. Centuries-old wharf fronts had been found a couple of streets back from the 1840s dock walls.

Later, over a coffee and a lunchtime sandwich – sitting outside – European fashion (the town had a continental feel), they talked ...

Ipswich was a very historic town. There was too much to see and they'd but only dipped into little bits on each visit. 'Several books would struggle to do it justice' both agreed: by the time they departed, too much had been seen, too many places of interest were visited and there was far too much to remember (or bore the reader with).

Sometime before that visit, the skipper, with their son as crew, berthed in the Wet Dock, close to the town. The dock was originally built in 1842 – though some say it was the first year of Victoria's reign, in 1837. The dock was the largest wet dock for many years and was a centre of the wheat trade, amongst many other commodities. The wet dock now housed several marinas and a yard offering repairs to both large and small vessels. Spritsail barges too had made it their home: the authorities were in touch with that community's needs. Alongside the dock, redundant buildings, granaries and the Old Custom House, opened in 1845, had been converted to a mix of flats and leisure facilities. On the whole, this transformation had preserved their outward appearance. The boy and the skipper found the 'town' marina too noisy though from late night revelries!

'It's all in all a pleasing aspect though,' the skipper commented, as they continued to sit, lazing over lunch.

The gate of Cardinal Wolsey's (Woolsey) college (College of St Mary) near the old end of Ipswich Docks. The buildings are derelict and await refurbishment.

Ipswich had had a maritime past as far back as Saxon times, probably the Romans too. The Danes used the River Gipping in 860 and settled, building a base at Rattlesden (Rattles-dane). For the period 650-850, Ipswich was described by Wade, a Suffolk archaeologist, as the 'largest known early trading centre in north-west Europe'. Stone for the cathedral at Bury Saint Edmunds, dating from 1065, was transported by barge from ships in the Orwell. The stone came from Caen, in France. By the 1500s, Ipswich became a King's Port and with its control of the River Orwell, given by a royal charter of 1199 by King John, it continued to grow, becoming a major shipbuilding port too.

Silting, that dreaded East Coast scourge, loomed. A dire need to dredge by the 1700s set in a decline: ships could no longer reach the town's quays. Shipbuilding declined too. Simper said, 'the last full-rigged ship was launched in 1855,' but a 'brigantine was built as late as 1885'. By the end, yards concentrated on spritsail barge building.

The opening of the wet dock and dredging of the riverbed created an impetus for a rebirth, but in the modern age, that too finally ended as ships again outgrew the facilities. Now shipping was limited to a few wharves out in the river. Harwich Haven had finally won! 'Though,' as the skipper was oft heard to say, '... still seems to be a busy river when we're sailing upon its waters ...'

Some years previously, the skipper and mate had sailed on a barge, the *Centaur*, owned by the Thames Sailing Barge Trust, from the wet dock. With a group from their yacht club, they enjoyed an interesting weekend sailing out of Harwich, down the Wallet and back into the Walton Backwaters for the night. For the skipper, it was his first sail on a barge for nigh on thirty years. That short trip brought back a

The Ancient House in Ipswich preserved and still in use after some 600 years.

flood of memories that culminated in a book about his childhood, living aboard the *May Flower*. For another old sea salt, one of the yacht club's oldest active sailors, a favoured old-timer, perhaps, had had a boyhood longing fulfilled too: he'd helmed a spritsail barge. He'd gazed upon these magnificent craft in his youth, along the London River, but had never boarded one ... Ah!

Defoe and Priestley visited Ipswich, as had Dickens and his band of fictional friends in *Pickwick Papers*: Dickens, it was said, modelled some of the characters found in *Pickwick Papers* on people met during his stay. Wool Merchants from all over Europe and beyond knew the town, during an earlier time too, for it was the very centre of that trade ...

'Come on ...' the mate said, '... we should move on.'

'I'm fit,' the skipper said, jumping up.

Refreshed, they continued their walk, initially concentrating on the town. In any town, it was above the shop fronts that the history of a place came alive, and Ipswich was a town full of the opulence of bygone era. New resources were being spent on redevelopment too, they noticed. One old building, in particular, near the Buttermarket area had stood out. It had a frieze, a series of plaster mouldings (pargeting), of the world's continents. Something struck them both: looking along the panels, Australia, New Zealand and Antarctica were missing. The building known as the Ancient House was still in use as a store. Pointing to it, the mate said, 'That's what keeps buildings alive.'

'Old and new intermingling,' the skipper added, nodding too, for he agreed, wholeheartedly.

Much later, tired and footsore, after finally traipsing around the Christchurch Museum, a building that was itself a museum piece, dating originally from the 1500s but improved and rebuilt later by a rich merchant family, the skipper said, 'Let's stop awhile. We need a rest,' he smiled thinly. The mate recognised the look and immediately acquiesced.

'It's all too much,' the skipper thought ... as he sipped a cup of tea, luxuriating in its refreshing zing. They were sat outside a pleasant tearoom down a narrow alley of timber buildings that leaned towards one another, creating a shade from the sun. The tea had quickly done its work: the skipper immediately felt invigorated and ready to carry their stores, which were about to be purchased ...

That evening, succulent local Suffolk pork sausages, served on a bed of pasta and tomato sauce, washed down with a glass or two of red wine provided their sustenance. 'That was rather delicious,' the mate murmured. The sausages and some fine cheeses were found in a very narrow alley of shops, near where they'd had tea. The cheese was sampled later: the skipper was then replete.

Later, a table outside the pleasant marina club, bathed by a pleasant evening sun was their reward. It had been a busy day and, what with all the walking and lugging back of fresh provisions, tiring too. Both felt contented. The mate had settled with her current novel, the skipper, browsed, with an absent mind, through a magazine but was soon looking around – soon wandering off looking at boats.

Returning, he sat down. 'Nelson,' the skipper suddenly said, the mate's head was buried in her book – she hadn't stirred. Undaunted, he repeated, 'Nelson ...' the mate's head moved, imperceptibly, but enough, 'Nelson was High Steward of Ipswich when that musket ball got him.'

'That's two hundred years ago,' she said, hardly lifting her eyes from her novel, 'so, what's it got to do with today ...'

'Just an aside,' the skipper grinned. 'Thought you'd like to know! Oh, I'm fetching another Adnams. Do you want anything else?'

'No,' she paused. 'We've an early start, you said earlier ... Oh, go on then ... cider please.'

Redgate Hard at Wherstead. Freston Folly is to the left surrounded by woodland.

The old dock below Cotton Creek.

A prompt start to take the ebb out into the North Sea and round past Felixstowe to the Deben meant breakfast underway. Once clear, the mate started by passing out a coffee, the skipper's second ... The wind, from the west, was a pleasant force four. It looked good for an easy passage. Warm sunshine enveloped the boat too as they ran down the river with the genoa pulling nicely. The mate, an admirable health and safety person, had already dispensed sunblock – routine stuff!

With the easy sailing, the skipper had time to look about as grilled Suffolk cured bacon wafted from the hatch, itching at his taste buds. Passing a buoy off Freston, he looked southwards to Red Gate Hard – commemorated by that buoy in the fairway – there, a small craft club was based. It looked very much like his own club's set up ... some old boys were already busy drifting around the waterfront ... getting set for the day's activities ... mainly based around their teapot? The hard previously served farms around Wherstead, a name corrupted from Anglo-Saxon 'Wharf Stead', an Anglo-Saxon wharf, according to the historian Skeat. Above the river here, up on the hill, below Freston church, sat a tower – a folly. It was now owned by a trust and was used for holiday accommodation – a folly no longer!

The skipper grinned as a plate with crusty rolls and that glorious bacon tucked inside was thrust into his hand. He beamed at the mate, 'you're wonderful.' They both quietly set to, munching their way down river.

Chewing on his bacon, the skipper said, spitting bread crumbs as he did so, 'There's supposed to be a tree near here ...' pointing to the Woolverstone shore and the 'Harwich' club, '... a local lady, Margaret Catchpole, was reputed to have had many a rendezvous with her smuggler lover.' Crumbs continued to scatter.

'Now if ...' the mate stopped, then said, 'weren't the pair of them transported?'

'Yes, I believe so!'

Later, as the mate had finished the domestic chores below, the skipper asked, 'Do you want to take over?'

'No. I'll just look around. You carry on.' It wasn't until much later, after rounding Languard Point, for the outside passage that she took over. The skipper was left quietly to his own thoughts, apart from keeping a look out and helming safely, and had not disturbed his mate – unnecessarily – remarkable!

On the Orwell, unlike the rivers in Kent and Essex, old, ramshackle barge wharves were sparse and there were virtually no wide expanses of marshland indented with deep, winding creeks. The huge acreage of private riverbank had prevented ad hoc building, perhaps. 'It had a Toyland quality ... a river in miniature, compressed between its green parks and wooded slopes, a child's toy land?' the skipper reflected.

Below Pin Mill, opposite Levington, there used to be a brickworks located near the thin, marshy edge of the river. The works had a wharf, last used around 1934 (says Simper) and around 1960 an attempt was made to build a marina here. The dock was still in evidence near Cotton Creek. The marina plans were quickly stifled by local opposition! Opposition, from incomers, had killed, in recent times, barge repair facilities at Pin Mill. The barges had gone elsewhere: the old blocks had disintegrated from neglect, decreasing any reason to come and the hard was disappearing under silt too – through a lack of use and other reasons.

Within a small area of marsh along the east bank of the river, below Collimer Point, a small creek ran into a landing. A few dinghies were moored off its entrance. Here, the hinterland needed the protection of a sea wall, unlike the greater part of the upper reaches of the river. The marshy inlet, Crane's Creek, was once the base for an Essex oyster fishery. Simper had said, 'The oyster beds were between Collimer Point and Shotley, but the Roach Company gave up in about 1920 after imported spat brought in limpets which killed the oysters.' It's something that had happened in many other places too – though some had survived to continue the trade. The rusting bottom of

Languard Fort topped with later Second World War buildings.

the oyster company's guard vessel sat on the shore nearby. Progressive and more recent rapid erosion of the saltings had destroyed many of the old oyster storage pits along the marsh. Recently, the skipper had found some old pits along the River Crouch. One pit still had its wooden sluice in place – 'with rising sea levels, how long would they last?' the skipper had mused at the time. For the Orwell, the problem of salt marsh denudation appeared to the skipper to be rather acute – there wasn't much anyway.

On the opposite shore, oyster works had existed in the marshes at Trimley. Those grounds had disappeared beneath the expanding port of Felixstowe though. But, as a foil, by legislation, an area of reclaimed farmland had been flooded and a fresh new habitat had been created, between Levington and the port. The new environment had become a great attraction to coastal birds. Salt was another industry. It was known to have operated from Roman times and the remnants, red hills – ash piles – created from the residue, were still visible. Red hills are common around the skipper's coast. Many have been ploughed in, on reclaimed land, and others lost to erosion. It was surprising how far inland some of the hills were – a sign that the wetter saline coast ran further inland.

Off Collimer Point, the skipper had to haul his sheets a little, as they came round onto a broad reach. It was held down to the entrance, where they ran east past Languard Point, gybing northwards, for the Deben.

The mate took over along the coast. Gazing behind, she said, 'None of those yachts followed us!' It was midweek so the waters were only sparsely sprinkled. Out in the open, they fairly skipped along. There was a low, soft sort of swell with occasional crests, and the boat curtsied from time to time as it had surged through them, throwing out a curvaceous wash trimmed with lacy froth. It was grand sailing and the skipper was extremely jealous ... of his mate's glorious trick at the helm.

Languard Point with its old fort was soon left far behind. The fort, on the end of the long shingle spit, was instituted by Henry VIII. It remained in constant use up

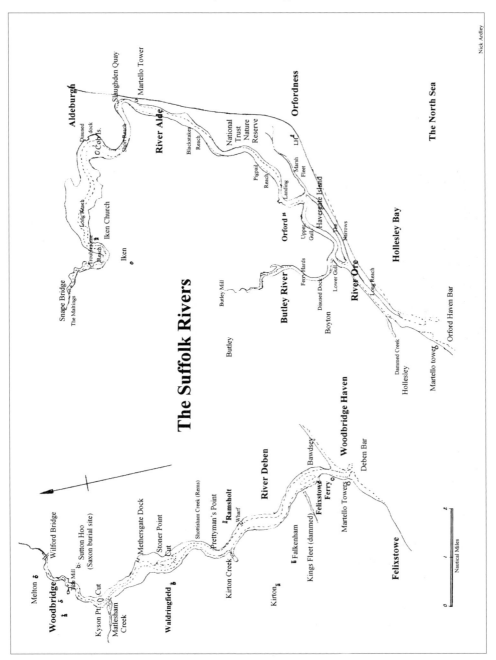

Chartlet of the Deben, Ore and Alde in Suffolk.

until the end of the Second World War. Now it was a museum. The fort has a claim to fame – it was captured, briefly, during the Anglo-Dutch wars of the 1660s. The raid was repelled. The war was about trade and its control rather than acquisition. The Dutch, though, gave up New York for a spice island in Indonesia at the cessation of those hostilities. The two countries have had a close association ever since. The skipper had just read a magnificent book by Giles Milton, *Nathaniel's Nutmeg*. It was an interesting account of exotic, far-away Spice Islands. The Dutch gaining of the island was probably the better choice, for within a hundred years, the New England colonies in North America had broken away from Britain. Who knows what influence a continued Dutch presence would have had? The historian Strugnell says that the name 'Languard' came from the Anglo-Saxon, 'a piece of land shaped like a spear'. It was apt. A lighthouse was established as far back as around 1666 too, indicating the great importance of the harbour within.

The Deben bar buoy was soon seen, away to starboard, but still some way off. It was near low water so the skipper rechecked the tides and a sketch chartlet of the entrance. He looked at the mate and smiled, 'Coffee?' he asked. 'I'll take over in a short while,' then he quickly disappeared below to put the kettle on. He knew the mate had had a long love-hate relationship with that bar … leaving her to get on with it a little longer would dampen her thoughts … Coming back on deck, clutching two coffee mugs, the skipper planted a peck on his mate's cheek saying, 'That's grand. I'll take over, shall I?' She relinquished the tiller.

Looking aloft, at the fluttering burgee, the skipper came round harder on the westerly breeze, hauling the main sheet in tighter. The mate wound the genoa in too, as they surged past the outer Knoll Buoy. It seemed dead water, though, as always, spume was being thrown up around the mounds of shingle that appeared as if from nowhere, metamorphosing from the golden-brown shingle backdrop that faded into the distance towards the next river beyond with its trickier bar.

As the tide reached its point of turn, its huge body gained an agitated look. That agitation, especially if a turn was made against the wind, was often spectacular. It could even be so on a quiet offshore wind day, like they were experiencing, but it was quiet. During strong onshore winds, it was a place to avoid! Many years ago, they saw a large yacht being picked up and dropped bodily onto that shingle. It was a horrible and thought-provoking sight. The mate, in particular, has never forgotten it: the yacht, from Holland, had children aboard. It later got off, fortunately, relatively unscathed, the skipper believed.

'Keep an eye on that buoy behind; tell me if it appears to drift off our track,' the skipper said. He had a surreptitious look too, but once clear of the coastal run, he was happy: the current, then on the flood, ran relatively true within the confines of the shingle. Wariness was the key! The suck and heave of the sea over the shallows was clearly audible; the grinding and grating of stone on stone as they clattered across one another, even though it was relatively quiet, drifted to their ears. The mate said nothing, impassively holding her thoughts within. The skipper was, as always, fascinated by nature's power, a power controlled by an invisible force.

Their shallow draft allowed them to go in shortly after low water, 'And …' the skipper said, '… at least we can see the shingle and enjoy its protection too.' Rounding the inner bar buoy, the skipper eased the sheets and sailed northwards, as if along the coast. The breeze had taken off too. A dry heat wafted off the land. It was like passing through an invisible wall. It suddenly felt a different world, after the coolness of their coastal passage.

In silence, they sailed up a valley of twice-daily-tide-washed shingle. Ahead, with just a whiff of an opening, lay the main river. The boat's momentum hardly caused a rustle at its forefoot, surging forward on the fresh flood with just enough steerage.

People moved about along the western bank, their footfalls audible in the quiet as they scrunched, waded even, through deep shingle. On the eastern shore, the Bawdsey side, others, they soon saw, lay soaking up the sun's warmth: it was holiday time. People loafed. Women and girls in swishing summer frocks, or not a lot at all, gazed at the skipper and mate as they passed by. Above the eastern banks was a low, wooded cliff upon which sat an old, red-brick, manor house.

'They'll have gone across on the ferry,' the skipper said, referring to the people. 'They'll have the full benefit of the sun too.'

A little later, they passed the ferry, leaving the Felixstowe shore, filled with more happy holidaymakers, giggling, laughing, chattering and pointing around. A feeling of great relief at being inside the bar enveloped the mate: she grinned, just a little, feeling more herself. Looking at the skipper, she pointed to the red building, 'That old manor was used by the government, wasn't it?'

'Err, yes' the skipper murmured, 'there's something in the pilot book about it – or was,' waving his arm in the direction of the book, where it sat, opened out for the area, stuffed, where he'd thrust it earlier, in the corner of the cockpit.

'It majored in the development of radar – the electronic means of detecting things out of sight. It was perfected here. Eventually, a ring of stations were built to warn of enemy activity during the 1940s war.'

'Margery Allingham wrote a detective story based up here too,' the mate added: Allingham was a favourite.

'That was up the next river – or rivers, the Ore and Alde ... over the other bar,' the skipper added tentatively, for later they planned to go that way too. The skipper had read the book too (*The Mind Readers*). It was a thoroughly good read. The story is about a detective, Campion, and his family. His child, and a cousin, had found how to communicate, by thought, using an 'iggy tube' they had been given at their school. Without their knowledge, surreptitious and evil experiments had been taking place on the children. It led Campion to a secret and mysterious establishment amongst a lonely, shingle, marshland 'island' that was cut off from the mainland. (That land

The traditional clinker planked ferry boat leaving Felixstowe Ferry with another load of trippers going to Bawdsey.

was now no longer a secret establishment and has been left to develop as a natural wilderness.)

'It's aboard with us,' the mate said, 'amongst our library of literary matter stowed below.'

Coming round onto a reach, the skipper saw that a few boats were on the move inside the river. From amongst the moorings, crowding the waters off Felixstowe Ferry, several sails were heading their way, engines running as the boats butted the young flood heading for the bar and a passage southwards with the tide. The skipper had waved in response several times – it can become monotonous – but out on the water, generally, politeness still prevails! The inner horse, a sandbank, was high out of the water and it was given a wide berth. Beyond the horse, they had to sail harder on the wind as the skipper worked the boat northwards.

The Deben River, with the Ore, had, generally, a north and south run. The former had a westward lean and the latter an eastward. Another was the Colne in Essex – all made fine sailing in a westerly breeze.

'The Deben's a very clean river,' the skipper said. 'There's not much debris along its banks.'

'What do you mean? What's that over there?' the mate immediately asked, pointing northwards.

'Oh, err!' the skipper had muttered, looking at his mate. 'An old ferry. What I meant was …' he paused. 'This river, well, in these lower reaches, it's like a canal. Look, the sea walls come to the edge; there's little or no marsh to speak of.' He looked at the mate. 'The Deben used to be much wider and deeper, but the marshes were embanked a long time ago, so natural scouring has been reduced.'

Grinning, the skipper had picked up their chart, 'Once creeks ran inland, especially to the west, beyond those walls,' waving an arm. 'Look, the road even now runs well

The evocative anchorage of Ramsholt, a famous watering hole.

back along the edge of the higher ground between the ferry, back there,' then pointing behind them, 'and Fakenham had a creek.' It wasn't on the chart.

'Kings Fleet ran deep inland. The flood walls ran with it. It's the expense of maintenance. I'm against cutting little creeks off. He grinned – as if he had a say! 'Sea-wall realignment has caused great changes to many rivers and channels.' The mate nodded: the skipper was away …

'There's a river, beyond the next, the Blythe. It runs out into Blythe Haven; used to be an important port too. Some land has recently been flooded. It was reclaimed by inning, that's sea-wall building around chunks of marsh, bit by bit, stealing, stealing, until there's nothing left to take.' He stopped to pause. 'It went on for centuries. Eventually, the loss of salt marsh caused a dramatic reduction in tidal flows and silting of the river.' He paused again to let his point lie a moment: his own creek had similarly suffered too.

'I've heard that sea walls protecting marshes between Blythe and Southwold have failed and haven't been repaired – though attempted. The authorities are content with the situation, it seems. I'm ecstatic!'

But, alas, the inhabitants of Southwold aren't! They're now worried about what the increased flows will do to the river: for any further failures will have a dramatic effect on the man-made entrance structures of the river.

'It's a funny old world … they're still arguing, I understand,' the skipper concluded.

The same thing, the skipper went on to say, had happened all over the East Coast: 'inned' land was found to be a fertile and a rich crop bearing treasure; this put further pressure on the marshes. The marsh is this land's natural defence. It had fluctuated back and forth over the centuries; now, in places, it had nowhere to recede as sea levels rose. 'The sea shall have its just reward,' the skipper said, grinning!

'The old course of the River Alde now runs out through a sluice at Thopeness Mere, well to the north of Aldeburgh, I read somewhere. The town too has shrunk from its sixteenth-century size due to sea erosion.'

'Oh yes' the mate interjected, trying to maintain interest!

Undaunted, the skipper continued, 'The original river was gradually forced south, naturally, by the southward drift of coastal shingle. It closed what was Hollesley Haven. The lower end became known as the Orford River.'

'Hollesley Creek, well, Barthorp's Creek, is just a ditch now. It ran inland during Tudor times – the Butley River ran out into the Haven too.'

'We'll be up there later …' He stopped. He needed to focus on the river they were actually sailing in. Ramsholt was being approached. The mate had breathed a sigh of relief.

Moorings lay thick around Ramsholt, their destination for the night. A tack or two was needed up the reach above Felixstowe Ferry, then they sailed easily through the moorings, stowing the mains'l on the way.

'Where do you want to moor,' the mate called out, from her position at the helm. She'd seen the skipper looking ahead as they approached the old quay, surrounded by pretty woodland and its friendly public house on flat ground beneath them. She waited for an answer.

'There's a buoy just ahead. We'll sail past, turn and run back,' the skipper said. 'Mind you ease the jib though …' he grinned.

'Tide's flooding … we'll be heading it,' the mate said, nodding her head.

In the prevailing conditions, this was their normal practice. With the jib spilling wind, the mate sailed slowly back until the skipper had hooked the buoy's trailing line. It was covered in weed, full of tiny marine life – shrimps and minute baby crabs and curly shells. 'You'll be alright, I'll wash you back overboard in a minute,' the skipper had murmured quietly. The mooring line indicated that its owner was either away, or that the mooring was not in use. 'This'll do us,' the skipper had called quietly to the mate, 'Leave the jib to me ... Oh, pass the dip bucket ... please.' The mate then disappeared to rustle up lunch from the galley.

The Deben was once a busy industrial river. It was hard to see much of that now though, except for a sprinkling of farm wharves, on the whole still in use. Further up river, at Waldringfield, there was a wharf that had been used for cement and lime production. At Woodbridge, there were many wharves and a greater diversity of industries had existed. Woodbridge had remained the area's centre. Beyond Woodbridge, the skipper wanted to find Wilford Bridge, a mile or so above the waterside market town, where there is a quay. One hundred years before, the skipper's old sailing home, the spritsail barge, *May Flower*, had delivered a 130-ton cargo of road-making stone. That was in July of 1902. The stone had been loaded at Rainham in Kent. The bridge was on the road to Sutton Hoo, the site of the 'ship burial' of an Anglo-Saxon king. It was a place they planned to visit: a new centre had been opened.

Later that evening, the skipper went off for a sail in the little lugsail dinghy leaving the mate to tidy away their supper things – a simple fare rustled up by the skipper from vegetables, tinned prawns and a tomato sauce, served on a bed of pasta – deliciously tasty. What a blessing pasta sauces were!

While lazily tacking up river, back and forth through the moorings, the skipper came across a yacht that hailed from their sister club on Canvey Island. He spilled his wind and 'jogged' over for a chat, keeping his dinghy stationary, breasting the tide. They were bound for Woodbridge too, on the morrow. 'We'll probably see you,' was their parting comment, coupled with a cheery wave. The skipper grinned, thinking, 'what a charming pair they were,' as he waved back.

Later that evening, sitting in the cockpit, the mate reading, or trying to, the skipper had interrupted her from time to time. He had related the first time that they'd visited the river when their son had been but a wee child of two. It was 1984 – Orwell's prophecy hadn't happened: but an ongoing miners' strike had humbled the nation, coal was being shipped into some very odd, almost-forgotten East Coast wharves, during that summer ... playing cat and mouse with flying pickets – Orwellian or not? Their enchantment with Ramsholt had not altered during the intervening twenty-five years either ... Their yacht had only recently been launched by her builder. She had remained their pride and joy. 'All in all, she owes us nothing,' the skipper had recently said to a fellow yachtsman.

The skipper, ruminating over a glass of red wine, had watched the skyline as the evening started to turn to night. He glowed with a feeling of happiness, with life, with what they'd done. With his mate too, who'd found the combined pleasures of reading and sailing very compatible. 'I'm a lucky man ...' he murmured very quietly.

Sitting, he suddenly noticed apparent changes to some trees on the skyline above and beyond the inn. On the ridge, a stand of conifers had looked, the skipper thought, 'like ladies with layered feather skirts', and too, it seemed, 'they floated as if dancing on their way to church – slightly up river.'

He watched, entranced: it was the setting sun. The beauty of it filled him with awe. 'You must watch,' he entreated the mate. She closed her book and watched too.

The sky displayed discordant, yet conjoined colours. Those colours ran from red to rose pink, above the distant horizon, in distinct layers. The river was tinted pink too. The colour shimmered on the wet, recently uncovered river edges. The saltings were tinged too. Above the cockpit, the sky still had the light of day: it was blue beyond a layer of thin, grey cloud. Those clouds were imbued, beneath, with streaks of pink blush and gentle orange. Both had gasped, 'What a wondrous sight!' They continued to watch, mesmerised. Coffee would have to wait. Slowly, the clouds above them had gradually darkened, bit by bit, yet leaking through were the last blue vestiges of the day. They were blue, yet almost translucent.

Some moments later, looking away from the sky, they saw that the conifers had lost their previous becoming look. They became, it appeared, puffs of smoke. The puffs, the upper fronds, appeared to float above the darkened skyline in a thin streak of light beneath the high cloud layer, supported by hazy, threadlike spirals – perhaps a distant farmer's field of burning stubble. Whilst that had been happening, there'd been an incessant calling, vociferous complaints; screams even, of a host of oystercatchers along the muddy, marshy edges of the river. It was enchanting.

'Coffee,' the mate said, the spell broken. The skipper nodded in an affirmative. Stillness had overtaken the anchorage, except for the babble of excited voices emanating from the waterside inn, from which lights shimmered across the now-darkened water towards the yacht, dancing in slow motion from the last of the ebb's swell.

The mate soon reappeared with coffee and some of the skipper's smelly cheese – 'Ah, that's just grand,' the skipper said, and as he breathed in deeply, his taste buds salivating. Belatedly, he thanked his mate.

The next day, they'd awoken in good time for a casual breakfast, which was enjoyed in the cockpit. They planned to be away a little after low water and be up off Woodbridge Tide Mill marina soon after mid-tide to slip across the sill.

The boat's head lay aslant the stream and the mate had merely hauled up their genoa, then slipped the mooring. The mains'l too soon rattled up the mast. 'Time is on our side,' the skipper said, confidently, watching their slow but sure progress with the fresh flood.

On the west bank, they passed an inlet, Kirton Creek; a landing used to be possible at its head, but whether it was still there, the skipper didn't know. The *Three Sisters*, an old spritsail barge, had been abandoned in the creek many years previously. She'd been built in 1865. Her hull had now collapsed, deck fittings sitting as if rightfully placed, lonely, forlorn, in her lingering death. The skipper had silently paid her his respects as they sailed past.

Passing a wooded bluff, the skipper had indicated some low ground; beneath it, a cottage could be seen. It seemed to drift at roof height below the sea wall. 'A creek used to run in there,' the skipper said. 'The *Cygnet*, the little barge we so often see, visited the sluice ... her skipper visits old docks ... wasn't the real creek though ... but as good as!'

The skipper reflected briefly, 'We saw her go up to Benfleet a few years back, and I saw her sail into Leigh-on-Sea too.'

Waldringfield, that pretty and pleasant place, a place that has more than a whiff of middle England about it, had eventually come into view. It was difficult to visualise the place with numerous belching chimneys – cement and lime kilns – which had once infested the waterfront.

Passing through the moorings, walkers on the beach below a stand of trees and a public house stopped to watch their passage past. The skipper knew that the tan sails set against the boat's varnished cabin sides and cream-painted hull had always looked a treat. Towing a similar-coloured simulated clinker dinghy behind only added to that allure. The skipper grinned broadly as he raised a coffee mug to his lips, as if to say 'Cheers!'

Abreast of the old wharf, the skipper had pointed, and at the same time nudged his mate, saying, 'There were cement works right onto the wharf. Doesn't seem possible, does it?' The works ran back inland and a row of chimneys belching noxious fumes would have deposited grey dust for miles around – washerwomen's worst nightmare too: if a breeze gently fluttering the nearly dry weekly wash had changed direction ... all would have needed doing again... 'Doesn't bare thinking of, does it?' the skipper was thinking of his childhood experiences on the Medway. 'There was a lime works too,' the skipper added. The cement works continued working into the early part of the 1900s, and like many small manufacturers, amalgamations and transport costs caused the demise of many of the smaller firms. Most of them ended up under the name of Blue Circle flag – a well-known cement brand.

The mate chipped in, 'Your Mother told me about washing and cement factories once. Didn't a cement works sit near your home, when in Whitewall Creek?'

The skipper looked at the mate, 'That's pretty good,' he said, grinning, and thinking, 'Wow!' She wasn't renowned for remembering immaterial facts! The cement works referred to by the mate had closed around 1963.

Pointing back at the wharf, with its ancient-looking crane, the skipper remarked, 'The Nunn family bought the old works and started wooden boat building. They did repairs too. Lay-ups seem to take up most of the room though.' The firm progressed and had to move around as they got bigger. They later became Seamark Nunn; they're still in Suffolk. Over the years, they've built many classes of fibreglass dinghies, and in their early days, they built Dragon's class yachts too. The company moved into chandlery in recent years. 'You know, our creek buoys, going into Smallgains, came from them, and as far as I know, a branch of the family still runs the yard here.' The wharf had by then long fallen astern.

'Coffee,' the mate said as she quickly grabbed the tiller, 'You make it – this time.'

The sail had continued in that lazy fashion. Nice and gentle: there'd been too many windy days by the time the summer was out; well, that August anyway!

The upper reaches of the river had soon come into view. Near Martlesham Creek, the skipper doused the sails as they turned into the wind, with the engine running. Their 'friends' from their other Island club came past at that point, waving madly, their boat's propeller churning the flood tide, as she cut past.

It was at the entrance to Martlesham Creek, off Kingston Quay, or Kyson Point, that an aging Maurice Griffiths, the long-time editor of *Yachting Monthly*, broke a leg after slipping on the foredeck of his last yacht, *Kylix*. Griffiths, a yacht designer, had designed her himself with the intention of a few years of gentle cruising. After the accident, he had to sling his hook. The man was a legend and had been the skipper's exemplar. God Bless him!

The mate loved Woodbridge. The skipper loved Woodbridge! The boat ... surely it did too? 'It has a certain charm,' the mate said. 'It's something so many other places have lost.' The shopping hub contained an abnormally high proportion of locally generated businesses of all types, a reminder of its distance from large towns and its independence too, perhaps.

They had an interesting afternoon walking about, after a late and hastily grabbed lunch, seeing things with a fresh eye. The skipper, in particular, had enjoyed a visit to the local museum, just across from the Shire Hall. The hall was a fabulous building with a Dutch influence, reflected by its roof. They were taken too with the entrance to the old abbey grounds, where it appeared that the buildings within had been converted into flats. 'A good use,' the skipper said.

Back aboard their yacht, sitting in the cockpit reading a book he'd picked up, the skipper suddenly erupted, 'Look, here listen,' he exploded. The mate looked up from her own book, smiling; the skipper's face had that expression that she'd come to know so well. It was his 'Constable Look' and she inwardly grimaced as she turned her own book over to await its passing. The skipper then had her attention, 'Robert Simper ...' shaking the book *Woodbridge & Beyond* '... has said about the approach to Woodbridge, "The first thing that catches the eye is the Old Tide Mill. ... and in the distance can just be seen the white sails of Buttram's Tower Windmill. ... It is a scene completely unscarred by industry." That's piffle.' The skipper waved his arm around. 'We've seen old wharves, barge remains; there's the old malting building, the windmill

Right: The Shire Hall in Woodbridge; close by is the town's lovely museum.

Below: Wilford Bridge with the mast of a yacht, and just seen, a Dutch barge, at the ancient quay, where the skipper's old sailing home came to, with a cargo of stone, nearly a century before.

above the town and, of course, that over there,' pointing at the Tide Mill, 'What's all that then? Aren't they industry? Weren't they the industry of their time?' He was exasperated, but grinned broadly, letting his questions rest awhile.

'Some of those mills were even moved around to new locations,' the skipper said. 'They were probably the first portable industrial buildings.' The skipper looked across at the mate. Had he expected an answer? Doubtful!

The mate smiled thinly and said nothing: she'd known what was to come ... and the skipper hadn't surprised her, for he soon crashed onwards: nothing would have stopped him, 'In Constable's day, had there been electricity pylons roaming and marching across the countryside, he'd have painted them, just as he'd painted locks, barges, ships, mills, fords, farms, and people working, repairing and doing industrious things – where does one stop? Weren't they industrial? It makes me cross this preserving in aspic and setting aside old industry as if it were something it wasn't ... something pretty, yes. Constable and others painted what they saw...' There was a long, long pause. He'd stopped. He was out of breath. He sat grinning – wryly.

The mate merely patted the skipper's knee gently, saying, as softly as possible, 'There, there, don't get so excited,' and had gone quietly back to her book. The skipper just shook his head.

The afternoon slumbered on. Both continued to relax beneath the awning, initially put up for a rain shower – the first for a week. It later came into its own offering shade as the skies cleared away, leaving it blazing hot.

The skipper had earlier met the folks from the other boat, inviting them aboard for pre-dinner drinks and canapés later that evening. At the agreed time, they arrived and a convivial time was spent, chatting about the area and ruminating over the lack of craft seen from their own locality during their respective cruises. Some, from the other club, had made an attempt to go 'foreign', but most had not gone, due to the weather.

Later, the skipper and mate went ashore to find a decent meal and think about their planned visit to Sutton Hoo the next day.

It was a long, sticky walk to Wilford Bridge and up the hill to the burial site, where two tired and thirsty sailors beat a rapid path to some welcome shade and refreshment.

At Wilford, the skipper had seen the wharf his family's barge had unloaded stone at, all those years ago. They lingered awhile, gazing up and down the beautiful river. It was a place where the sea wormed its way in, slowly, barely visible, meeting the fresh. It looked so natural, but man's hand lay close. The river had a look, the skipper thought, 'of betwixt land and sea', something he'd said before about another creek.

At Sutton Hoo, a ship burial discovered in 1939, and hastily covered back over for the duration of the coming conflict, had been found to contain an amazing array of treasure and common artefacts – treasures themselves. One of the most exciting discoveries was the imprint left by the hull of the ship in the light, sandy Suffolk soil. It was thought that it was the burial place of Raedwald, an East Anglian king. However, the local historian Simper says, and others too, that the burial was thought to have been a memorial to Aethelhere who died around 655 in a war against the Northumbrians. Historians, however, may never know the king's tre identity. 'Does it really matter?' the skipper commented to the mate.

Both had found the exhibition astounding, the more so for seeing exhibits within their local setting. At the British Museum, a place oft visited, the 'Hoo' artefacts are just bits and pieces, beautiful as they are, but very much out of place. 'Those things should be in a museum in Suffolk,' the skipper had muttered at the time. Seeing the actual site, he'd not changed that view at all!

The forecast for the next day, although it was to remain sunny, was for increasing winds; the two listeners had looked at one another in dismay. The skipper had begun to think that they wouldn't get up to the Ore and Alde – though he'd kept his thoughts guarded. The summer was about to turn. It led to a fairly dire month!

That evening they visited their yachting friends for pre-dinner drinks. Strange as it may seem, it was sometimes nice to meet others from one's own locality when cruising. In general, the skipper and mate were quite content with each other's company. Following the meet and greet, which was easy-going and full of bonhomie, the skipper and mate headed shoreward to a fine French restaurant near the bottom of the town. It had been recommended.

On the way, the skipper commented, 'It's funny,' with a wry grin, 'the chap was a long-time friend and crew of the bloke, from our club, who disappeared off to Cyprus (with his wife) to live. He shipped his boat out too – he had the *Morakena*, she's *Lucy Too* now.'

'It's a small world,' said the mate.

During the meal, which was absolutely delicious, the two road-weary sailors sat chatting. The mate talked at length about Sutton Hoo and finally said, 'I thought all those other graves found near the mounds quite sad. They were felons' graves – just shallow cairns – scattered around the site, and beyond too.'

'Yes,' the skipper added, 'that's why I feel the British Museum display is so devoid of feeling.'

'There were other graves,' the mate added, 'just ordinary burials, further away.'

'I was interested in all that stuff about shipbuilding in the museum yesterday,' the skipper said, changing the subject matter. 'Some large vessels were built during the sixteenth and seventeenth centuries. The Pett family were big. One of them married a local girl,' he grinned. 'The Pett's were a dynasty within naval dockyards.' He stopped for a sip of wine. 'There's a funny tale – well, it's sad really – it took place following the Dutch raid on the Medway ...'

'That was in 1667,' said the mate.

'Err, yes – a Peter Pett was reprimanded by the Privy Council, arrested and removed from office.'

'What had he done?' chipped in the mate, quickly.

'Well – he saved a load of ship models ... probably the most valuable bits of military design then available,' he grinned. 'How the Dutch would have loved to have got hold of them ... the Privy Council thought he should have been stopping the Dutch!' The mate had skipped that bit of the museum.

'I was interested in the area's old industries. The cement works, though, I don't suppose were missed! Fertiliser manufacture took place – used that stuff dug out of the fields around here.'

'Coprolite, wasn't it?'

'Yes, that's it – was used to make a phosphates fertiliser – used to increase farm yields. It was particularly important because parts of Suffolk have a very poor-quality soil. The industries had all gone by the 1920s though.'

'Why?'

'Well, fertiliser was shipped in from abroad at a much lower cost.'

'Remember that shipwreck in the Thames,' the skipper added, 'she'd got fertiliser aboard.'

'Wasn't coprolite dead animals?' the mate asked.

The skipper nodded and sat back to appreciate a draw on his wine ... a delicious red from France. The choice had had the assistance of the waitress, a fragrant young thing who'd actually lived near the château (she said). The wine had gone well with the gorgeous piece of fillet steak. Then he was aware of the mate, trying to grab his attention.

The sad sight of the intact bottom of the spritsail barge *Westall*, burnt out some years before. It will eventually spawn a fresh patch of marsh.

'Choose a sweet ...' The skipper had grinned and gone for a selection of cheeses. As their last course appeared ... a quiet descended over their table until coffee appeared.

Remembering that the skipper enjoyed walking past the yacht yards, the mate said, 'Weren't a lot of yachts built here?'

'Er, yes ...' but that was as far as he got.

'And ...' she said, '... weren't those flowerbeds and rafts of plant pots lovely along by the house barges,' adding, 'It was sad seeing that barge though, but...'

'Yes,' he murmured, sipping his coffee and thinking of the burnt-out barge remains up river. 'Her bottom seemed in such good condition too – shame,' he said reflectively. 'She's the *Westall* – came to Woodbridge for repairs.' The project had failed.

Then remembering the mate's last comment, 'Oh yes, those sea-wall gardens were very pretty – a splash of summer colour.' Then they talked about boatyards – how romantic!

Woodbridge had been well endowed with boatyards, but some such as Whisstock's yard down by the Tide Mill had closed in recent times. Robertson's, on the site of an old lime kiln (the Lime Kiln Yard), was still operating. There's another lay-up yard, higher up river, at Melton Dock. That was full of interesting vessels.

'Of course,' the skipper said, 'Whisstock's built a class of little yacht – the Deben 4-tonner – turned out for a price. They're still sought after in some circles – generally need lots of renovation though.' He paused. 'The yard built craft for the war departments too, like many yards on the coast. It was their lifeline.'

Simper writes of a Sun Wharf and Gladwell Dock, they were part of the old Lime Kiln quay. It was known as Hart's Dock though.

'There's Everson's, of course,' the skipper added, 'down near the yacht clubs. It's only a little yard on the wall. The boy and I landed there a couple of years ago.'

Getting up, after dealing with their bill, the skipper, feeling replete, said, 'You know, Defoe, that great traveller, stopped in Woodbridge too, he said something ...' but the skipper couldn't remember what exactly.

Defoe wrote, 'Woodbridge has nothing remarkable...'

The skipper said, 'The food was remarkable. Defoe was above food, however. He'd probably say the same now: Woodbridge remains a sleepy little hollow – pretty, comfortable and it has an easy-to-feel-at-home feel too.'

Later, back aboard, they sat out with a nightcap ... the skipper remarked, 'We'll not be leaving tomorrow.' The mate merely nodded.

'The lady on the boat we were aboard earlier was worried about the weather. Still, I can think of worse places to be cooped up in. Do you remember our enforced stay at Queenborough a few years ago, out on that mooring, being tossed around like peas in a pod?'

'Yes,' the skipper said, offering not a jot more!

The next day, they awoke to a howl in the rigging, even down inside the protection of the marina. During the morning, a walk around the town and a look at areas not previously visited kept them occupied. It was interesting, but the skipper was concerned about time ... about their plans ... especially a visit up the Thames to London – where a play at the Globe had been booked, during a spring day out, earlier that year. It would be a day or two off their spare time.

Sitting at a waterfront establishment at lunchtime, enjoying a plate of crab and fresh, crusty local bread, the skipper looked at the wind ripping across the tide lapping a few metres from them. 'It's only one day,' the mate said.

'Yes, I know.' Thinking though, it might be two.

Close by their luncheon place was the Old Tide Mill. It was in desperate need of money: the base of the building was in poor shape, a notice said. 'Perhaps it should have been dealt with when first renovated,' the skipper had said, imperiously, walking past earlier. The mill had its own small pond, fashioned from around the edge of the original tide pool, for operating the waterwheel. They'd seen a demonstration some years earlier. The old tide pool, now greatly excavated, was the marina lagoon. The area had a purposeful and functional aura: maritime paraphernalia had always been part of the town's make-up and it would be sad to see the mill close, or go even!

Down near the waterside, they looked at the local cinema. It served as a theatre too. The films then showing were mainly child-orientated – the summer season! 'It's a lovely building,' the mate murmured softly.

'Yes – it's a treasure!'

The building sat near the station, a place the mate had travelled to a number of years before. She'd then had to go on a cross-county bus that wound through picturesque villages to Orford, where he, the skipper, and the boat were ...

The skipper, with their son, were sailing – an annual event for a number of years – on a week's cruise. They'd worked up to the Ore in stages, stopping at Queenborough, West Mersea and Pin Mill, leaving a few days for the Ore and Alde. On one of the days, they'd picked up the skipper's brother and two of his children for a sail. 'The Windy River,' the skipper's brother had said: he'd sailed these rivers with his family, in his elderly, cold, moulded, wooden Albacore sailing dinghy.

When approaching the entrance, the skipper and the boy had watched as a spritsail barge sailed out – a grand sight. Then, they themselves were hurtling into the river, on an urgent flood tide. The skipper saw for the first time the lonely stretch that was Long Reach separated from the sea by an exceedingly narrow shingle spit and then the protracted channel, the Narrows. 'That was boring,' the boy had said. The skipper, at the time, could only agree as they sailed past the marshy Havergate Island. The island had a sprinkling of huts and hides: it was a bird sanctuary along with the lower edge of the Orfordness wilderness. Havergate Island sat between two distinct channels of the Ore. The other, on the inland side, was the Gull channel. Leaving the island behind, they'd made for Slaughden Quay. The skipper had always remembered the frustration: they were unable to see over the high sea walls that ranged along the river's edges. It wasn't until above Slaughden that a decent view was found.

The entrance to the Ore was a little more complex than the Deben, but providing the basic rules were adhered to, difficulties were likely to be avoided. Over the short span of one hundred years, the spit had progressed ever further in its south-westerly drift – over half a mile. At times, the river's mouth must have been virtually closed by strong and prolonged easterly gales. On all the times that the skipper had passed this way, conditions had been benign. It must be said, the skipper hadn't lessened his reverential appreciation of the entrance's latent dangers.

Of the Ore and its entrance in particular, Strugnell has said, and it was something that caused the skipper angst, '… the river today is a deserted place except for a few enthusiastic yachtsmen, and indeed, with the hazard of the bar, it is hoped that only the experienced will venture out to sea. For the inexperienced such waters are best shunned; the lifeboat service has plenty of worthwhile tasks on its hands without wasting time and dissipating its energies in pulling half-wits from a well-deserved watery grave.'

'What pomposity. What ignorance, from an educated man,' the skipper had hollered across to his mate. 'The lifeboat service is no busier in these waters than others. Sailors on the whole have far more sense than landlubbers – a quality bereft in many, but rarely in sailors. One only had to digest the facts behind the figures: the greatest need of help around our coasts comes from day-trippers …'

After 'the boy' had departed ship, the skipper had had several days sailing on the river alone. Two were spent in the Butley River, once a river in its own right discharging

The gnarled transom of the *Tuesday*, drawn by the skipper. She sits by the ferry landing onto Orford Ness, rotting slowly away. Note: she was tiller steered.

directly into the sea, but now a tributary of the Ore. The skipper anchored above the old barge dock, at Boyton, then sailed his dinghy as far as the tide would allow. The Butley River had remained an oyster river, so care in the upper reaches was needed.

The mate had said, on the day she'd joined ship at Orford, 'While I was waiting ... for you ... I looked about.' She'd grinned! 'The castle was built by Henry II. It was part of a series built to keep his barons in order.' The period had been the beginning of a desire for democracy – down to their level only ... for many more years – but the seeds had been sown! 'The quay was constructed for the castle works. Wool was the important export ...' The castle was completed between 1165 and 1173.

'... was in Ipswich too – so it's not surprising,' the skipper quipped, quickly adding, 'Coal and wheat followed.' Like many coastal ports, predominantly, wheat was shipped out, coal came in.

Ashore, they'd savoured the sights and collected a chunk of smoked ham from Orford's famous 'smokery' tucked down a little lane.

The quay that day was busy with ferries. The bird protection society's boat, a small boat that ran foot passengers across the river, and another, able to carry vehicles, ran to Orford Ness too. Finally, a prettily painted old fishing vessel came alongside; she'd disgorged a host of sightseers, as another line, lined up, had boarded for a river trip. The sides of the quay, the skipper saw, needed some attention: they weren't yacht friendly! It had been frenetic. Their own dinghy became buried in a melee of tenders. The skipper had to dig their dinghy from the shambles by a set of steps to get back aboard their own little ship. 'Crikey,' the skipper had said, grinning.

Later, aboard, the skipper had said, 'We'll drop down to the Butley River and swing on our anchor there for the night. We'll come back here, if you like, later in the week.'

The skipper added, after a pause, 'It's a delightful little town. It's exceedingly picturesque, but something seems to be missing.'

Skipper's sketch of Orford from the Upper Gull channel, pencilled as the boat gently made over the tide.

'Chocolate Box,' the mate said! 'But there are a couple of good stores,' she added, being ever the practical one.

They'd soon been under way, on a run: wind was in the west. The mate had enjoyed the solitude of their anchorage above Boyton Dock. The dock had had 'brickworks' written all over it! 'Was it a brick dock?' the mate asked. The skipper didn't know. Mills, though, had operated at the top of the river, and a brickworks. That evening they walked ashore, landing at the brick quay and ambling inland enjoying the scenery. Close by, across the low fields, is Hollesley Prison – a place that used to be a colonial college.

Over the next two days, they'd gone up to Slaughden Quay and Snape.

The town of Aldeburgh was a fraction of its original size, though modern growth had added to it. After the demise of its old access to the sea, the Alde crept southwards, the lower end became the Ore. The river had run, it was said, out along Thorpeness Mere, a stream still discharging through a sluice some way north of the present town.

In Aldeburgh, a short distance from the beach, was a sixteenth-century Moot Hall. It once stood in the centre of the Tudor town. Slaughden Quay, the waterfront entrance, was a separate entity then; it later became the centre of Aldeburgh's trade. Another old wharf, used by the brick industry, sat inland behind the town. Since consolidation of the seafront, land loss to the sea had ceased. Instead, the sea devoured land elsewhere, as was its want.

'It's strange,' the skipper said when rowing ashore, 'just a thin strip of sand separates us from the North Sea.'

The mate nodded reflectively as they came alongside the yacht club pontoon.

From the quay, they'd walked into Aldeburgh to dine amongst the jet set, worldly and all knowing. The skipper had remarked about some posh narks' very rude children 'in town' for their summer.

Later, sitting in the cockpit, the skipper said, with a wave of an arm, 'Dear Libby (Purves), your story is so apt!' It was said with some venom. The coffee came laced with something nice – the skipper had needed it!

'Hmm,' the mate said over her coffee, 'I didn't like the attitude of some of those people … either.' It was an unusual thing for the mate to say, but she'd been greatly upset by some extreme rudeness.

'Let's not be judgemental,' the skipper said soothingly. 'I'll make another coffee – then bed!'

They left Slaughden for Snape on a rising tide. Everyone they knew had said, persistently, 'You must go to Snape.' So they were going!

The skipper, during the few days on his own, had anchored for a night below the derelict dock that sat on the river's eastern bank behind Aldeburgh. The dock, a quay, was used for the export of bricks made at a local works and farm produce. It was a forlorn sight.

A swish fibreglass yacht motored past as they'd tacked, against a generally westerly breeze, back and forth across the shallow, muddy channel. The people on the other boat had persistently waved, enthusiastically too. The skipper had lifted his arm, in polite salute.

'Do they know us?' the mate said, keeping her voice low, 'they seemed to!'

Later, at Snape, they'd found that the boat had had the author of *East Coast Rivers* aboard – the skipper had corresponded (about changes) with the editor, one of Jack Coote's girls, for a number of years. She'd recognised the clinker yacht! Sadly, it was learnt months later, the boat's skipper, the editor's sister's husband had died quite suddenly that year. 'His soul will be riding the waves, flowing amongst sea aster and purslane … amongst the marshes …' the skipper had thought, reverentially, when he'd heard.

Eventually, a little exasperated by a series of very short tacks, the mate had

The little farm barge *Cygnet*, built in 1881, alongside at Snape, by the famous Maltings buildings converted into a concert venue in memory of Benjamin Brittan, who lived locally in Suffolk for many years.

sarcastically commented, '... forgotten the pin number ... again,' (for the engine) and '... what's the use of an engine ...' with a cross look!

The skipper surprised the mate and immediately started it ... then he called, 'ready about ...' and again, for some distance further.

The mate had fumed: she was on the jib!

Finally after bumping around a reach, Troublesome Reach, with barely enough distance to tack – just short of a nice reach with the westerly, the skipper had said, 'Okay, I'll stow the sails, you steer ...'

'Thank you ...' the mate said grinning, killing her grim look!

They'd reached Iken Cliff.

'One day ...' the skipper said much later, over dinner, at a little place ashore, 'I'll ... well, we'll sail all the way up, or out ...'

'Yes,' she said, 'I expect YOU WILL!'

Anyway, that had been a long time before their present voyage up into Suffolk, and they were still near the railway, leaning on the parapet of the sea wall, gazing across the choppy water, wave crests breaking in tumbling white foam, towards Sutton Hoo.

The coming of the railway, sweeping right along the bottom of the town, must have been a godsend for local farmers and producers: shipping fresh produce had suddenly become so much easier. The railway, too, helped in the demise of waterborne transport, but it had, of course, been the rapid road-building programme of the 1920s that completed the job. Roads built from materials carried in those near-obsolete, ubiquitous, tan-sailed spritsail barges became the arteries for lorries – wonderful!

That evening, they dined at the Steel Yard, an old inn. It had on its upper story, a wall crane for lifting produce into the lofts and warehouse floors above. The building had had another use, of course. On the way back, they ambled past the old malting building. It sat at the lower end of the town. It had a noticeable forlorn, tired and neglected look. 'Hope it's renovated,' the skipper murmured. 'It'll probably be flats, but at least the building will live on,' he continued quietly, for the streets were silent and the wind of earlier, too, had diminished greatly. With that singular thought on his mind, the skipper had added, changing the subject completely, 'We might be able to get away tomorrow and drop down to Ramsholt.'

'Let's wait for the morning forecast,' the mate said, squeezing her skipper's hand and pulling him closer ...

He nodded: he was always mindful, well nearly always, of his mate's caution, which was greater than his own!

It hadn't been dark: it wasn't late. They sat out; with the cockpit cover flapped back, to view a starry night. Clouds had, from time to time, scudded across, high above Woodbridge. A wind was still blowing up there, the skipper noticed, but had said nothing of his observations.

Over coffee, sitting quietly, a disturbance in the wooded slopes across the river below Sutton Hoo caught their attention. It was a woodpecker's screech, then another further away. 'They're Green Woodpeckers,' the skipper said softly. 'Its laughing call is completely opposite to the bird's beauty,' he added.

The next morning, the skipper awoke early. The wind was still relatively quiet in the rigging, but the treetops across the river were waving, however, not wildly ... the forecast was eagerly awaited. It spoke of a brisk breeze and lighter conditions by the evening, and the next day too. Okay for Harwich Harbour, but the Ore was definitely off the agenda.

It was still cloudy and grey. Some sunny breaks threatened, but it was decidedly chilly. Oh, for a return to the previous few weeks of relatively fine weather.

'Departure?' the mate asked.

'It'll be around late morning' the skipper said as they discussed it all.

A last shower was enjoyed at the beautiful facilities within the marina, and after breakfast, the mate disappeared up to the town for some fresh meat, whilst the skipper topped off the freshwater tank.

Departure was mundane and they soon had their sails aloft, the mains'l with a single reef, for it was still gusty outside. The little dinghy had tugged at her painter and skittered obediently behind after its little rest. The mate had started to tack out of the bight below the town, until she put the skipper on for the stretch round past Kyson. 'You're better at it,' she had said.

Sailing down towards Methersgate Quay, making long and short tacks, they spied a friendly boat moored off the old barge quay. The quay was still in use – by a dinghy club. The river was unusual in that respect, for the way so many old wharves had gone forwards into other successful uses. Passing the boat, they'd waved excitedly, at one another! A camera was seen snapping away. The 'snapper' was an original crewman on the skipper's sailing home when his father had purchased the barge in 1950. The crewman, his own master now, was a cheerful, crusty, old ship captain, who was always ready to swing the lamp and tell a salty tale! Now he was happily reliving boyhood dreams, cruising with his lovely mate! Much like the skipper, he had not quite grown up ... even approaching eighty ...

The little yacht's crew had a cracking sail, via the cut, inside Stonner Point and its adjacent patch of saltings, where they'd tacked freely within the limits of their draft, and on down to Ramsholt. The cut at Stonner Point was excavated to allow barges and schooners better access to Woodbridge. The mud was used in the cement industry. The skipper chose to moor just below the wooded point above Ramsholt where the wind was across the river, alleviating any wind-over-tide tendencies.

Over lunch, the skipper said, 'There were only a couple of boats at anchor under the cliffs,' she looked at him quizzically, so he added, 'The place back round the point – The Rocks,' pointing back the way they'd come. 'It looked jolly uncomfortable

Whimbrel sailing, with a reef tucked in, on a squally day near Methersgate Quay. (Courtesy of I. Kemp)

– there was a boat having difficulty anchoring too.'

'We're alright here, aren't we?' the mate had quickly interjected.

'Oh yes,' the skipper quickly said, adding, 'the forecast is for more settled conditions … we're on a buoy …' reassuring her.

Later, over a pot of tea and cake, the mate said, 'We'll not be going ashore here, tonight?' The water was still disturbed.

'No, no point. We've had a good run for our money up river. A rest from a nightly jug of Adnams would do me good!' His taste buds had rapidly salivated though, which was only to be expected!

'No, we'll have a quiet night and look at the conditions tomorrow for a run down to the Walton Backwaters or the Stour.'

'The Stour first,' the mate retorted gleefully.

'Then we'll go and find our quiet anchorage up Landermere Creek – far from the madding crowd,' the skipper said, pinching from Thomas Hardy.

They both settled, heads still, apart from the gentle, almost imperceptible flicker of their eyes as the pages of their books were consumed one by one.

Looking up sometime later, the skipper had seen his mate looking shorewards, so he said, 'The Ramsholt Arms was once a farmhouse. I believe there was originally an inn up the road, closer to the population.'

'It … wasn't it different years ago?' the mate asked.

'Yes, a lot different. It's been extensively modernised since the early 1980s.'

Later, the skipper had learnt more: Simper says that with the greater use of the area, from tourists and visitors, a local gentleman converted the farmhouse into a pub. He said, 'Lord Rendlesham, aware of the growing number of people coming into East Suffolk on holiday by railway, adapted the Dock Farmhouse into the "Ramsholt Arms Hotel" … it did not have a pub sign until 2001.'

For supper that evening they enjoyed a brace of succulent lamb cutlets each, served with gorgeous local new potatoes and a salad – 'That was lovely,' the skipper said, licking his lips afterwards. The mate smiled, visibly more relaxed: earlier she'd been feeling somewhat apprehensive at the morrow's bar crossing … the evening's forecast was good.

The next morning, they were underway straight after breakfast, the tide had an hour to ebb and by the time they reached the entrance it would be slack or just on the turn. As it happened, it took a little longer to make that short trip down: the skipper had left a reef in the mains'l, as a precaution. The breeze was nothing more than gentle upon departure but had picked up as the hamlet of Felixstowe Ferry hove in sight.

'Right,' the skipper said, 'I'll stow the jib and we'll motor, sail down, past the shingle. We'll have to tack, as you know, outside.' He left the mate to navigate down past the ferry. The tide, the skipper saw, had turned. 'Tide'll be with us outside,' he called to the mate as he lashed the jib down.

All looked well … then passing round the inner buoy, the Mid Knoll, they saw that there were rollers outside … the mate had looked at the skipper, he looked ahead … as the mainsail had drawn properly. All around them, the tide was pouring through the Knolls. Spray was thrown up on the outer sides and skittered across the shingle.

'Tide's running hard,' the skipper said. He glanced at their echo sounder and looking at the mate added, 'We're fine …' Within him, the skipper had felt coldly the vitality of the North Sea. Its heartbeat pulsed, and in the shingle shallows, a million pebbles ground and grated in response. He said nothing.

The boat had started to move from a heave coming inwards from the entrance … then the yacht's bow rose up and crashed down. The depth sounder showed two and a half metres … the skipper frowned, hard; 'thank you,' he said, looking skywards!

'You alright?' the mate said weakly: she hadn't been. It was written strongly across her face.

The whoosh and roar from the tide ripping through the submerged channels between mounds of almost-fluid shingle was stupendous. The grinding of stone on stone and their rumblings, were eerie indeed. They were nearly clear, and then the outer buoy shot past on their port side. 'Right oh,' the skipper said, clipping on his harness, I'm going forward to set the jib.'

Whilst removing the jib lashings, a wall of water came crashing across the foredeck, leaving the skipper dripping from head to toe. Looking up at the masthead burgee, the skipper saw that they were sailing broad on the wind with the engine going too. 'What's going on,' he'd thought. He looked back at the mate and gesticulated – their normal engine signals – the mate slowed the beast to an idle, coming back onto a reach. A sense of normality soon returned, and the boat rode the seas instead of trying to dive through them. Those seas, though, out in the open, were of far greater magnitude than anticipated. The skipper hadn't dallied with the jib '... a roller jib would be a boon ... perhaps one day,' the skipper had thought.

'Sorry about that,' was the mate's greeting! 'I'd brought the boat's head round ... wasn't concentrating ... was watching you,' she exclaimed! 'I was worried about you ...'

Comforting! '... nearly drowned me ...' he said laughing and hugging her tightly.

'It's a good job we put our oilies on,' the skipper said, continuing to grin broadly at his sheepish mate while tidying things around the cockpit.

They then settled onto a close reach, an outwards leg. The boat intermittently smothered in spray, bashed and crashed through the wind over tide rollers and ragged water. The cabin rang with noise! At times, seas sluiced along the side decks too. The skipper enjoyed the sailing, but not the rolling waves that had thrown them sharply about. The mate had hung on grimly, but their boat had looked after them. It was, in some respects, exhilarating stuff – for the skipper!

They sailed a mile out. The next tack took them down past Felixstowe pier, and then another outward leg put them near the ship channel, where they had to sail back

... the outer buoy shot past on their port side. (Drawn by Gwendoline D. Ardley)

and forth for two ships to clear away. Eventually, after crossing the channel, they bore away for Harwich Haven. Sailing in from the yacht crossing, the wind, closing the shore, had more south in it. 'That'll be useful,' the skipper thought: discussions had not been the order of the day. The mate had need of a recovery time.

Turning past the breakwater, they went onto a run with the rollers behind them. The dinghy gamely tripped along behind, surged and shot forwards in a headlong rush before snapping back on its painter. It had bashed into the transom ladder, but only once. Then, as if by some magic switch, the peace of the haven enveloped them. It was a wonderful feeling.

Gybing round the nose of the old naval pier, they crossed the channel to stay clear of ship movements, and reached along the north side of the Stour. The sky had broken too; the sun shone thinly at first, gaining in power as time went on. That sun, when it had appeared, dappled the hills on the Essex and Suffolk shores, lightening and darkening them in a variety of shades, greens – blues even – and wheat-ripe yellows. Those dapples were cast between darting shadows by high, fast-moving, cauliflower clouds. The sail, though, was glorious: the wind diminishing as they went, its strength sapped as they moved further inland.

Closing with some moorings under the cliffs of Wrabness, the skipper had stowed the mainsail and they ghosted onwards, slowly – very sedately. The moorings were privately owned, but owners away weren't adverse to visitors hanging on for a while. The skipper always looked for a weedy one – a good indication that it was, at least temporarily, vacant.

'There's one,' the mate called back from the foredeck, 'that orange one.'

'They're all orange ...'

'No they're not! That one, over there,' the mate indicated, pointing a few boat lengths ahead and away to port. Their own mooring line was soon run through the buoy's ring and the boat swung to it, at rest.

'Tea,' the mate had quickly called, as the skipper finished lashing the jib along the guard-rail, before sluicing weed and tiny shrimps from the foredeck.

'Grand,' he called aft: it seemed hours since lunch, which they'd enjoyed, coming up river.

The skipper had sighed, 'the heavy sailing' (of earlier) 'has given me a few aches,' he murmured. 'It lasted less than an hour and seems an age ago.'

'What's that?' the mate called.

'Nothing, I'm hanging the damp stuff up to air ... then I'll set the cockpit table in place.'

'Okay, cake?'

'Mmmm, yes please.'

Over their tea, the skipper had watched the sun, by then out most of the time, but well on its downward path. It shone on the multicoloured sandy cliff, heightening the curving strata of differing coloured sands. The sun, too, glinted on many windows, for a profusion of summer chalets sat dotted amongst overhanging trees. It was picturesque. It was comforting.

The skipper, re-energised, by his tea, said, 'I think I might snatch those hues,' as he dived below to grab his watercolours and cartridge pad.

The mate smiled.

5

The Borders and Backwaters of Essex

The tide was rising. Close to the beach and the remains of a steel Humber barge, the boat swung to a light southerly breeze scuffing the water under the picturesque knoll of Wrabness. The skipper hoisted the sails leaving them to shiver and shake harmlessly until ready. The mate dropped the mooring as the jib was held aback. They were underway, both quietly thanking whoever for the mooring loan as they sailed gently westwards along the wide open river, framed on either side with tree-covered hills. Ahead, away in the distance, a smudge almost, was Mistley and Manningtree. They were bound for Manningtree at the head of the tidal waterway – the Manningtree River as it used to be known.

It was an idyllic morning, with some welcome sunshine too. They discussed the breeze: although a southerly still, it was forecasted to become a north-westerly by the morrow and remain settled for a few days. 'That'll be nice,' the mate had candidly remarked, thinking of the previous day.

'Yes, we'll drop down into the backwaters tonight, or if the breeze is light, we'll fetch up under Ewarton Ness.' The mate nodded as if in agreement ...

Manningtree was an Essex gem. It sat just below the Cattewade, a river control system for the Stour and its tidal limit. The skipper's old sailing home delivered stone here when the Cattewade was under construction towards the end of the 1800s. The countryside was typically Constable, and it should be said, he'd painted in Essex as much as in Suffolk – though Suffolk folk like to think that 'they own Constable'. In the skipper's view, one of Constable's finest paintings was of Hadleigh Castle – in Essex – of course, overlooking the Thames. Its home was at the Yale Centre of British Art in Newhaven, Connecticut, in the United States of America. The skipper had seen it during a London exhibition. Manningtree had a sailing club, filled daily with an eclectic band of boatmen, maintaining a friendly, open and inviting atmosphere. On a previous visit, the mate had been given a marrow and some runner beans ... just for being there, by a gangling old boy, hailing originally from the south of Essex.

Off Stutton Ness, a place that they'd fetched up in before, there was a shallow, protected creek at low water, where once they'd sat out a northerly blow. The skipper remarked about some old wharves hereabouts. On the east side of the Ness there was Graham's wharf, built originally by a coal exploration company. None had been found! (Coal had been mined in the 'south' though – pits existed near Canterbury, in Kent, and the coal was shipped out of Whitstable.) Graham's wharf was then used for the import of coal, and probably other commodities too. Across the bay another wharf, where a dinghy was moored, was seen. 'That's Stutton Mill. It's as much a Ness as the actual Ness – look,' the skipper said, pointing.

Leaving Stutton Mill behind, they had to concentrate, for the water got appreciably shallower. A turn too was needed, heading away from the middle of the river, towards the quickly looming waterside town of Mistley.

'It's strange,' the skipper remarked, 'there were numerous wharves on the Suffolk shore, but few on the Essex side – between Harwich and here – strange. There's an old hard up Jacques Fleet ... always a dinghy moored there,' he nodded backwards, 'and by those old barge remains we've just passed, there was another hard. The barge was the *Victoria*,' he added, staring thoughtfully at nothing in particular.

'Concentrate,' the mate barked – an order almost – not wanting to end up on the putty. He was ... dreaming again ... at the helm too!

Gradually, to the south, the distant river edge across an expanse of mud, rapidly being covered by the flood, had drawn in. The confined and limited channel zigzagged on its approach to Mistley, but it was well buoyed: commercial craft still used the quays here. At a quay, marked on some charts as being public, there'd been a recent furore over access. It had been recently fenced off – the battle continued. It was an ancient right of way, it was said.

Below Mistley a rusting collection of old craft were jammed ashore, all at the end of their lives – '... awaiting the oxyacetylene torch?' the skipper remarked not expecting an answer ... It looked horrible, scarring the beauty of the surroundings. Beyond was a new mud marina where a rigged spritsail barge, the *Victor*, was seen, perfectly in keeping with the area's maritime past.

'Wasn't she on the Medway?' the mate asked as they swept past.

'Err, yes, that was before she spent some time down on the south coast – Portsmouth ... the chap who's got the little *Whippet* now owned her then. He rebuilt the *Victor* after she finished trading (as a motor barge) and kept her at his yard – by the pub – sold her years ago though.'

'Oh yes ...'

'Horlock, a local family, operated a fleet of barges from here,' the skipper began. 'They built up quite a fleet and had a clutch of steel barges built, many of which are still sailing. They'd their own yard.' Shipbuilding had indeed taken place at Mistley from around the late 1770s. 'The boatyard and marina are descendents,' the skipper added.

A misty-looking view down Mistley waterfront and the still-busy commercial wharves.

Mistley towers – all that remains of Adam's church.

Sailing past the quays, they saw that many of the old maltings were being transformed into waterside apartments. 'Better than pulling them down,' the mate quipped. The quays dated back to around 1720 and had been continuously extended as trade grew. All was now quiet except for delivery of timber and building materials. 'Did you see those bricks,' the mate said, prodding the skipper.

He looked through the binoculars. 'They're from Belgium!'

'The *EDME* carried a token cargo from here to Maldon a few years ago. It was about fifty tonnes,' the skipper murmured while still looking.

'Concentrate!' the mate said.

Passing the quays, they lost the wind from time to time but the tide took them on. Then the river bent away, it seemed, towards Suffolk. 'It's always so fascinating to come up on the early flood. It gives you a feel for a place. Creeping up on the tide with the lowered plate acting as a depth sounder ... scraping from time to time ...' the skipper said. 'It has a charm!'

Looking back at Mistley, the twin towers of a church designed by Adam, the eighteenth-century architect, stood alone, its 'house' missing. The church had been part of a grand plan. Robert Rigby, a rich gentleman, was inspired to build a spa town to rival all others of the time. It failed, but the towers had remained, as had the quays which Rigby first formalised. The town of Mistley was a model of what small places should look and feel like. The skipper and mate had visited by road, some years before, and again recently too, stopping for tea.

At Manningtree, they rounded up under engine and hooked a buoy off the sailing club. The skipper cleared up on deck while the mate busied herself below collecting bags and her little list of stores. She reappeared as the skipper pulled the dinghy alongside. 'Good timing!' they both chimed.

Although the club and town have a friendly, comforting feel, some of the riff raff were as bad as any that the skipper had come across. On a previous visit and wanting to place their bags of shopping in the dinghy, they found that their tender was nowhere to be seen. The skipper was about to explode, his anger volcanic. Amongst a group of children, of around nine or ten, playing on the beach, a cheeky voice had chirped, 'wern' me mate it wer' 'im,' as they'd scampered, guiltily, away. The skipper wasn't at that moment interested: his capable schoolteacher mate would deal with them …

The skipper spotted the tender drifting amongst the moored yachts, bobbing on its lonely passage to Suffolk. Fortuitously, a chap from the sailing club, quickly learning of their problem after coming ashore from his own boat, immediately gave up his dinghy. After a frantic spell of rowing the skipper caught the drifting tender … well, it had stopped: its painter had caught on a mooring – a stroke of luck! At that moment, too, the Essex River Police rolled up in their giant rib – they were out patrolling the borders … Two of the crew recognised the skipper, from when they'd kept a larger patrol launch near Canvey Island. After a few consoling words … content that nothing had been stolen … they'd gone on their way. What more could they do? The skipper had had his own thoughts …

Back ashore, the skipper was met by the mate, 'I've had words with that little group,' she said, indicating a gathering along the shore and grinning, 'they've threatened to fetch their dads, so I said, "Good" and continued to harangue them – they're not happy bunnies at the moment!'

The skipper immediately brightened, 'Well done!'

'Oh, the chap said, "could we put his dinghy in the pound" over there,' waving with her arm. That done, they'd repaired to the club for a shandy.

'Good timing,' they both chimed. (Drawn by Gwendoline D. Ardley)

The skipper had still been angry when they left the club. The boys, thought to be those responsible, had run off as he approached the dinghy. The mate grinned at her skipper and ruffled his hair, as he bent to untie the painter, 'no harm done,' she said … But that was history. Their present visit was much happier!

Again they sailed off the mooring, always a grand thing to do. It calmed the skipper – especially as he felt the itch of watching binoculars from the sailing club. The tide was well over the flats, so the bows were pointed almost directly east, towards a distant Wrabness, its greens looking dark and almost black in the afternoon sunshine. The wind was gentle, more from the west than south and they were carried as much by the ebb as the breeze.

'Think it'll be Ewarton Ness, tonight,' the skipper said softly.

'We'll get anchored and have tea – well, you will,' the mate said, gently nuzzling her skipper.

Some time later, around three hours after departing, they picked their spot; just off the ruined barge wharf now just a few gnarled timbers. As the mate came round into the breeze, the skipper let the anchor splash overboard, paying out cable to his desired length. Then he dropped the mains'l. 'Depth's okay,' the mate said quietly, before disappearing below to put the skipper's kettle on to boil – tea and cake.

In the anchorage were a couple of old yachts. The old yachts held the skipper's attention. They looked pristine – 'probably from the classic yacht club,' the skipper commented. 'They do the work and you sail the boat.'

'Wouldn't suit you,' the mate said, smiling, 'ours is as much your hobby – well – after me – she's your life!' She grinned deeply, her eyes twinkled too as she lowered them back to her book.

Whilst they sat reading, a spritsail barge came up from Harwich, 'She's the *Hydrogen*,' the skipper said, confidently. She was too. She passed, motoring with her topsail set. 'Airing the sail,' the skipper remarked, 'for the punters.' She'd continued up to Wrabness and anchored.

Earlier, passing the wide open Holbrook Bay the skipper and mate had talked about the Royal Hospital School. It sat up on the hill in Suffolk. It had once been for children of seafarers, but was now a fashionable private school. Some students had been out

She'd passed, motoring with her topsail set, 'airing the sail,' the skipper remarked, 'for the punters.' (Drawn by Gwendoline D. Ardley)

on the water, sailing. Safety 'Ribs' had buzzed about, shepherding their flock. 'It was grand seeing those kids – future sailors? Possibly,' the skipper said.

Whilst sailing on his own, a season or two earlier, the skipper had sketched the school during a monstrous downpour. He'd come up to Wrabness as the heavens had opened. A man had leaned out of his boat, calling, 'that buoy's alright.' The skipper had smartly moored and rigged the boom tent. The boat had swung with the aft end open to the Suffolk shore, giving the view. Later, to the mate, he'd said 'I've only seen rain like that in Singapore – thick, silvery rods of water, coming down as straight as a die.'

Up Holbrook Creek, beneath the school, and also up another, Gallister, in which they anchored the boat during a north-easterly blow some years ago, were the rotting remains of a several wharves. There'd been a brick workings too, still working into the 1960s. There was another wharf to the west of their present anchorage. All trace had gone following sea wall realignment. 'The number of wharves on this river was massive in comparison to the Orwell,' the skipper remarked, thinking back to a recent visit.

'Do you remember that night at anchor in Gallister?' the skipper asked the mate. She nodded: for they had a most uncomfortable time of it. 'This is not a river for the prevailing winds, probably why it's relatively unspoilt,' pausing, 'Let's hope it remains that way.'

'Yes,' the mate said, smiling, 'it's so beautiful here – I love it!'

Over on the Essex shore was Copperas Bay. The bay was bird reserve owned by the Essex Wildlife Trust – the woods too. The marshes, inundated too often by sea-level rise, had become mounds of bare clay, running inland for a good distance. A picture, from the air, looked weird to the skipper when he'd seen one some time beforehand – a muddy desert. 'It's a prelude to what awaits huge areas of marsh around the East Coast in the coming years,' the skipper had muttered: over a fifteen-year period, a recent study had confirmed, saltings loss in the Stour had been recorded at around 40 per cent. (*The Essex Coast ... beyond 2000*, published by English Nature).

Later that evening, the skipper went off in the tender for a sail while the mate did duty at the sink: he'd cooked! Their repast, deliciously tender pork cooked with cider and onions, was a boat favourite.

Returning after a short, quiet sail, they sat out awhile, as evening had drawn in, with a coffee, enjoying the tranquillity of this quiet anchorage, its atmosphere seeping into them ...

The next morning, with a fine south-westerly tugging at the burgee, they left promptly, quickly passed Parkstone Quay, with two towering ferries alongside. 'The quay was built on what was once an island,' the skipper said, adding, 'Ramsey Island – only a name now.'

Reaching out through the Harwich Harbour, the skipper set a course for the Walton Backwaters. Well, actually, they tacked ... finally dropping anchor in the Walton Channel, to the south of Stone Point, in waters that were quiet and placid. The mate had a 'fond' memory of this channel. During her first year of sailing, they'd tacked up to the Twizzle in their engineless Yachting World People's Boat. Then, the very next day, because the wind had gone round, they'd tacked back out. 'Ha! ... must have known you needed the practice ...' the skipper always chortled when this episode was raised!

This place had been immortalised by Arthur Ransome in *Secret Water*, a story about a group of children who were allowed to camp on the main island of Horsey Island from where they'd explored and mapped their little world. The beauty and magic that exuded then, during the 1930s, and was loved too by Maurice Griffiths, had not diminished with time, even though there were innumerable moorings up the

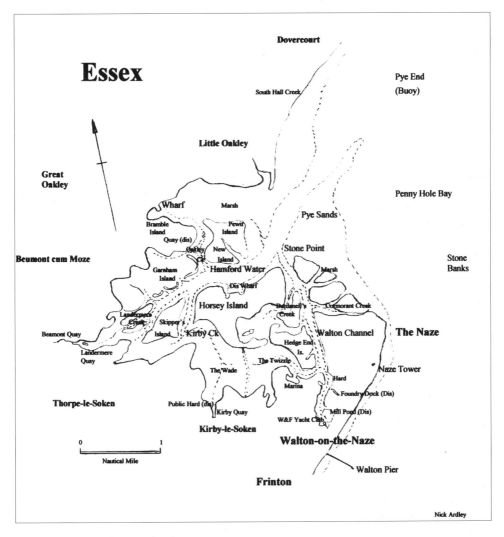

Chartlet of the Walton Backwaters.

main channel towards the town of Walton-on-the-Naze and round to a marina up the Twizzle, a creek that peters out in a flooded mere, known as the Wade. From that marina, at weekends in particular, shiny, plastic motor craft, with glinting chrome fittings, burbled and spluttered leaving wash waves that careered into the crumbling marshes. Arthur Ransome, the skipper was sure, would not approve! 'It's their speed,' the skipper said; 'it's the type of wash they leave in their wakes ... harsh and vicious.'

During the afternoon, over tea, they watched a group of people, two families it had seemed, setting up 'camp'. The skipper, mostly, watched the group play beach games, enjoy mud sliding and swimming ... Both had giggled at the youngsters' antics, and ... too at the parents ... disappearing across the grass-covered sandy point ... Later returning, from different directions, the couples displaying a marked closeness ... !

In the evening, preparing vegetables at the cockpit table for their supper, the group were seen collecting flotsam and jetsam. Soon a roaring campfire was seen. A barbeque was lit too. 'That's what family sailing should be like ...' the skipper commented, happily sipping his beer.

After supper, the skipper nipped off for a dinghy sail. He tacked up to the head of Walton channel, to the Twizzle, and then enjoyed a lazy run back, nodding to various 'yotties'. It was a tranquil evening, an almost blue sky, but 'night was rapidly approaching,' the skipper thought as he neared his little clinker yacht, glistening gold in the last of the sun as it slipped towards the horizon.

Back aboard, the mate had lit the cabin lights. The wicks turned low. The gentle light glowed around the varnish work, seductively. The skipper smiled, turning away as he remembered something. 'Heck, the riding light,' he said, immediately hooking it out of its stowage, checking its fuel level, lighting it and setting it aloft from the forestay. So many boats don't seem to bother these days ...

'Coffee ... and something?' the mate asked, grinning sweetly.

'Ooh, Yes Please...'

Settling back on their cushions, they watched and listened to the world. Ashore, the flickering embers of the campers' fire blinked as youngsters, barely seen, rushed to and fro. Excited voices drifted clearly across the smooth water as those children splashed along the beach. The lower tones of the adults reached them too. Above them all, the first stars had appeared in a darkening blue. The sun had gone, yet its glow tinged the skyline with shades of yellow, orange and purple. Those merged with deeper mauves and blues as a sort of darkness came. Along the beach were flashes of light, searching out belongings. 'They're clearing up,' the mate said in a hushed tone.

'Do you think they're Swallows and Amazons?' the skipper asked. The mate giggled: they'd both enjoyed those stories and reading them, too, to their son, when a youngster.

Down at the water's edge, the youngsters were still busy kicking up water at one another. The moon glinted on those splashes – phosphorescence – caused by tiny sea creatures in the rich tidal waters. Then a whistle struck up, a penny whistle perhaps, the sharp, but harmonious tunes trickled down to the yacht, where its two unobserved observers sat silently in appreciation.

The group's dinghies, a day boat and another smaller dinghy tethered astern rode to an anchor near the low-tide line. The line was long covered by the fresh flood. One of the older children, a boy, swam out to bring the little ships into the shore. A mast was seen to move against the low skyline as he clambered aboard. Shortly afterwards, an outboard, after a few stuttering purrs, crackled into life. 'It's an old Seagull,' the skipper said knowingly. That dinghy soon came past, coughing and spluttering, seemingly enveloped in its pall of exhaust fumes, carrying two adults with a couple of sleepy young children. None noticed their quiet watchers, in the yacht's cockpit.

Then it was quiet. Curlews and oystercatchers could be heard; Canada geese honked and argued along the mud flats, soon to be covered by the rising tide.

Slowly, the larger dinghy came up with the flood, her sails dark, in silhouette against the sky, gliding along with the night air. As it had wafted past, ghost like, the skipper, without any warning to his mate, called out firmly a challenge: 'Swallows or Amazons?'

The answer, with a cheerful chuckle, had been swift: 'Eels for Ever!' Were they awaiting that challenge? It was a true resonance of Ransome's yarn in *Secret Water*: the Eels had been local children (a tribe) who'd camped on the very same shingle and sand of Stone Point. The boat had soon disappeared into the night, leaving the skipper and mate chuckling as one or the other had nipped below to put the kettle back on the stove ...

Rising late the following morning, the skipper stumbled out into the cockpit. 'The riding light,' he exclaimed at his mate's murmurings. The sky had a summer look about it, 'Let's go round to the top of Landmere Creek today,' he called below, lowering the lamp, 'might see the seals up Oakley too.'

... a challenge: 'Swallows or Amazons?' The answer had been swift ... 'Eels for Ever!' (Drawn by Gwendoline D. Ardley)

Breakfast was soon done with – cereal and toast that morning. As soon as the skipper started to shorten the anchor cable, the mate appeared on deck with their life jackets ...

Reaching out of the intricate, narrow, buoyed entrance to the Walton Channel, they set to, tacking westwards down Hamford Water, passing a line of sunken lighters that acted as breakwaters to protect the weak, open northern head of Horsey Island. Reaching the entrance to Oakley Creek, they crossed the shallow bar, then well covered and reached comfortably deep into the marshes between Pewit (and New Island) and Garnham islands. An old wharf in a creek running under Bramble Island, but no longer an island, was passed. Rounding a bend they found the seals, dozens of them, basking up on the marsh edges and upper mud flats. Seeing the yacht, the younger ones slipped down the mud, they then popped up, inquisitively, sniffing and familiarising themselves – sensing no danger, they floundered up out of the water to wag their tails at the yacht ... it seemed to the watching mate!

'There's the end,' the skipper said, as a wharf, with a big sign that shouted 'No Landing' was seen. The engine had been started on the last stretch (much against the skipper's ways – but it was too narrow to tack). The wharf was used regularly by small coasters shipping raw materials to a fertiliser factory. Before that, ammunition had been manufactured in that remote place amongst the marshes. The skipper and mate had had a night in the backwaters on the spritsail barge *Pudge*, during a weekend with sailing club members some years before. It's one of the few times that they'd actually seen a coaster motor up into Oakley Creek on the tide – many of the barge

At the head of Oakley Creek is a lonely wharf where coasters still come and go.

crew hadn't believed the skipper's assertion about these creek crawling coasters – it was grand – 'does away with lorries,' he'd said!

Leaving the creek, they continued to tack up Hamford Water, working right up, with the tide, above Landmere Quay. At the quay, dating from the early 1800s, were several old buildings. One, just beyond the quay, was once a public house, closed since 1950, another, a cottage. All sat in an idyllic setting above the high-tide levels, surrounded by a stand of trees. A group of spectators, the inhabitants perhaps, stood and stared, chattering to one another. Their voices were clear to the yacht's crew. A voice cut across the placid surface, marked only by the yacht's ripples, 'Do you think they know what they're about ...' The skipper had grinned at the mate, and laughed quietly, shoreward!

Shortly after, as a maze of marsh with barely discernable openings, appeared to block their way, the skipper quietly called to the mate, 'We'll run back to the little anchorage we use. You tack. I'll drop the main as you come round – ready?'

With that, he'd gone forward. The mains'l soon rattled down the mast and was stowed along the boom, while the mate navigated backwards to 'their' anchorage. It was an anchorage they'd rarely seen other yachts use. At low water springs it had a comfortable two metres within it – mid-length – plenty for their shallow draft, though they'd often brushed the mud laying to the wind at the bottom of the ebb. It wasn't a worry!

Off the marsh, as the tide started to recede, came an almost astonishing scent, a powerful pungency, strong and saline. They both sniffed at it over a late lunch. It mixed well with the sweetness of some tuna that had appeared on plates, passed out to the skipper moments earlier.

'Do you remember your sail round Skipper's Island,' the mate asked, pausing. 'You did a circuit – one afternoon a year or two ago – I had a nap ...' she added, colouring a little: she was prone to little sleeps in the afternoon when afloat. And why not?

'Yes,' he said, 'it was very marshy round the back between the island and the land.' He paused, in thought, 'almost impassable on a lower tide. I wriggled through though and eventually worked back against a rising breeze, up Kirby Creek and then back down Landmere. You'd awoken and found your skipper still absent ... "Not resting from looking ..." you said, "until I got back." I remember!' Both grinned.

Reflecting and looking thoughtful, the mate started to say, 'That wasn't the first or the last time ...' but she stopped!

The island the skipper sailed round, Skipper's Island, was used by the Essex Naturalists' Society. A watchtower had been erected for the purposes of studying birds – the feathered variety – it was well used, the skipper understood. Although largely an island flooded at high water, mostly consisting of salt marsh and mud, an area of high ground had a block of deciduous trees upon it. It was a fascinating and beautiful place – very much a true interface of land and sea in miniature.

The skipper had sailed, on another time, through an opening to the north of the 'fingered' western end of Hamford Water, into an inland sea of water and marsh. He remembered sailing round tufts of grasses in a riddle of channels. That water, the flooded centre of Garnhams Island, was Ransome's 'Northern Sea' in *Secret Water*. The opening, the skipper had seen at low water, had been dammed, ragged rotting posts with sharp heart-wood points remained of the vain effort to control nature in the past.

In *Secret Water*, the Amazons, Nancy and Peggy, had gone off early on the last morning of their holiday, to map the last bit of 'their wilderness' before they and the Swallows were collected by, said Wardale, 'The Busk family who appeared ... as missionaries' when sailing into the backwaters on their yacht *Lapwing* to fetch the tribe back to Pin Mill. Could you imagine a group of youngsters, of between nine and about fourteen, being allowed to do that? Unlikely!

There was another opening into the inland sea opposite the entrance to Kirby Creek; it too had old stakes set in the mud. Kirby Creek wound its way southwards to a dock at Kirby–le–Soken. The dock was once a hive of trade and activity for the local community. An old warehouse had been converted into a dwelling and the dock was now private – limiting access. A public hard still existed close by; it had been inundated by marsh, but was still useable on the tide. Titchmarsh Marina close by had more or less ended the use of these old landings ...

Sitting nattering, they reminisced. They'd had so many days here in these marshy creeks sitting at anchor just enjoying a night to a few days, *far from the madding crowd*. They both remembered dinghy trips up to the old quay at Beaumont. They'd sailed, on one occasion, up the cut, a channel dug through the marshes to allow easier access to the quay by spritsail barges. The quay was built in 1832, by Guy's Hospital, using stones from an old London Bridge. During the 1600s, Guy's Hospital bought up a large number of the manorial rights locally and needed a sturdier quay to ship out produce. Lime making was an industry situated on the quay too. Some years ago, most of the buildings, old warehouses, were pulled down, but one was refurbished and remained as a token remnant. On the edge of the marsh, just beyond the quay, the bottom of a spritsail barge, the *Rose* of Maldon, once used as a home, sat shattered and broken, her rudder standing proudly.

Later, after supper – a pasta dish, concocted from a mix of fresh vegetables, tinned seafood and a sauce, enjoyed out in the cockpit – they mulled over their next move. The evening's forecast had given warnings of winds for the next two days. 'Look,' said the mate, 'let's have a couple of nights in Titchmarsh, then leave for the Colne from there. Be an afternoon high tide by then too.'

'That's fine by me,' the skipper added quickly, knowing that the mate's plan was

Above: A view down the man-made barge cut with the skipper's dinghy alongside Beaumont Quay. The last warehouse, now preserved, is in the background.

Left: A typical East Coast sight, the rudder and stern timbers of the *Rose* of Maldon sit just beyond the stone quay.

sound. Scratching his back and twitching, 'A shower too … !'

'And we need a fresh bottle of gas …' the mate reminded him. It was settled.

They spent the two days' enforced wait restoring and cleaning ship.

On a windy, blustery second day, they walked into Walton town. A strange place, almost old fashioned. It had a charm, but it too needed more. For lunch, they walked down to the Walton and Frinton Yacht Club, a place visited many times, often by water. It had a heavenly situation on a fork of land at the head of Foundry Reach, a muddy creek with small craft moorings along its twists and turns. The club dated back to 1908. The present building, much changed, was originally built elsewhere and was moved to this site in the 1920s. It was erected on stilts – on the remains of a windmill. Its reputed origin was a coastal submarine listening post. The inimitable Maurice Griffiths used the Walton club as a base after his first marriage, living aboard a large old smack. He and his wife commuted to London daily. The club had its own peaceful marina, owned by a trust associated with the club, a twee grass banked pool with a tidal sill. A couple of boatyards had survived at the head of the creek too. It was a place where the skipper, and the mate for that matter, felt very much at home.

Adjacent to the club were the remnants of a tide mill basin and beyond was a sprawling caravan park. Lower down, nearer to the Twizzle, was a hard and a walled-off creek – The Foundry Dock – from where fishing boats. Light industry was situated inland here, where a steel barge, complete with spars, was built in sections. It was later used in the film *Atonement* abandoned on the 'Dunkirk beaches' – filmed at Redcar, way up the north-east coast. Another old hard, Eagles Hard, private but open to the public, gave access to the shore. The skipper hadn't used it for years.

Recently, the skipper had heard that some sort of development had been mooted up the creek. A dam and perhaps a marina re-dug from the silted-up mill tide pool

The Walton & Frinton Yacht Club at the head of Foundry Reach. To the right-hand side can be seen a Martello Tower, and to the left-hand side are the broken banks of the millpond.

to enclose the creek for long-term flood protection for the rear of Walton. What a scheme! Marsh loss would be minimal. Moorings could be reduced in the channels – 'I'm for it,' the skipper had mentioned in a few more words, 'it would solve your mud problem ...'

The mate, who'd been using the marina's laundry facilities on their last full day, met a very miserable lady ... The lady's husband had had a dream. A boat! He wanted to traipse around the south coast and beyond. The trouble was that they (well, he) had only just learnt how to sail, on a course ... The wife wasn't enamoured ... 'My husband has said "We can't go anywhere ... wind's against us ..." I just want to go caravanning ...' she said to the mate.

The mate said softly, 'There's lots of day sailing you can do locally,' and smiled. 'Why not go up the Orwell, to Pin Mill or Ipswich. Even round here ...' waving her arm across the expanse of the backwaters.

'He's not interested in any of that – wants to go deep sea.' The lady sighed. The mate had nodded, grimly, feeling for the lady's predicament.

Leaving together, the two had parted beside a swanky, new, French-built yacht: the lady's home of at least twelve metres. Reaching her own yacht, half the length, nearly, and probably a quarter of the volume, the mate stroked the boat before recounting her conversation to the skipper.

'Bloody fool,' he said, referring to the other skipper, 'he's jolly well ruined the sailing life of his mate,' he'd paused briefly, 'his too now!' grinning. 'What's wrong with the creeks and rivers ...' He left it there ... shaking his head.

'Yes,' the mate said, adding vehemently, 'If you'd done that to me twenty-eight years ago ... I'd not be here now ...' The skipper nodded sagely: he knew that. He'd 'nursed' his mate's fears a few times in the past, and heard about those of others – he'd listened and learned – it had worked.

On that third evening, after a convivial dinner at the restaurant overlooking the yacht harbour, a harbour gouged from the surrounding fields, they'd been in good fettle. Earlier, a favourable forecast, a north-westerly of no more than moderate winds holding for a few days had been announced. It would be a prompt start, so they'd not dallied over coffee, or a nightcap.

The next day, with three hours of ebb still to run, they departed the marina for the Colne. The skipper had set the genoa, the mate walked the boat out of their mooring finger near the entrance and the sail had pulled them silently away ... Guiltily, the skipper had glanced towards the marina office, the window blinds had twitched, but the radio remained silent. The skipper had raised an arm, in a wave: he'd recently been 'told off' for sailing away from a berth up the Orwell. Marinas didn't like it or dinghies for that matter; the skipper then looked astern at it, as it had tugged at its painter, tripping along behind ...

As they gybed, to head across the flats of Pennyhole Bay, the mate said, as she handed out some bacon rolls, 'Thanks, I've really enjoyed it up here,' she smiled. 'These backwaters are akin to being on the Swale, but not as lonely.' She loved the loneliness of the Swale. 'It's beautiful,' but pausing awhile and obviously deep in thought, she finally added, '... but I've had enough, for now ... I'm looking forward to all those other places.'

6

Tendring Bottom

Around the buttocks of the Tendring Peninsula, the eastern bulge of Essex, a delta of creeks, mud and marshy wastes meandered inland, like a sprig from Darwin's evolutionary tree. The dominant tendril was the Colne river itself, running up and through Colchester, that most ancient of towns and on, inland, as a freshwater river. The skipper and mate had touched upon the area earlier that season when anchored for a night in Pyfleet, that evocative channel between Mersea Island and the mainland, opposite Brightlingsea. The area was another favourite of the skipper and mate, a place of many memories.

Brightlingsea was the hub of the marsh-riddled web; it sat in the entrance of its busy creek. Sat at the entrance was Bateman's Tower, built as a watch tower for a past need. Before the land behind was reclaimed and drained, the tower stood on a marshy promontory. It was now covered with car parks and caravans. The town had an ancient connection to the major Cinque Ports: it was a satellite port, providing ships for the navy in past times. Ashore, places of historic interest such as the town's museum near the central green and amongst Victorian terraced houses, near the waterfront, a Cinque Port Board of Trade Wreck Warehouse was found. An old Custom house situated near the hard was still in use by a sailing association too. The hard itself, well kept and used, signified the port's past prowess as a maritime base for fishing and as a trading point for spritsail barges and sailing coasters. It would once have been thick with vessels. Smacks and barges can still be seen on the hard. In recent times, the skipper had seen the steel barge *Fertile*, converted from a lighter, and the powerful Skillinger Smack *Pioneer* following her relaunch after transportation from an inland farm where she'd been reconstructed.

They'd bowled into the Colne after a quiet, comfortable sail down from the Walton Backwaters the previous day, anchoring off Stone Point for the night at the eastern tip of Mersea Island. It had been very different from a passage the skipper made, alone, earlier that season, when voyaging homewards from the Orwell, when he'd bashed his way down the Wallet through short, steep seas whipped up by a sharp south-westerly. On a more recent occasion, they and many other craft were well and truly 'Walloped in the Wallet' on a day that was forecasted to be fine. Such is life afloat! The mate had said about that passage, when gazing at the mass of new wind generators being constructed and tacking out by the Old Gunfleet Tower, 'It seems tamed – fenced in … even' then added '… but it's not.'

'Yes,' the skipper had grimacing, adding, 'a fenced in look may give a comforting feeling – but it's still bloody, if it chooses!'

The next day was a mixture of cloud and sunny spells. It was a good day to potter on the tide up the Colne to Wivenhoe and Rowhedge, and then drop back down to Brightlingsea later in the afternoon. Their plan was to use the pontoon berthing as a base for a dinghy visit to St Osyth the following day. The skipper had had other plans

The Cinque Port Board of Trade
Wreck Warehouse in Brightlingsea.

too: he wanted to go up beyond the waterside town, inland, exploring the marshy interior.

'That was nice,' the skipper said, looking up from his book, his tea to hand '... a gentle meander up the Colne, a gorgeous sunshine sail ... a fair breeze back too.'

The mate nodded: she liked that type of sailing.

'Sunshine has brought out the day-trippers too. Did you see those hoards ambling along St Osyth Stone?'

'Yes ...' she said, looking across the water towards Brightlingsea hard, '... the ferry's busy too.' It was seen loaded down to its gunnels again.

During their sail up river they'd passed numerous creeks running into low marshy land, which dominated the lower stretches. To the west, the domain of the British Army, it was a barren waste used for infantry training. To the east, they passed along the edge of a high sea wall protecting the backside of Brightlingsea; here, not such a long time before, had run a railway, the Winkle Line. It had been dismantled. In places, the line had run on stilts above the marshes. The walled shore was then further inland. Further up that bank they passed Alresford Creek. The creek wandered inland up to an old tide mill at Thorington. The mill was still in working condition as a museum and was a place that the skipper and mate had not yet poked the bow of their boat into. That creek and the larger running past Brightlingsea almost encircled the town. Opposite Alresford Creek, on land covered with scrub and low trees, sat a nature reserve, amongst old gravel diggings. On the shore, an old jetty mouldered away, and close by, the bottom of a spritsail barge sat aslant the beach, dumped after her last voyage. Her hull had long rotted away. The riverbanks had, by then, a different feel: they closed in. The eastern side was pretty with wooded, rolling slopes, and a real cliff that fell to the water's edge.

Fingringhoe Wick nature reserve with remains of ballast jetty to left-hand side and bottom of a sailing barge to the right-hand side – dumped at the end of her days.

Passing Alresford Creek, the channel strayed westwards, more or less, so they handed the sails rather than tack in the shallow, narrowing waters and continued under their trusty diesel. On the Fingrinhoe shore was a busy ballast quay with two of Prior's motor barges alongside. Sand or ballast was being shot into the hold of one – building materials destined for London – and on the other, the crew were battening the hatches. 'They'll be away on this tide,' the skipper said, confidently.

'Back away,' the skipper murmured. 'There are plans to build a new wharf, just below Alresford Creek.' The mate had looked inquisitively at the skipper and he continued quickly, 'I've heard that it's the most economical and environmentally friendly way to move it away.'

'What?' she said.

'The aggregates,' the skipper added.

'Oh yes,' the mate uttered with just a modicum of interest.

Just below Rowhedge, there was a little river, thick with marsh and mud. It was known as the Roman River. Further inland, at the back of the village of Fingrinhoe, the river was fresh. There it meandered, in a tranquil fashion, across the lush, green meadows in a rural idyll.

Passing the little river, Brown's old boatyard, where RNLI craft were maintained, was seen. Its remnants looked forlorn and sad. Further on were two pretty waterside public houses with strips of open green space alongside the river. It looked idyllic! Beyond the village of Rowhedge, above a new pontoon for the Wivenhoe ferry, they turned. The skipper had recently visited Rowhedge with a friend, an old neighbour, who'd found a love for the water some years earlier after the skipper had taken him sailing: the chap was a born sailor too. Since then, they'd enjoyed two annual cruises, aptly named by the wives, 'The Jolly Boys Outings.' The mate hadn't wanted to dally

Left: The Thames Sailing Barge Trust's *Pudge* shortly after major renovation work had been completed (at the time, further costly work was still required). She was moored at Rowhedge.

Below: The glorious – because it has remained active – waterfront at Wivenhoe.

– preferring Wivenhoe – so dropping down stream, they moored off Wivenhoe Sailing Club, below the tidal barrier, and rowed ashore for a pleasant lunch.

Rowhedge and Wivenhoe especially, had once supported boat and shipbuilding of some magnitude. The last vessel to be built at the old yard of James Cook of Wivenhoe was a sail training ship for the Jubilee Trust. The ship, the *Lord Nelson*, was designed to carry wheelchair users as full members of the crew – a mighty event of inclusiveness at the time. The town had had a flourishing maritime history since early times. In more recent times, the yachts of kings, princes and the rich were outfitted by men from both villages. Fishermen predominated amongst the racing crews during the season. Now though, both places sat sleepily and quietly by the flaccid flow of the Colne's silt-laden waters. Some old smacks and a few rustic yachts had remained in traditional moorings along the river frontages, giving each a special charm. The skipper had heard that a new dock was planned for fishermen as part of a riverside redevelopment at Wivenhoe – glory, glory!

After berthing at Brightlingsea, the skipper had spent some time ensuring that their boat was well fendered: here, irresponsible people charged past creating heavy wash waves. Settling down, a pot of tea with the obligatory slice of cake had appeared. Draining his first mug, he found it necessary to disturb his mate … 'It's said that oyster shells from these parts have been found as far away as Rome – amazing isn't it?'

'Not surprising,' the mate said, quickly, 'the town up the river (Colchester) was the capital for their British domain,' pausing, she added, '… the Romans. The area was very busy with all sorts of trade to Roman Europe, I expect. Saint Helena was reputed to have been born here to King Coel. She was in the forefront of Roman Christianity.' She paused, smiled briefly and continued, 'You've read Evelyn Waugh's *Helena*. He spun a yarn about it.'

The skipper, nodding had looked skywards, as if for inspiration. 'That book was a difficult read, I remember.'

The mate then started to say, 'Do you remember …' pausing awhile, '… when we visited Colchester sometime ago we saw the Flemish area.'

The skipper was listening.

'Like other places, Flemings came here. They brought their cloth-making expertise with them, helping to make this country great.' (The Flemish people had come here after the Zuider Zee had progressively flooded during the fourteenth and fifteenth centuries. Later, Huguenots followed for different reasons.)

'Yes,' the skipper said quietly, 'people today forget the industriousness of those influxes – the country has always soaked people up. It's what makes us what we are.'

'It's sad about Colchester no longer being a port though,' the skipper murmured, 'the Hythe Quays were once such a bustle of coastal trade – housing now – on the whole.' The port had been deregulated by an Act of Parliament in 2001.

'Didn't you say that, last century, Colchester only had spritsail barges and small coasters trading up to the Hythe?' the mate added.

The skipper nodded: coasters of up to 500 tonnes had used the River Colne, and as recently as 1984, a million tonnes of cargo came up to the three places. At Wivenhoe, where once there had been vitality, a string of waterfront houses sat on barren, once busy, wharves. Rolling swathes of mud and silt had infested the old berths.

On the following day, after a visit to the shops for fresh stores and something frozen for the morrow, they went up to St Osyth in the dinghy on the first of the tide. It had been a threatening day. Clouds traversed slowly across the sky, blocking the sunshine, but by the end, remarkably, it had remained dry and become warm and sunny. On their passage up the creek, winding through banks of mud and marsh, they were reminded of the closeness of farming to these muddy waters. Unseen tractors hidden

The partially rebuilt hull of the school ship *Thalatta* at St Osyth. *Thalatta* is a large mule-rigged spritsail barge (her mizzen is set with a gaff instead of the traditional sprit).

A spritsail barge at St Osyth Mill. She was the *May Flower*. She arrived on 13 September 1931 with a cargo of flints from Hoo Creek on the River Medway. The *May Flower* departed on the 16th, light, after a Board of Trade inspection. (Print courtesy of Ron Green)

beyond the grassy sea walls were heard, hard at work. It seemed familiar, like sailing up Faversham Creek, 'twixt land and sea,' the skipper commented.

'Look,' the skipper said, pointing at the gooey mud banks, 'there's the stern of a barge up in that old dock.' It was largely out of sight from their position down in the rill. The remains were of the spritsail barge *Bluebell*, he knew; she'd been abandoned in the dock at the end of her life, latterly as a houseboat. The dock was built for shipping out shingle, dug from the surrounding fields. Those fields on that side of the creek were now largely used as a nature reserve. The area had once supported brick-making industry too, but they were nearer the village. The manufacture of bricks was a very local industry – mainly for transportation reasons.

Soon after came the wharves, ancient buildings and a morass of houseboats that sat up on mud flats, cord grass sprouting in patches around them. The last part of the passage was slow going – at the speed of the tide. Eventually, they'd made fast to a rustic old fishing boat that had seen better days, but nonetheless, a welcome transit platform. Soon after getting ashore, the skipper was away, mooching about the yard.

There'd been a yard at St Osyth since around 1215. It had remained a thriving place where boats were repaired and spritsail barges rebuilt. Years before, the skipper and mate had come into St Osyth, in their boat *Whimbrel*, to look over the *EDME* then recently arrived from Maldon where she'd been largely rebuilt. The yard's owners had completed the project – now she was a picture of perfection, dominating the annual barge championship. Cocooned inside a tent, perched on a giant, steel pontoon, was the *Thalatta*, a large, powerful coasting barge undergoing a rebuild. Unfortunately, the money had run out. The *Thalatta* had been converted, many years before, and fitted out for taking school children afloat. The works completed looked splendid and would, it was hoped, eventually allow her to sail onwards towards the next century. 'She looks new!' the skipper had exclaimed.

The priory at St Osyth.

The creek, above the yard, was dammed and a road ran across it. A pool beyond the dam was once used for a tide mill, but now it was used for paddle and row boats. It was a wildfowl haunt too. A mill had reputedly been located here from around 1285. The last was badly damaged during a storm in 1962, being demolished soon afterwards. The skipper's old sailing home, the *May Flower,* had traded to the mill during the early 1900s. Lime works, brickworks and maltings were other activities that have been and gone, leaving the land rural and picturesque.

After some lunch at a local pub, a casual walk was taken up into the village. The village was named after Osytha, the daughter of a seventh-century East Anglian King. Osytha set up an abbey after running away from an arranged marriage, but met her death soon after at the hands of marauding Danes in 653, being beheaded for not accepting paganism. The Priory, presently owned by the de Chair family, was an interesting place to visit. Peacocks strutted about the grounds – their calls loudly announcing their presence. On an earlier visit, in 1990, the skipper had seen that one of the de Chairs had relieved Baghdad during the First World War – the First Gulf Conflict had just erupted with Iraq's invasion of Kuwait. The mate had said, 'Do you think you'll be going out there … ?' she'd been worried by events and the posturing of world leaders. The skipper had worked for the Royal Fleet Auxiliary and knew that his chances of 'avoiding' the conflict were slim – indeed! (He'd later been with the 'invasion' fleet.)

Opposite the priory, on a prettily kept green, was an obelisk, 'The Bury', with a plaque. It detailed a recent voyage around the globe by a local lad of a mere twenty years. 'That's lovely …' the mate said, '… such a wonderful local touch.'

Before heading back to the dinghy, the skipper had gone off to explore the seaward side of the creek, leaving the mate talking to a couple of old boys, artists, busy painting. The creek was straddled with a morass of floating homes; a mixture of Dutch barges; a spritsail barge, the *Vigilant*, looking like the skipper's old *May Flower* when in her twilight years during the late 1970s, and a motley collection of others, all reached by rickety jetties running out from the yard. Against the far bank, a hulk had caught the skipper's eye. She'd the look of an old working vessel, 'I'm sure you're from down west,' the skipper murmured, as he stumbled across rough grass and marsh.

Reaching it, he saw that the hulk had the look of a Tamar barge. She looked largely sound and some recent work had been done, prior to her being abandoned. 'What tales could your old bones tell?' the skipper murmured again, as he walked away, in another world. He promptly fell down a hidden rill in a patch of long grass! It brought him back to his senses: his mate was waiting …

The mate, who had become restless during her wait, said, as the skipper reached her, 'Come on, time we're on the move.'

The dinghy was by then afloat in a wide open sea that had spread across the mud flats. The skipper tentatively broached the idea of sailing back down the creek … it was quickly vetoed by the mate, '… use the outboard …' she muttered.

Bright sunshine rained down and it was gorgeously warm. It was a pleasant trip and they soon returned to their moored yacht. The mate climbed aboard, and handing up various bits and bobs, the skipper announced, 'I'm off for a sail.' Readying the dinghy, he'd soon left the mate to her book. She'd looked up briefly, smiled and waved …

Passing round the western end of an island of marsh that sat in the middle of the creek, the skipper sailed eastwards past Brightling   …uttering at the monstrous flats built on the site of an old shipyard. 'Tho   of the land in a modern way,' he reflected continuing to loo   of the yard …' The new businesslike floating hard, recently b   hai   ority, from which a ferry ran across to the shingle beach of Po   n   shore was busy with people.

Houseboats are now moored at St Osyth, the old spritsail barge *Vigilant* languishes amongst them. The view is taken from almost the same spot as that of the *May Flower* some seventy-five years earlier. Note roadside handrails.

'Oh my poor tired hull …' She rests in her last berth, but what's her history?

Sailing briskly, with the wind on the beam, he raced past a collection of smacks and bawleys sat tied up in a dock. The dock was the site of the Aldous yard, a famed smack builder. It was now a heritage site. The dock sat next to Oliver's Quay, where preparations were taking place for its use as a base for building a wind farm out on the Gunfleet Sands. The quay had caused some strife some years before when it was used for the shipment of livestock to Europe. Protesters had converged on the sleepy little town of Brightlingsea. Old ladies in twin sets joined the usual campaigning crowd to fiercely express their opposition. The skipper had silently agreed: other than for breeding, such transports were unnecessary. The trade eventually dwindled and ceased. The quay was also used during the famous 1984 miners' strike to import coal – too distant for the angry miners to blockade – or they'd not known about it!

Leaving Oliver's Quay behind, the skipper began to revel in the sail. He was moving fast, but easily. Fronting the river was a boatyard with a marina full of sleek, shiny, white-plastic motor craft. Then all of a sudden, it was all open, unspoilt, low marshland running across to a backdrop of wooded hills. In the distance, a little cluster, still a blur, was seen on the marsh edge far ahead.

Behind the skipper was the marshy island that cleaved Brightlingsea channel in two, known as Cindery Island. The islands were once one, but erosion ate through a narrow isthmus some years ago – though a local legend says that it had a helping hand from a man who'd got fed up with rowing round it! The western end had a long shingle and stone spit reaching into the heart of the harbour. Inland, all was mud.

The skipper continued at a pace, the dinghy leaving a trail of foam in its wash. It was exhilarating stuff! The creek, strangely, was in that part known as Flag Creek: only the entrance was known as Brightlingsea Creek. All the time the skipper's grin was a fixed picture, a picture of sheer enjoyment, a boy in his element.

The little cluster seen earlier was a little ramshackle yard, of an old-fashioned type. It sat on the edge of the marsh. Its look was beguiling: it had an industrious feel too.

The old and new ... a disused farm wharf and an aggregates quay (Martin's Farm ballast jetty) up Flag Creek, beyond Brightlingsea. Both sit redundant.

A modern yacht was up on the slip. Alongside were a colourful group of live-aboards and upon one, strung on lines, multicoloured washing, mainly of the female variety, fluttered in the breeze, cups spinning in the wind!

The marsh, beyond the outer tufted fringe, had by then become a flooded mere that ran back to a steep hillside. It was bounded by a low, broken sea wall. 'A fairly recent flooding,' the skipper thought. Some walls ran in strange directions – '... attempts to hold back the sea?' the skipper murmured, thinking aloud. A scattering of yellow-flowered gorse thrived on bits of the old wall that sat above the tideline.

The skipper sailed on. He gazed around at the environment and smiled broadly: it was all new to him. On wooded hills, houses peeped from between trees and interspersed were open fields of yellow, ripened cereals. It looked ... looked ... idyllic ... as the patchwork ran away into the distance. He almost became transfixed.

With a start, he returned back to the watery world upon which he was traversing: ahead he'd spotted something different. 'That's strange,' he thought, 'the channel seems to be marked.' Ahead was a line of stout posts, 'leading to where?' he added, speaking aloud, 'And they're topped by radar reflectors too.'

Soon all was revealed. Beyond, on the St Osyth's shore, a ballast quay with the paraphernalia of cranes and conveyors for loading little coasters was seen. As he got closer, he saw that it had a look of disuse about it. But, before reaching the quay though, something else caught his eye – an old barge wharf. Later, the skipper found that this was probably Wellwick Wharf, a farm wharf once used by Wellwick Farm and others around, a little inland. The ballast wharf, opened in 1961, is currently mothballed.

The channel by then had curved away to the north and the skipper was on a run, 'I'll have to tack back along here,' he said, grinning, in anticipation.

Ahead, he saw, the channel split. One, the shorter leg, was Thorington Creek. It was dammed off years before. An old barge dock had existed on its banks too. The creek went up to a park for caravans and chalets. They sat snugly behind the sea wall, dressed with pretty, flowered arrays, lit up by the afternoon sun. There was a ramp for speedboats: a couple had gone past earlier, skimming the surface up on a plane. They'd kept clear of the little dinghy, the skipper saying a silent, 'Thank you ...'

After leaving the smaller creek, the skipper had sailed into the other, a continuation of Flag Creek, turning sharply westwards. He'd not gone far though: time had gone on. The tide had turned some time earlier. It was time to return. The creek, though, ran for nearly a mile onwards, curling around the back of Brightlingsea, where a mill was once sited along with an obligatory quay.

Turning for home, he tacked, initially, against the southerly until able to bear away for Brightlingsea. Away in the distance, another small dinghy, larger than his own, was seen turning up towards St Osyth, against the falling tide, 'It'll have a beam reach ...' the skipper murmured softly. On his voyage of exploration surrounded by such unforgettable scenic beauty, it was the only other sail seen.

Reaching 'home', he quietly stowed the dinghy and moored it astern, tucked in close to the transom, all along, grinning avidly. The mate was asleep ... snuggled down in the fo'c's'le. Gingerly, he made himself a pot of tea.

Heading for the cockpit, he murmured, 'Ah – cake.' He licked his lips, 'it'll go well with my tea ...' turning about, he reached into the locker. Settling down with his book, his repast to hand, he released a long satisfied sigh ...

7

'The Barge River,' They Say ...

The skipper and mate had been 'on the Colne' for long enough, nice as it was, it was time to move on. They'd had time to sit and stare; to read and ruminate; to chill and, in the skipper's case, to potter casually in their lug-sailed tender. The skipper seeing that the breeze was a southerly quickly decided on a sailing departure. So, with the tide nearing the bottom of the ebb, they walked the boat round, head to tail, as it were, before ghosting away from the pontoon under genoa. The mains'l was hoisted shortly after, when clear.

Leaving Mersea Island's eastern shingle point astern, the skipper set a course across the extensive flats that lay to the south of the island towards the gaping entrance of the Blackwater. The estuary looked inviting in the sunshine, Sales Point and the Nass stood open before them. The Nass, to the north, was a long shell, shingle and sand spit that extended from the marshes south of Tollesbury, reaching some distance eastwards protecting the Mersea channels. It was a barely visible blur. To the south, the land climbed gently from the sea from behind a sea wall, fringed on the whole by salt marsh. It was a sea of differing greens and golden browns of ripened cereals. On that south side too, amongst a patch of trees, sat the Chapel of Saint Peter built on the site of a Roman fort, Othona. Their course put them clear of an isolated beacon, marking an old wreck – the skipper had a plan though: the tides were near springs.

'We'll skirt the shallows, keeping two metres under us,' the skipper said as he disappeared below for a reason only he knew. 'Don't forget it's around low water – springs ...' he called back.

'What, towards that beacon?' the mate asked, pointing for her own benefit.

'Keep the beacon just to starboard ...' had been the call from below. The mate had sailed across these flats numerous times, but not that close in, on the bottom of the tide. Her skipper's intentions were a mystery. She shook her head and settled down.

On returning, the skipper had a sheepish grin and the mate knew that he was up to something – or about to be.

'As we close that beacon,' he said, 'I want to go off in the dinghy and have a closer look over there ...'

'Why?' the mate enquired, interrupting him, 'There's nothing to see.'

'There is ... look over ...' the skipper said coolly, pointing to a nondescript weedy piece of debris being swished by a swell.

The beacon marked the bomb-shattered remnants of a little piece of maritime history – the remains of the *Molliette*. Her sister, the *Violette*, now a hulk at Hoo on the River Medway, was all that remained of a brief experiment in concrete shipbuilding. That was apart from the later oil and water barges which were still in use in varying guises, and, of course, the Phoenix caissons for the Mulberry Harbour constructed on the French beaches following D-Day in June 1944 (where many still lie). In many respects, the shape of the two concrete coasters was futuristic: within

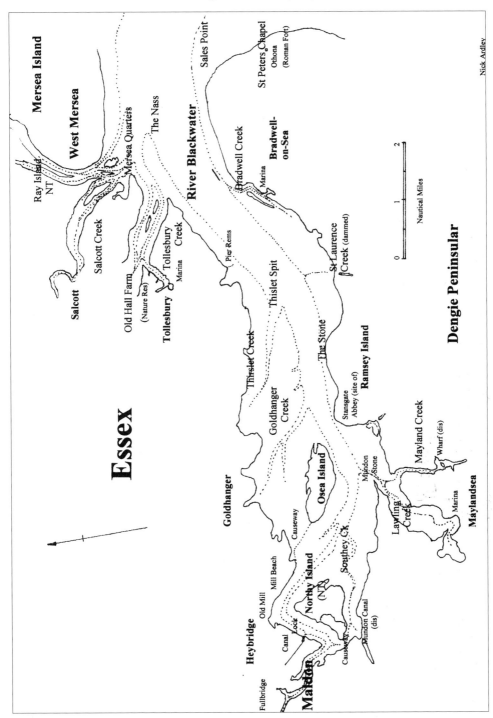

Chartlet of the River Blackwater and offshoot creeks.

The motor gaff schooner *Molliette* stretching her sails upon completion in 1919. She was launched at Pollock's yard in Faversham in November 1918, as the First World War closed out. (Courtesy of Patricia O'Driscoll)

… his mug … leapt skywards leaving a trail of coffee … as it had gone clean overboard. (Drawn by Gwendoline D. Ardley)

twenty to thirty years, the hull shape, refined somewhat, had been adopted for motor coaster design and remained little changed for many years.

Luffing up, a short distance off the beacon, the skipper pulled the dinghy alongside and abandoned the mate, leaving her to sail up and down. Rowing purposefully across the water ... her last words echoed inside his head – 'be careful'. As he moved further away, his yacht diminished rapidly in size, seemingly on an open, empty expanse with nothing for miles, reminding him forcefully of his mate's words.

The skipper soon reached his quarry and closed with the area of the wreck. The surface became decidedly oily looking, with swirls and eddies indicating unseen dangers close to the surface. Rising above the surface was a piece of the old ship, covered in weed. It looked dark and foreboding. The low swell breaking around the area spoke to the skipper, or were they his mate's last words? He moved away, pausing to say a few words for her builders and the old ship herself, then, with vigorous stokes of the oars, he pointed the dinghy's bow towards the yacht and probably his highly relieved mate!

'Right ...' she asked, sarcastically, '... Bradwell? Or have you some other excursion up your sleeve? Here, take the helm ...' At that, the mate, pulling a face, had disappeared below to put the kettle on.

The skipper was reminded of an earlier sail that season across this stretch of water ... He'd had a different mate aboard. A friend was crewing, enjoying a weekend away from family duties! It had been a blustery sail from the Colne, which helped to clear cobwebs from a sojourn ashore the previous night – where they'd met several members of the skipper's club. The skipper, taking a mug of coffee from the crew, had placed it on the cabin top. Moments later, the boat had taken a lurch into a deeper sea and his mug, a mug that had sailed many miles, leapt skywards leaving a trail of coffee, which was whipped across the cockpit, as it had gone clean overboard! The crew had had a more recent cruise to Faversham and had, laughing, reminded the skipper about 'his' mug!

The present trip was very much more docile.

Bradwell soon hove in sight. Coming into the wind off the creek's entrance, the sails were stowed and then they slipped under engine into the creek. Passing round the end of Pewit Island, they crept past the remains of the old half tide quay where once a fleet of proud, well-kept spritsail barges worked, before berthing within the marina, just beyond.

As soon as they'd berthed, the mate, with a pile of washing, disappeared off to pay their dues then deal with their laundry, leaving the skipper to tidy up. The skipper had soon done that and over a coffee he watched some ongoing work to an expansion project within the marina. It reminded him of the previous season when he'd come into this place to await the arrival of his mate who'd just completed her end-of-term duties at her school. Their kindly son had delivered his mother after he'd finished work – 'for a meal at the Green Man,' he'd said!

The skipper was then sitting back in the cockpit with a coffee, relaxing and watching the world go by. The basin was being excavated by huge, tracked 360s with an incredible reach, scooping and shaping, fashioning even, the clay banks. Spoil was being spread and compacted, too, around the perimeter. They'd worked the banks into a stepped escarpment. The clay, laid down eons ago, was being moved with impunity.

The skipper's gaze was stopped by a man who came shuffling down the mooring finger to talk ... He and his wife had had a large motor cruiser but had recently put her up for sale. 'We're downsizing,' he said, 'getting a smaller ... sailing yacht.' The skipper was quite taken aback and it must have shown! It transpired that the couple lived up in Norfolk, but where the new boat was going to be moored wasn't indicated.

'Yes,' he said, 'we've come down from Lowestoft for a nostalgic visit. I used to sail from here when a lad. Dad had a boat in the creek – no marina then. I used to love sailing on this river,' he said, waving his arm in a broad sweep, '... love to do it again.' He paused. 'Oh yes,' the chap added, grinning broadly, and looking at the works going on, 'I used to catch eels in the shallows here when they first dug the marina.'

'I enjoy this river too,' the skipper said, thinking of the chap's earlier remark, 'especially places like the Quarters and Lawling Creek.'

The old boy nodded, remembering perhaps, called to his wife that he was coming, and ambled away.

The skipper's reverie was broken by the voice of his mate, 'Here, where's my coffee ... ?'

'Just making it ... !' he said, rapidly disappearing below with a comment about the washing taking an hour ringing in his ear.

Later, after pegging an array of colourful smalls, summer shirts and two duvet covers around the rigging, they set off for a walk to St Peter's chapel. It was hot so a bottle of water was packed – a blessing it was too, later on.

Their walk, round the sea wall, took them past the decommissioned nuclear power station ... 'It was a damned sight more productive and sensible than those bloody wind mills out there,' the skipper said, with some feeling, waving his arm at the distant sticks being erected on the Gunfleet Sands. He did, though, believe 'they' had a place within the nation's power sources. Certainly, he didn't fancy increasing the burning of oil and coal. 'Build another generator here,' the skipper said grinning.

His mate remained stony-faced.

Inland, running away from the sea wall, the fields were deep below the outside marshes, but surprisingly, rose quickly upwards. The fields were filled with level swathes of cereals and other foodstuffs. This high ground is the tail of the Dengie

Within Bradwell Creek are the remains of the half-tide quay. Half-tide berths were once commonplace around the East Coast. Barges were held off by tall posts – loading took place, by hand, from carts. It is a great pity that the quay has been allowed to crumble.

spine. Amongst the fields, during the 1940s, was a large air force base, one of many that dotted the countryside. A farming family, the Parkers, once owned many acres of this land. They had a fleet of spritsail barges to ship out their produce and bring in waste to spread on the fields. Their barges worked in various trades. Parker had, for a time, a contract with Essex Council to deliver walling stone and road stone to numerous places around the Essex coast and rivers. Sea walls during the 1920s were heightened and strengthened after a period of regular flooding problems.

The skipper thinking about this had muttered, quietly, '... and a huge amount of that stone now lies in heaps, lost forever, around abandoned grazing islands.'

The mate looked at him – saying nothing.

Before St Peter's chapel was built, the Romans had visited. They were followed by the Saxons and probably the raiding Vikings later too. It was a place to wander, to gaze across an unspoilt marshland, to sit and luxuriate in a quiet so pure: whatever one's religion – it had remained a special and spiritual place.

A large portion of the original Roman fort had disappeared. It lay out over the marshes – now a bird reserve. Following the demise of Roman influence in Britain, the fort area became a centre of population named Ythancestrir. In the fourteenth century, the populace moved inland around a new church built in the present village. Bede, that venerable monk from his monastery on the banks of the Tyne, at Jarrow, referred to this place in *The Ecclesiastical History*.

The mate had looked at the skipper. She was remembering a week she'd spent up with him when away on 'his' ships. He'd been standing by a refit at a lonely shipyard in a field of Tyneside desolation. They'd visited the Jarrow monastery and enjoyed seeing the connection to their own part of the world. She said, 'I loved that time ...'

'What was that ... ?' he asked.

'I was remembering the Bede exhibition ... and we had snow ... Do you remember those young girls wearing next to nothing in the depths of winter waiting to get into the night spots near where we dined one night ... ?'

The skipper smiled too – pretty little things!

It was here, in 653, by invitation of King Sigbert of the East Saxons, that Cedd came down from Lindisfarne to build a church and convert the people. He landed at the now-lost Roman quay. The building used the debris of the old fortifications and it sat across one of the fort's walls and its main gateway, hence, the Chapel of St Peter-on-the-Wall. The greater part of the building remained as Cedd had it built, except that a low tower, used to warn ships of the shallow St Peter's Flats, was attached to the western end. It's long gone and it is marked out, as were other parts of the building, for people to see. Following the building's restoration as a chapel in 1920, after 200 years of miscellaneous use, and subsequent archaeological excavations, the old walls of the fort were marked out too.

'It was used as a barn for many years,' the mate said to the skipper, as they walked inland towards the village, adding, 'where did you disappear off to while I was sitting on the grass?'

'Oh, I wanted to take a look at an old wooden cottage that used to be lived in by an ancient wildfowler.'

'Who was that then?'

'Walter Linnett,' he remarked. 'He worked on until well into the 1950s.' He added, 'his cottage, now used by bird-watchers, is surrounded by damson and bullace trees – looked enchanting.' He scratched his head and said, 'My mum used to make jam with those berries too!'

'Yes, I'm sure,' the mate quipped. 'Those people upset me ... in the church. Did you see? Reading the newspaper they were. No respect.' She grimaced sadly, shaking her head.

The skipper stayed silent.

The Chapel of Saint Peter-on-the-Wall. It sits at an iconic spot 'guarding' the Essex coast.

Wildfowler Walter Linnett's traditional clapboarded cottage on the edge of the high ground as it falls naturally into the saltings. The building is now used by bird-watchers.

Later, after a thirsty trek, they returned, tired and well walked, to the marina and flopped into their cockpit, where the skipper immediately murmured something about tea ...

The next day, passing the Thirslet Spit, the skipper piped up, 'Do you remember that picture I showed you years ago?'

'What picture?'

'It was of a barge up on the spit,' he grinned, 'she cut inside the buoy, or could have been the beacon then. She ended up perched ... sorry balanced, across the spit after the tide ebbed. It caused great hilarity ...' He laughed! 'It ended happily, fortunately, for on the flood she'd lifted without any damage. She'd been a steel hull though.' Then added ruefully, 'An old wooden one would've taken up the curves of the spit beautifully, and probably would've stayed put!'

'There's a beacon in the painting we have of smacks drifting down past the spit – isn't there?' The mate asked rhetorically: she was certain of this.

Off Osea Island the boat was set towards Lawling Creek where they intended to enjoy a quiet night or two before moving up to Maldon.

Osea Island had had an interesting past. The mansion was once owned by a brewing family and it was used to help inebriates off the demon drink. It's been in private hands for quite some time, but recently, the skipper had heard that the building was again to be used as a rehabilitation centre. People renting bungalows on the island were being forced to leave! During the Second World War, a shipyard was set up building coastal patrol craft, in wood. It was away from pre-war building sites, yet close enough to a labour pool. Along the beach in front of the main house are the remains of a stump against which Bentall's yacht *Jullanar* sat when not away racing. The yacht, built in 1875, was a radical design with a cut-away forefoot and run aft. Bentall, a Heybridge iron founder, was a keen Victorian yachtsman and he messed around, with designers, trying things out! The island was also the location of a television dramatisation of a book, the *Mystery Mile*, by a local author, Margery Allingham, who wrote detective novels, many set within the estuary marshlands. She lived, until her death, in Tolleshunt D'Arcy, near Tollesbury.

'This'll do,' the skipper said as the anchor splashed overboard – then, as he let the mainsail rattle down, 'a bit of peace and quiet before we attack Maldon – the heart of "the Barge River" they say!' He'd grinned in affection down at his mate.

Lawling Creek was a little gem. There were a few moorings in its outer reaches, sheltered inside a long shingle and shell spit known as Mundon Stone. Passing the point, the skipper had said, 'We'll run the boat up there tomorrow,' pointing to the spit, '... at the bottom of the tide and scrub off.' He added, 'The weed growth from our time in the Orwell and backwaters is pretty ghastly.' From the rudder, long tendrils of green weed could be seen swaying in the tide flow and from the hull below the waterline too!

'Does that include me ... ?' the mate enquired slowly.

'Too right – I'm not doing it on my own!' the skipper ejaculated.

Looking at the skipper, she nodded in a reluctant acquiescence and shivered: it didn't feel like high summer at that moment.

They'd used the anchorage here for many years now. When their son had been little, they'd walked into Maylandsea. The marina was not as developed as it now was – it too had provided a safe haven – especially during periods of inclement weather and was on the boat's list of coveted places ...

'Do you remember me taking the boy ashore here and picking sea spinach?'

'Yes,' she said, her face expressing her disgust!

'I was the only one that ate it.' The skipper smirked ... his family hadn't appreciated free food!

During the afternoon, while sitting relaxing, the skipper remembered he'd painted a

The picturesque Osea Island set deep within the River Blackwater. It is a natural island, much of it above the wash of the twice-daily tides flowing round it.

'... at the bottom of the tide and scrub off.' ... 'Does that include me?' the mate enquired slowly. (Drawn by Gwendoline D. Ardley)

The sun glistened across the Blackwater from Ramsey Island, and the site of Stansgate Abbey, in 2006. The spritsail barge *Wyvenhoe* had just broken out her anchor to sail slowly past the *Reminder*, which also got underway – a timeless, iconic East Coast sight.

picture some time before. It was a view looking across to Osea Island – he went below to fetch it out. Looking at it, he spent a few moments pulling it apart – much to the mate's annoyance: for she liked his sketches, pencil or watercolours.

Looking at the picture of Osea Island reminded the skipper that there were many islands up this river. The skipper had made a remark about this and then said, chuckling, 'most have gone though.'

'What do you mean ... ?'

'Well, you know the big ones – Northey, further up river; Osea out there; and Mersea, the largest, in the river's entrance – they're Danish names apparently.'

'Yes, but ...'

'Okay, okay, let me finish,' he pointed to a tree-cloaked peninsula out in the river, 'that's on Ramsey Island – well, it was an island. It has those two sailing clubs fronting the river around Stone Point.'

She nodded.

'The trees hide the remains of an old abbey – Stansgate Abbey. It's said that part of the old walls are in the present farmhouse. It was a Cluniac priory – got done over during the Reformation!' He paused, scratched his head and added, 'There's Ray Island up the Mersea Quarters too.'

'Northey Island belongs to the National Trust. Most of the land has been let back to the sea with only a piece of high ground and the old house left. There are a couple of spritsail barge hulks up in those marshes – they went up on big tides and became trapped.'

'Ray Island ...' the mate asked tentatively, '... isn't that where Mehalah lived?'

'Yes,' the skipper confirmed.

Mehalah was the fictional character in a book by Sabine Baring-Gould about a young Mersea girl who became trapped in a dirty marriage to a local villain, Elijah Rebow of Red Hall. She fell in love with another – it all ended very unhappily. It remained a wonderful, evocative yarn, first published in 1880, set amongst the marshes and of the people who lived within them. Ray Island was now owned by the National Trust. Gould was a prolific writer, as well as one-time vicar of West Mersea. He wrote many Christian hymns too, was a keen archaeologist, collector of folk songs and historian amongst many other achievements.

'Probably,' the skipper said, 'there are many little marsh islands that have been inned,' adding ruefully, 'lost in the general landscape.' Dammed off creeks still existed and can be seen when walking the sea walls. They run out through sluices after the tide has ebbed: the land behind often sits many metres below today's tides.

'There was a canal over the marshes pointing westwards towards Maldon, 'it ran inland up towards Mundon – was dug by the local farmer – abandoned now though.'

'Okay' the mate said, 'I'm reading for a while ...' her look saying, 'now leave me alone.'

So he had.

An onlooker would've seen that the pages of the skipper's book weren't turning very fast. In fact, they'd stalled. He'd looked up and seen a dinghy coming out from Maylandsea with three people aboard – needed too – for there was a stiff breeze blowing. The people were thoroughly enjoying their romp, laughing and chatting as they flew past. It reminded him of a couple of days he'd spent recently in this anchorage, alone, waiting to pick up his mate at Bradwell.

On his first evening alone, after his supper things had been cleared up, the skipper had slipped away for an evening sail.

He'd luxuriated in the quiet, the dinghy barely making a noise or leaving a ripple as she slipped along. He'd had time to gaze and take in the surroundings. Beyond the creek, the low, green hills of the Dengie spine lay undulating in a gentle series of almost erotic curves, their sides dappled from broken cloud and sunlight. The tide was near the bottom of the ebb and the evening sunshine glistened on the mud banks, darkly accentuating too the low marshland fringes.

Slipping past a shell point that separated Mayland and Lawling Creeks a seal had popped up. Inquisitive, doglike eyes gazed at the skipper, before, with a snort, as if to say 'you're in my patch', it slipped effortlessly below to continue its search for food. The shell bank was covered with waders skittering about – it was feeding time.

The skipper had sailed slowly on, in the fading breeze, up the creek until he'd had to turn. Mud banks showed around him. Fish plopped too. The ebb was about done and so was the day: the sun was approaching his horizon: the low sea wall to the west. Bright orange rays cut across the surface, now all but unruffled by the last of the breeze. Lower down the creek, the skipper turned for his yacht, it glowed golden in the sunset.

Nearby, some seals lazing on a mud bank had flopped into the water. Arm-like flippers flapped, as if a baby attempting to crawl, as seal after seal whooshed down the slimy mud into the water. The tide had made its turn, bringing with it a fresh stock of fish. Some of the seals had, though, just watched and stared; 'so human,' the skipper had thought. He'd nodded a good evening to them, before finally having to pull out the oars to gently row back home.

Over a warming mug of coffee, in the gathering gloom, he saw a heron alight close by. Standing still, the skipper had watched, silently, as it stalked its prey. By then, the busy little terns had ceased their frantic forays for food. Earlier, around the dinghy, they had dived for small fry, before darting back into the saltings to feed their young. All had gone quiet.

From the land, to the south, the scent of oilseed, or was it wheat, wafted gently

... he saw a heron alight close by ... watched ... as it stalked its prey. (Drawn by Gwendoline D. Ardley)

across the creek on the zephyr of an air. Earlier, the skipper had watched as a combine had wended back and forth across the field gathering in the harvest. Out in the river, a barge had motored up against the last of the ebb. It fell from view as it disappeared behind Mundon Stone, the point at the entrance to this creek, but the skipper knew it would've brought up shortly afterwards. As the light faded over Osea Island, the Colchester-registered skillinger smack *Pioneer* slipped into view sailing under her jibs and large mizzen on the first of the flood. The skipper, enchanted, had watched through his binoculars as she brought up off the Osea shore.

The skipper, over a final coffee, this time with some flavouring, had sighed, deeply, saying, whilst gazing up at the stars, '... cheers, darling ...' He'd missed his mate and the evening had been one to savour. The clouds of earlier had all but dissipated, leaving wandering vapour trails of long-gone jet aircraft that glowed from a sun, well below the horizon. Around that horizon hovered the remnants of the days clouds, they were thin and hazy and were coloured almost purple against a little light. A gentle southerly had filled in – 'that'll be the change promised' said the skipper to himself, '... and a bit different from the brisk north-westerly of earlier ... God, I fetched a good dollop of the river's briny over me too ... off the Stone!' He'd laughed: his mate would have enjoyed that spectacle!

Suddenly his attention had been attracted by an orb of fiery orange creeping up from the Stansgate peninsula. They were the lights from the myriad of holiday caravans, which inhabited the low land around Ramsey Island, with their noisy music halls full of life and gaiety. It looked alien, but the light shone across the flooding tide, flickering on the ripples, as it crossed the shallows.

'Bed,' said the skipper!

The following morning had dawned very hot with a gentle breeze, enough to flick the yachts burgee back and forth in a lazy lackadaisical wave. 'How different from yesterday morning,' he'd thought, remembering his blustery sail up river.

Later that afternoon, he'd started reading *The Children of Men* by P. D. James, a story about the inability of man to procreate: the breed was heading for extinction ... ! Picking it up, with his coffee, and settling on a cushion in the cockpit, he'd buried himself in the book's pages. Breakfast, of cereal and hot toast with home-made Seville marmalade, had long gone, as had several more cups of coffee ... when he'd put the book down with a satisfied smile.

He'd finished. Looking about and shaking his head, as if to return to a reality, he saw that there was an hour or two of flood to run – time for an explore ...

He'd headed for Mayland Creek; a creek not investigated other than a short excursion a few seasons earlier. Settled back in comfort against one side of the dinghy, a leg up on the opposite gunnel, he took in the panorama sailing at a moderate pace with the wind on an aft quarter. Passing a marshy point between the two creeks, he'd looked in awe at how much had crumbled in recent years. A section of wall seemed to have been abandoned. It had collapsed. Behind was a patch of high ground. 'Perhaps it's being allowed to go naturally,' he thought. The creek ran south-east then southerly up to its head the skipper knew. 'Be a tack out,' he said, grinning, 'it's about a mile (land mile) inland to its dammed-off headwater,' where he knew a wharf had once been sited.

'Strangely,' thought the skipper, 'Maylandsea was fed by Lawling and the village of Mayland, inland, had no access to the water now.' Mayland Creek was full of marshy islands and mud. Yet, only the very top end of Lawling creek was like this, up past Maylandsea. A season earlier, while they had berthed for a couple of nights up at the marina, the skipper had found that a sewage works discharged a large volume of water, which, when the tide was out, created a constant scour to the bed, helping to clear silt.

Maylandsea was one of those places that were developed in the postwar (1920s and 1930s) period as a plotland. Plots of land were bought and people either put up a holiday bungalow or a permanent residence. Often the development became scrappy, but this one had become a thriving community, largely separate from the village of Mayland nearby. In places, it still had a raw, new feel. It was a place often enjoyed by the skipper and mate. Not least for their domestic services!

Steeple creek was another waterway that had all but disappeared. A small section still ran through a patch of marsh set deep in the bay below Stansgate Abbey. The

The head of Mayland Creek and an oft-seen dam, shutting out the sea – how much longer?

creek had run southwards before it was dammed, round the underside of Ramsey Island. Further up Mayland Creek, another smaller waterway ran eastwards towards Steeple Hall and the village of Steeple; the skipper aimed to find that one on his way out – he was looking for an old wharf.

Passing a slipway by a caravan park, the scene of the polluting light and noise of last evening, the skipper saw that a few water bikes and speedboats were being readied for the water. 'Each to their own,' the skipper murmured softly, smiling. Later, he would be less easy about them.

Beyond the slip, the creek narrowed slightly, but was still wide open. The banks had suffered from serious wash erosion and the skipper reflected on this, wondering if the authorities were aware. Areas of sea-wall facing had collapsed where walls ran into raw marsh, the marsh having gone. 'Needs attention – that lot,' the skipper chuckled as he sailed swiftly past.

Around the mid-creek point, the skipper came across areas of lower level marshes that were dying. 'Sea rise is affecting these marshes,' the skipper muttered, 'they're being covered too often for the salt-tolerant plants to survive.' The last was said with feeling. His eyes then alighted on patches of purple-headed sea lavender 'floating' amongst cord grass and other plants; their brightness brightened his sadness at marsh loss. There were asters too, but they weren't then in flower.

Eventually, rounding a shallow bend, it became obvious that he'd reached the head of the creek. The marsh disappeared and land fell directly into the water, fringed with sea purslane. A bank that could have been an old wharf ran up into scrub trees, where a lady sat, while her dog cavorted about, exercising itself. She waved, probably a little unsure about the strange man in his tan-sailed dinghy!

Sailing back out, in long and short tacks, gave the skipper some much-needed exercise!

Later, he found his offshoot to the east, towards Steeple Hall. A man-made hill lay beyond it. Sheep grazed its sides and some scrub had taken hold, but its look was unmistakable, 'A rubbish heap!' exclaimed the skipper, as he ran off into a mass of marshes, the way barely perceptible. Then he saw the old wharf. Rotting and gnarled remnants of its piles rose out of the water, some at angles outwards having come to rest after giving in to the pressure from behind many years before. The collapsed walls showed clearly the 'stuff' used to build it: chalk, Victorian or Edwardian rubbish and clinkers. None were natural! The wharf sat hidden by a marsh island, but even that had had its purpose. Within the marshes stood rotting hauling posts, yet substantial-looking. They were once used to 'wind' a barge one way or the other, to or from the wharf. The skipper had grinned! It was a thoroughly enjoyable find, because on 11 September 1931, his old home, the *May Flower*, had sailed into the dock with a cargo of flints, departing two days later.

Clear of the little backwater, the skipper had been met by several rapidly moving projectiles, one careering round his transom, throwing the dinghy every which way ... 'Bloody Hell ...' he'd shouted, shaking a fist. Then another, an RIB-type craft, had sped by. The driver set it on a course and then stood up on the driver's seat, arms outstretched, as the craft weaved across the water ... 'Fool,' muttered the skipper. He wasn't wearing a life jacket either! To add insult to injury, the next projectile bore down on the skipper as he cowered low down in the dinghy. Two water bikes came round a corner, heading directly at his bow. They careered down both sides, their wash waves meeting in a volcano of water. The dinghy was thrown about like a top. Water spilled inboard. 'BLOODY HELL!' he'd shouted. 'I've had enough ... The sooner I get out of this creek ... the better,' he said, his voice wobbling. With venom, he shook his fist at the diminishing craft, crying loudly, 'there's supposed to be an 8-knot limit ...' before sponging the bottom of the dinghy out ...

Deep in the marshes, the skipper came across a disused wharf. How much longer will its existence be evident?

'Err ... what was that ... you were shouting?'

Coming to and realising that the mate had spoken to him, he said, 'Oh ... did I? I was thinking of something ... sorry ...'

Later, sitting back in the cockpit over a late lunch, the skipper remembered a piece written by Maurice Griffiths, an East Coast sailor, now, sadly, deceased. Griffiths, in *The First of the Tide*, complained bitterly at the antics of a group of ski boats that wove in and out of a line of anchored yachts, creating mayhem. His crew had wanted to use a twelve bore on them – fortunately for them, it hadn't been aboard! The skipper had always remembered that piece of writing.

Everyone is entitled to use the water, but the rules were, sadly, being flouted more often as the rivers had become busier. 'Never mind common sense – let's show some decency for others!' the skipper thought.

Leaving the creek early, the morning after scrubbing the boat's bottom, they'd motored in a flat calm to Maldon, coming to a halt in the silt build-up a boat's length from the yacht pontoon alongside the Hythe. A friendly face appeared, as if prompted. He'd propped his bike against the quayside railings and called, 'Want me to take a line ... ?' The grin was very familiar.

'Isn't that ...' the mate said.

'Yes ... it is. His boat is down river. I'll throw a line.' In the eagerness of the greeting, the skipper's first attempt fell, embarrassingly, into the tepid, muddy water. He'd grinned saying '... sorry!' before completing the exercise.

They'd nattered for a short while. The chap soon departed, heading for his own sailing yacht moored opposite the promenade that runs downstream from the Hythe: tide waits for no man!

Maldon was a premier Royal Borough in Saxon England, then known as Maeldune. It was a defensive settlement. It gained a Royal Charter in 1171 under Henry II, requiring the town to provide a ship for the navy. There have been developments going back to Roman times: on the river, near Heybridge, the remains of a Romano-British

The Moot Hall at Maldon is now used by the town's council.

port have been found, now well away from the present river's course.

While at Maldon, the skipper and the mate enjoyed seeing some of the town's delights and on one of the days had walked round the sea wall to Heybridge, returning along the Chelmer canal. It had been exceedingly hot!

The canal was built in 1793, or there about: it took longer to build! Traders in Chelmsford disliked paying dues to Maldon and goods were transhipped from ships lower down the river into spritsail barges and lighters, discharging in the basin at Heybridge. A smaller class of lighter took goods up to Chelmsford. Maldon's maritime demise then set in – yet it had survived – as a base for the modern spritsail barge charter trade.

The skipper had spent a short period of his childhood in Maldon, while his sailing home, the *May Flower*, had had large, at the time, repairs carried out. The old yard still operated, repairing barges, and in a newer shed, wooden boat building still took place. The steaming shed and workshops of the skipper's childhood had gone though – only part of a slope that was the shed floor remained – at its top end sat a pile of seasoning timber, waiting for use. A picture on the inside of The Maldon Salt Company's current brochure had an ink sketch of the skipper's old home at the yard from that time. The old shed with its wicket-type gate is clear. The sketch used to adorn the products' packets some years before.

The skipper and mate had walked past the salt factory many times; interestingly, it was now one of the last places to make salt from seawater, in the traditional manner. It was good stuff and was revered by chefs and home-side cooks alike. Salt had been produced on the site since medieval times. Marshland salt panning had taken place from the early Roman period. Those panning sites were known as Red Hills, from the burnt debris left behind year after year and an archaeological study had traced many surviving remains around the Essex and Kent coasts.

On their last evening, over a glass of ale for him, and one of a wonderful selection of ciders for her, the skipper and mate had reminisced about their stay.

'The place is full of such fascinating history,' the mate said. 'It's a friendly place too ... and there's such a diversity of shops.'

'Self contained – nearly,' the skipper replied. 'Nice!'

The big food stores, though, had migrated out to Bentall's old factory site across the Fullbridge in Heybridge and on the site of one the town's old stations: Beeching, the mid-1960s head of the nationalised (British) railway system, effected the demise of many a rural line, and not-so-rural ones too – all in the name of saving money (how much had those 'cuts' since cost?), took the town's rail links away – a short-sighted and stupid action in the light of Maldon's expansion afterwards!

'The old town used to be away from the river,' the skipper said. 'The Hythe and Fullbridge were hamlets in medieval times. All were joined up as trade grew from the seventeenth century.'

'And ...' said the mate, 'there's Beeleigh Abbey – well, the abbey suffered its demise under Henry's (VIII) Reformation. We've walked through the area many times – it's just a large house now,' she paused, 'albeit an important historic one – it's owned by the Foyle family – I think.' The buildings and grounds had in fact been owned by the

Angled sprits, evocative tan sails and snapping bobs lined the Hythe at Maldon in August 1987. The shapely *Vigilant* sat outside the *Edith May* – both were built by Cann at Harwich. Compare view of the *Vigilant* in chapter 6. The *Edith May* was on the blocks sporting a new suit of sails – she went to Liverpool and nearly perished at the maritime museum. She will, once again, after a long restoration at Lower Halstow, be sporting another new suit of sails in 2010.

family since William A. Foyle, the bookseller and founder of Foyle's bookshop, bought it in 1943. The original abbey had been founded in 1180. An owner, Sir John Gate, was beheaded for supporting Lady Jane Grey, who suffered the same fate. A painting in the National Gallery depicting the last moments of Lady Jane Grey, looking beautiful, calm and serene as she went to her death, is a picture that always caused the skipper to 'swallow a little' whenever he looked at it.

The skipper said, 'I looked at an interesting write-up about the place while wandering round the gallery beneath the Plume Library earlier.' Later that year, the skipper heard that a group of Norbertine 'white' monks (to do with their habits – outer clothing), the abbey's original inhabitants, who'd a base at Chelmsford, had returned for a visit for the first time since their expulsion, hosted by BBC Radio Essex.

The mate nodded: she'd been doing something different. She then said, 'Don't forget the Battle of Maldon – it was an epic moment in British History.'

They'd been down to the end of the promenade for an amble and looked up at the giant memorial to Byrhtnoth, Earldorman of Essex. The skipper had thought that this man's feat of offering a level playing field for the Viking invaders to do battle in 991 was perhaps a defining moment for what is euphemistically known as English fair play!

The Vikings had occupied Northey Island opposite Heybridge Basin and in full view of Saxon Maldon. They were being hacked down one by one trying to cross to the mainland. Byrhtnoth didn't think it fair – so he'd invited them across do

An Essex legend – of far greater importance to British History than Essex girls! The statue of Byrhtnoth stands proud, defiant in its commemoration of his stand against the Danes. Was his sense of fairness the first record of what became a very 'English' trait?

battle after the tide had dropped – and lost! England was, after that, divided in two. One half Saxon, the other under Danelaw, and a payment to prevent invasion and subjugation (Danegeld) was paid too, until finally it was smashed by King Harold at Stamford Bridge – he'd then traipsed south, to meet his fate at the hands of William the Conqueror.

'We'll have to visit the site and Northey Island too,' the mate added as they drank up.

'Yes, another time,' the skipper said grinning, remembering their recent Easter-time holiday in Norfolk and a visit to Ely cathedral, 'the Ship of the Fen'. There, they'd seen the tomb of Byrhtnoth.

After breakfast the next morning, they watched as several barges prepared for sea. The Hythe was alive with milling brightly clothed people, ladies with chiffon dresses, floating in the breeze, mixed with those wearing more sedate costumes (the sensible and knowing – perhaps). Then after repeated calls, '*Hydrogen* sailing in five minutes …' the barges had been filled with the happy punters – all about to enjoy a couple of hours out on the tide, or longer.

'That's three away' the skipper said, adding, 'we'll be off very shortly too,' looking the mate's way.

So they had. Slipping the last of the lines with sails set, they'd sailed away – the engine silent beneath the cockpit sole: the wind was a pleasant south-westerly. They were bound for West Mersea.

Maldon as it has always seemed to be: smacks, barges and the sailors' church, with the tide ebbing away leaving the mud glistening.

Looking back, as they'd left, the skipper gazed at the sailor's church set prettily amongst cauliflower-like green trees perched up on the hill above the Hythe. 'That chorus of bells was something else ...' he said softly '... started as I handed out that rather nice bacon with scrambled eggs for our breakfast.' Their breakfast had been enjoyed in the cockpit under a full sun. It was Sunday morning and the bells had resonated in tuneful song above them. 'The bells are timeless – an intrinsic part of this maritime town,' he added, 'as are the tall masts and the gaily coloured fluttering bobs of the russet-sailed spritsail barges.'

The mate nodded, saying, '... a beguiling reason to visit.'

It was indeed.

On the way down, the skipper had pointed out to the mate the old shingle-loading point and later a base for ship breaking that they'd walked past on their walk to Heybridge Basin. Along the shore sit two old spritsail barge hulks and a myriad of other remnants of smaller craft. The skipper had looked up into Saltcote Creek towards the old malting and mill buildings. The creek was now full of marsh and the tide mill pool is no longer. It had remained a place the skipper desired to investigate by the dinghy – another day, perhaps. The dark-green-hulled little yacht owned by an old 'eastcoaster' wasn't in residence. 'Must be away ...' thought the skipper. The boat, a russet-sailed gunter cutter of around seventeen feet, had been sailed just about everywhere locally and many places further afield too. The boat had often been passed by along the coast, and once in the skipper's own waters sailing on Benfleet Creek.

Sailing past Mill Beach, a long length of shore that enjoyed good, clean landing, the skipper remembered, with affection, Maurice Griffiths. This venerable man, author of many yachting books, had kept several of his numerous craft moored off here during the 1920s and 1930s.

Clearing the end of that shore, the causeway to Osea Island hove in sight and the shore beyond. The skipper pointed out a barge away in the distance. 'It's up Goldhanger Creek – there's a hard up there which can be used for scrubbing off.'

'Didn't we dawdle that way one year ... what is it you say? ... Oh yes ... with time and tide on our hands?' the mate asked.

The skipper had grinned broadly ... thinking of time and tide: here they were again ... sailing quietly, ever so quietly, down with the ebb: the wind had taken off, slowly overhauling Osea Island, with time on their side.

'Did you see those seaweeds,' the mate asked, 'amongst the black "popable" stuff ... don't know what it was ... looked like sea urchins or the heads of alliums.'

'The black stuff is wrack,' the skipper said, 'the other ... I haven't a clue!'

They never had found out either.

Many craft were out that day; it was glorious. Barges and yachts glided onwards, sometimes putting in a tack, sometimes on a reach, for the breeze had become fickle and changeable. Reflections were strangely elongated and the mirrored surface occasionally rippled, the pictures flickering, as the gentle wash from other boats motoring rolled by. From across the water there floated the sweet dum ... dum, dum ... dum, dah ... of a peel of bells. They emanated from the church in Goldhanger village, nearly hidden amongst trees. Then, as if the bells had been a signal, the breeze filled in and order was once more restored to the antics of craft – well, those that hadn't given in and were still enjoying the lazy Sunday drift down with the ebb.

Later, they fetched into the Quarters. The tide was, by then, well down, and while dropping the mains'l, the skipper saw the remnants of the Kings Hard. 'It was built as a landing for access to the big yachts – they sat out in deeper water – deep keeled they were,' he said, as he put lashings round the sail, adding, 'it's unused now.'

'What was that?' said the mate, as she took a bemused look at an apparent nothingness in between concentrating on threading through moored craft, looking round a dropped sail and easing the jib sheet as she began a run into Mersea Fleet.

In reflected glory, her image gently rippled. The lovely *Marjorie* stemmed the tide off Osea Island on a hot, sultry day.

The skipper saw this and grinned! 'Good girl,' he thought, then, 'It's that black line over there,' he said.

All he got was, 'Oh!' and one of those looks.

After finding a buoy and sharing a beer, the mate said, 'For once, we've had two passages on this river without having to bash into short, steep, waves – it's been lovely.'

The area and Tollesbury, like the Colne too, had provided numerous men for the big yachts of the late Victorian and Edwardian eras through to the late 1930s. Much has been written about this past era. Probably only a few modern yachtsmen were really aware of this and the area's historic influence on their sport or pastime. The skipper, thinking about this, had said, quietly, 'let them read about it ... and enjoy, as I've done ... it would take a book to tell.'

Smacks: it was as much a smack river as a barge river and a mass of traditional yachts inhabit the Quarters, mixing with their sleek, fibreglass sisters, interspersed with many modern fishing vessels. It was one of the joys of visiting the Quarters – its diversity, vitality and its sheer saltiness: West Mersea lived, breathed and exuded yachting and fishing.

During Cadet Week, young children, some barely old enough to walk too, can be seen happily engaged in sail training, chattering and squabbling with each other as they pass by. In the past, the skipper had heard all sorts of conversations as their little boats, Optimists with brightly coloured sails, had ghosted past.

'Pull that in' and 'no ... go that way' and 'watch out for the boat ...' and sometimes a more meaningful, 'why's he (or she) going faster ... ?' or there'd be a shout from a safety boat, 'Felicity ... Jamie ... watch what you're doing ... this way, please.'

On one occasion, the skipper, varnish brush in hand, had said to a little cluster vying with one another, 'ease your mainsheet – you'll go faster.' He'd received blank looks from some, but others had listened and quietly forged ahead! The skipper had, too, saluted the crews of the safety boats, keenly giving their time, as they buzzed about like busy bees, incessantly!

A unique round-the-island race was run each year. But, behind the island, the waterway was crossed by what was known as the Strood. It sat at the junction of the Mersea Fleet and Pyfleet channels. That causeway onto the island was, strangely, covered during mid-range tides and above – fairly frequently, in fact. It was understood by the skipper that the Islanders' were content with the status quo! During the race, when the dinghies reached the Strood, they were hauled out by willing volunteers and carried across, allowing the participants to continue gaily onwards. The race had been running for years. They're a hardy lot in the Quarters!

It was reputed that the first causeway was built by the Romans who'd garrisoned the island – oysters were probably the draw. Later, in Tudor times, the eastern end of the island was fortified as a line of defence for Colchester. During the siege of Colchester during the Civil War, between the Crown and Parliament, the fort was occupied by Parliamentarian troops, their ships and troops prevented the Royalists from entering the river.

Over a number of years, the skipper had continually promised the mate that, when in this haven, he would treat her to dinner at the premier club in the area, the West Mersea. They'd been by road, for a naval association meet, but not from the boat – yet. The food was renowned too – Ah! In earlier cruising days with a child aboard, they'd rarely eaten ashore – but as the years had passed by, a bite ashore was enjoyed more often – and why not?

Another of the joys experienced by the yacht's crew in this anchorage was fish. An abundance of locally caught fish and shellfish was always available. Oysters, too, remain a viable enterprise and the upper ends of many mud creeks around the

The last remaining wooden oyster-packing shed on Packing Marsh Island. The remains of an old wooden lighter sit on the shore, and beyond, the ribs of a smack and rudder of a spritsail barge moulder away. The island is in danger of being overcome by the rising sea level.

Quarters had oyster-layings marked out within them. A simple supper of some fish, new potatoes and a salad had graced the yacht's table from time to time, as had seared scallops finished with a little reduced wine on a bed of rice. Yummy!

The fish could have been enjoyed with a bottle of local wine: wine was produced locally at a vineyard that had been described as looking like a piece of Tuscany – 'Why do people say that ... why can't they say that Tuscany looks like the vineyard on Mersea Island?!' the skipper had said when he'd seen the article: wines had been made in the rolling Essex valleys since Roman times and many vineyards were dotted around the Blackwater's salt marsh-bounded hills.

While in West Mersea one year, the skipper had had a surreal conversation with a lady beside a bank cash machine – she'd noticed that he was a sailor – his waterproof jacket was a dead giveaway! She'd asked, in a cut-glass voice with a trace of rural Essex, if the skipper was racing.

'Oh no, we're visitors,' he'd said, grinning widely.

The lady had explained that usually she'd be sailing with her husband, but it being a regatta race day she was shore-bound looking after the kids while hubby was afloat with a group of beefy men to haul on the ropes. They'd got an old boat – the skipper had guessed – but she'd told him!

'Ours is a Finesse 24,' he'd said, trying not to grin at what he'd just heard, 'she's a clinker sloop – iroko hull – built by Alan Platt – she's called *Whimbrel*.' But he'd wanted to say '*Whimbie* ...' to mimic the lady's affectionate naming of her joy ... a look from the mate though, who'd just sauntered up to his side with a bag of stores, and had heard too, said 'NO!' very clearly. So with mutual good lucks, they'd then parted ...

Passing the lovely parish church, the grounds of which were always beautiful, the skipper said, 'There's a little museum down that road – we should visit sometime.' The mate had looked, interestedly, in its direction, but had kept walking. They'd not visited yet – but would. It had always been out of season when on the island on an autumn day ... closed.

Pausing on the way back down a hillside road, they looked over what was called 'the cricket field' and gazed onwards across the Quarters: it was a delightful panorama to be enjoyed. The field was left to the people of West Mersea by a benefactor. The land, though, was a little rough now and was closer to being a marshland habitat – 'cricket is unlikely to be played here,' the skipper commented, as they walked off.

Continuing their walk back to the dinghy, they'd looked over the strange, yet pretty-looking fleet of old yachts being used as houseboats along the saltings. The road here, on the approach to the 'City', as the waterfront was affectionately known, sits barely above the tideline and often floods. 'Many of the old yachts that used to be here have now gone,' the skipper commented. Close up, some of the remainder showed signs of being well past it, but they lived on. A reminder of a different era of yachting when a rich owner had a crew in whites! Not so long ago, one yacht hull was hauled out and taken away for rebuilding. It was now enjoying a fresh lease of life. Some pretty-ugly steel things had arrived with other assorted old craft.

'No doubt,' the mate said, 'in time they'll take on the atmosphere of the older craft.'

The skipper had other thoughts. The saltings, though, were now an official houseboat dwelling 'station' and moorings change hands for relatively high prices.

All too soon, it had been time for the mate and skipper to depart those waters. A night up in Tollesbury fleet was to be their last Blackwater port of call before heading away into the Burnham Rivers, southwards.

Tollesbury was a famous yachting village and had pretensions to greater things. A light railway was built across the marshes to a pier running out to deeper water in the Blackwater. The line linked through to the country's main network. For a very

A view across the Mersea Quarters to the hills above Essex Wildlife Trust's Abbots Hall marshland centre.

An old-timer, the *Othona*, serving out her life as a houseboat on the edge of the saltings at West Mersea. Will this be her last berth?

short period, a steamer service ran, but it was not successful. The skipper had always thought that if the Southminster line, over the other side on the Dengie Peninsula had come out to Bradwell, the deep water of the river and its natural shelter could have provided the impetus for creating a port – thank God it hadn't occurred! 'But the railway should still be extended!' he'd muttered regularly at the mate. Remains of the Tollesbury pier were still evident on the mud flats out in the Blackwater. The skipper had pointed them out to the mate earlier in the week.

The two channels that lead off the Quarters and ran towards Tollesbury Creek and further into Abbots Hall marshes were a gloriously quiet paradise. At the creek's headwaters, the low fields of Abbots Hall farm had been flooded for a marshland regeneration project. Within two years, marsh had re-established itself. Now the tide laps the edge of the rising ground beneath the hills beyond the creek.

'It's akin to the South Deep,' the skipper commented.

'I like the back of the Swale,' the mate added quickly.

Yes, both were a mixture of land and sea. Birds abounded too. At night, especially, the bleating of sheep or the mooing of cattle had been known to awake the crew – no bad thing: the remoteness of the area, especially when low below the sea wall on the ebb, allowed on a clear night the sight of a myriad of stars.

Within the creek, a large number of moorings exist, barring most of the area for anchoring, but a mooring was often found and on one the skipper and mate had had many peaceful days over the years. The skipper was prone to go off in the dinghy to investigate the marsh channels on a rising tide. Doing just that one year, he came across the rotting remains of a barge, the *Saltcote Belle*, mouldering in a gully off Tollesbury Creek. She'd been sailing as a yacht barge during his childhood. The barge had been built for the mill owner, up river at Heybridge. Up a different gulley was another of those fine vessels, the *Memory*. She sat abandoned against the saltings close by a line of yacht moorings within the marshes. The mooring rights in the marshes were ancient and controlled by a society.

During their present visit, the skipper and mate had sailed, well motored under outboard, in the tender up to the old village hard, close by the entrance to the modern marina. There was a good butcher in the village – it was their destination.

Within the creek sat an old lightship used as a base for a Christian outward bound sailing school; there, a mass of little craft were being prepared for use. Moorings abounded, with boats snuggled into rills in the marsh. There was a littering of wrecks too, ancient smacks, old yachts and converted ships' lifeboats. Planking, rotted and falling away hung with tendrils of weed. Parts not submerged by the twice-daily tides showed signs of faded, flaked paint still. The old lifeboats were from the days when they were still a useful shape and size for conversion by cash-strapped, keen young yachtsmen unable to afford anything else: wooden lifeboats were regularly condemned by ship surveyors as useless after spending most of their lives slung in davits on ocean ships, cracking in the hot sun on distant passages.

Mooring the dinghy, the skipper was accosted by an old boy. The man's face was lined and coloured nut brown from years of being beside and on the water. After he'd commented on the handiness of the dinghy, the skipper asked a question about the old granary building standing atop the hard. It was like a signal ... the old boy started talking and nothing was going to stop him!

In a voice full of the local accent, dialect even, '...it weren't no granary, it were an ol' coal 'ouse. Oi remember the ol' *Tollesbury* (a spritsail barge) used to fetch coal up this 'ere crick.'

The skipper could only nod: the old boy was flowing.

'She was unlowded into the shed by us fishermen,' he added.

'Probably his father's generation – perhaps,' the skipper had thought silently.

'... it weren't no granary, it were an ol' coal 'ouse. Oi remember the ol' *Tollesbury* (a spritsail barge) used to fetch coal up this 'ere crick.' (Drawn by Gwendoline D. Ardley)

'There were ninee smacks in the fleet in them days – ooh – that be sevenee year ago. Of'en be twen'y-five up 'ere on this 'ard,' he said, canting his head sideways and screwing up his heavily wrinkled face.

At that point, they parted. Many of the old lofts and warehouses along the road into the village had remained in use. Converted and modernised, they made excellent offices for various local firms.

Walking up towards the village, groups of gaily clothed children were seen crabbing from a wharf that went up to a boatyard. Shrieks of delight, laughter or pain, were heard as lines were hauled in, crabs clinging, stupidly, to chunks of bacon. Little fingers delicately lifted the orangey-brown creatures off, to be dropped into the victor's bucket. Those kids were well trained though and seemed always to return their catches to the creek.

On the way back, the skipper needed to stop for a pint of refreshing ale: it was again warm ... the mate hadn't argued! When they returned with their prized pieces of pork, the old boy was seen still loitering on the waterfront. The skipper had grimaced.

He walked up to them and started yarning again. 'I's remembered sumin as yer went off earlier,' he said, his eyes glinting. 'It were when Oi were in a smack. Oi needed some milk,' he paused. 'Moin 'ad gone off.'

The skipper nodded benignly; the mate smiled sweetly.

'Oi 'opped in the dinghy and sculled towards a yacht – goin' t' ask for some.' He paused again, grinning, well, almost a laugh, 'out pops this 'ead and a Lunnon voice says "Oh hello my man – come for the mooring fee have you?"' He stopped and looked at the skipper and mate. 'So Oi said, "yus, that be five poun' please sir." He paid it too. So I's sculled up to the next then the next – Oi filled my pockets – that Oi did! Never did get me milk though!' The old boy's face was a picture and his eyes twinkled, full of life.

Groups of gaily clothed children were seen crabbing from a wharf ...
(Drawn by Gwendoline D. Ardley)

Leaving him, they motored slowly away from the hard, the man's twinkling eyes and ruddy face firmly imprinted on their minds.

'Bit of a tall story ...' the mate said, grinning.

'Yes ... maybe ... but I bet he'd done something roguish though – it's probably been embellished with time!' the skipper commented.

During the afternoon, the skipper had put a coat of varnish on the two deck hatches while listening to a crucial test match between England and Australia – an Ashes-winning year!

'Tea,' the mate called at some point, breaking his sojourn at whatever cricket arena 'he was at'.

Over tea, he watched as a fleet of fuchsia-pink-and-white sails appeared away in the distance from behind the two marshy islands tacking up the narrow strip of water. The islands were by then surrounded by mud flats and were a piece of privately owned 'land' now nothing more than salt marsh and mud.

'They're the outward bound lot,' the skipper said.

The mate nodded – she was reading and wanted to continue.

The skipper watched alone. The dinghies collected round a motorboat that had moored close by a little earlier. The crews, one by one, released the sail sheets and rolled them up by rotating the masts. Eventually more boats appeared – slightly larger GP14s, a solid and sturdy day-sailing dinghy much adored by many.

'More tea?' the mate asked, giving him a prod too: he'd nodded off. His book, propped on his front, had fallen onto the cockpit floorboards.

The jostle of boats and the sounds of excited, but tired young people had all but gone by then. Most had been dropped ashore at the fishermen's hard that came down from the sea wall close by. The last were disgorging from a couple of rigid inflatable craft and walking gingerly up the hard, giggling and chaffing. The last crocodile trail was soon receding into the distance. They were crowned by a largely blue sky that had fluffy summer clouds, tinged grey in their underbellies, slowly passing by.

'It's what summer should be about,' the skipper murmured quietly.

Later, after supper – that wonderful piece of pork, grilled to perfection – the mate said, draining her glass of wine and heading for the galley to clear away, 'We'll have an early night tonight,' adding, 'what with setting off for the Crouch – the forecast looks okay,' adding, 'be checking again, won't we?'

'Yes, of course,' the skipper said, feeling a little irritated; they'd had that conversation earlier! 'I'll go for a potter in the dinghy – though the breeze has almost gone.'

The mate wasn't hungry in the morning and barely ate. The skipper munched through his cereal and then his toast greedily, anticipating a good sail. They'd soon been underway.

'You know' said the skipper later, with the Nass well behind them, 'there's too much history in this river – well, too much for one person to know –'

Then he added, '... like most rivers really.' He grinned boyishly.

'Yes,' she said, 'I like what I know ... and ... I like the way we pick up ... no ... see more ... year by year.'

'A deeply fascinating river ...' the skipper said, as the boat curtsied to the little waves off St Peter's Flats, his head nodding in unison with the boat, not finishing what he was saying ...

8
The Essex Archipelago

The Burnham River and the Roach in particular with its myriad of creeks was a network of canal-like waterways threading through low, marshy islands, protected, on the whole by grass-covered sea walls. The skipper referred to this combination as the Essex Archipelago. The 'sea', for sure, was not as wide as that of the Aegean, and its islands were more densely packed. They had a special beauty. They had a feeling of remoteness and an abundance of wildlife existed within.

The skipper and mate had not been into these waters for some time. The skipper, though, had had a few sails on a friend's yacht enjoying day sails and a run up to Brightlingsea via the overland route, and it was that route, from the swirling silt-laden waters near the confluence of the Colne and Blackwater, that the skipper and mate had decided to take.

They reached deep into the Swire Hole, a deep tongue at the end of the Wallet that became a shallowing channel, tacking on the approach to the hard, steep edge of the Buxey Sands. They then worked, back and forth, in a generally south-westerly direction, past a gaunt beacon that had marked this channel for many years. A yellow buoy indicating the best water for the overland route to the River Crouch was their target. The buoy sat over a strip of sand. The sand, the Ray Sand, connected the outer mass of the Buxey to the Dengie Flats (when the tide had gone!) stretching out from a deeply sunken land hiding behind its sea-walled buffer.

The overland route down the famed Ray Sand Channel, the Rays'n, was in past times an open swatchway similar to that which now ran through to the Wallet from the Swin – now the main artery up and down the coast for yachtsmen and a few motor coasters. On the day that the little yacht's crew tacked down its length, the wind was generally a southerly, necessitating deep tacks into the Dengie Flats.

At first, along the edge of the Swire and Blackwater, a little lumpiness had been experienced, but as the passage progressed, the waters had quietened, turning almost flat and docile. Before long, they sailed close by their yellow buoy and were happily in the Crouch, reaching with the wind nicely on the beam towards the still-distant entrance. It lay amongst a murky blur along a seemingly solid, low coastline.

'That was good,' the mate said. 'We did it. I'd been worried earlier … before we left I mean … I can still feel those bruises from the Wallet!'

The skipper had smiled, affectionately: he'd seen those blue marks daily! Continuing to gaze at her, he said, 'Well, we're here. Well done you,' pausing and adding, 'you've done most of the sailing down the passage …' Giving her an affectionate squeeze, he said, 'I know how you felt.'

'You navigated!' she said, looking his way, looking pleased with herself too.

Leaning against the cabin top, feeling pleased, the skipper said, 'It saved us some seven miles – even after tacking …' he paused, 'Heck,' he called out, 'that bloody yacht … she's not going to give way … Tack!'

'I was watching him …' she said indignantly, adding, 'We had right of way,' and with some passion, 'he could have come round our stern too.'

'Thought you hadn't seen it,' he said quietly, winching in a bit more jib sheet and staring back at the other yacht – the helmsman, bless him, waved! The skipper hadn't responded. 'Bloody cheek,' he said, grinning, and adding, 'Perhaps he was mesmerised by our passage across the sands …'

'Bigger than us,' she said, 'treated us as if we weren't here – typical.'

Sometimes larger yachts 'disobeyed' the rules, often coming at you with engines running too – always expecting the smaller to clear a passage for them.

'Best to give way …' the skipper said, trailing off: he'd been caught recently.

The skipper had then taken over for his hour. He'd peered ahead from time to time, while maintaining strictly the charted course towards the unseen entrance. The entrance, though, had soon become apparent, right where expected. The little yacht whooshed past the sand and shell banks off Foulness Point, the tide firmly helping them on their way.

Later, when inside the entrance, the river itself, sandwiched between its high sea walls, was seen to run away before them into the distance, curving round northwards, east-west, on its run up towards Burnham-on-Crouch, the Mecca of east-coast yachting, some have said.

Without sounding priggish or being detrimental, the outer reaches of the river had always been of little interest to the skipper and mate: they felt they were barren and virtually featureless. 'It's like sailing along a wide-walled canal,' the skipper had said before. Not until the Roach was reached was there any sense of the existence of real land!

'You did say that's why the racing boys like it,' the mate interjected, passing a mug of coffee out through the companion-way.

The skipper, taking his mug, merely nodded.

They were passing along the edge of Foulness Island, close to a place called Clark's Hard. The skipper had looked that way briefly then turned to his mate. He was grinning too, and said, 'Here's a bit of interest for you. The *May Flower* probably anchored over there many times 'cos her skipper, Captain Crix, lived at the village across there,' pointing southwards and adding, 'You can just see the village church amongst that patch of trees.' The skipper had found in the barge's cargo records a long period over a Christmas, a hundred or so years before, when the barge's skipper had been ashore … presumably leaving his mate aboard!

The mate smiled: she knew, all too well, that the barge had been the skipper's childhood home.

'We sailed into this river a few times back in the early 1960s,' he added, remembering a childhood visit to Burnham with his parents – they'd needed provisions.

Passing the entrance to the smaller, but more interesting (local sailors say) River Roach, the skipper had pointed ahead, 'We'll be up to the first moorings soon,' he said, adding, 'We'll dispense with the main when we pass the "Burnham" and run back under jib to a buoy along the town shore – bound to be some along there …'

That's what they did. The boat was soon tethered to a buoy and they swung with a gentle breeze across the tide in warm sunshine. The sun lit up the largely red-brick front in varied hues, glinting on glass and colouring the whites. A weather vane topped the view too. It all looked charming, pretty even, across the gently rippling water, from the boat's cockpit.

The mate quickly had some soup bubbling atop the cooker, calling out, 'this'll keep us going,' whilst preparing tuna and cheese melts – a toasted speciality of hers.

Sitting on soft cushions at the cockpit table, munching, the skipper said, 'That was a gorgeous sail – made up for our wallop in the Wallet of last week!'

'Yes ...' she said, '... but I'm not better yet ... I'm getting there.'

The skipper had smiled, saying, 'I know.'

Later, as they sat back with their books enjoying a peaceful afternoon, the skipper had looked up from his book, saying, without a glance at the mate, 'That beacon on the Buxey – it's been abandoned – well, it's going to be.' Her face had registering nothing. 'Trinity House is no longer going to maintain it, I read. It's hoped that local river authorities and possibly local yacht clubs will do something.'

'Oh yes ...' she murmured wanting to get back to her book, but added, 'Will they?'

'I hope so!' he said with a wry, unbelieving look, feeling that in time the beacons would collapse and then become a hazard – as had happened to other old piles out over the sands.

The next day, they sailed up beyond Hullbridge, returning later to moor at Fambridge for the night.

On the way up, they'd passed such places as Lion Creek, once a busy barge port with a dock under the edge of Canewdon Hill; the famous Creeksea Cliff, a crag that rose up from the top of a beach, rising to no more than fifteen metres, but nonetheless a mountain in these parts; and Bridgemarsh Island, once a place of industry and farming, but its interior had been out of sight, hidden by an intermittently broken sea wall.

Coming up through Fambridge Yacht Station, the skipper, grinning, thought, 'Why station?' Well, it went back to a time before marinas and such: here were good, safe moorings where even anchored yachts were left for a week or two, looked after by the station. The village, inland a little, had had a railway station since the coming of the line during the mid-1800s, so it had been ideal. The river was now crowded by a forest of tall spires – those masts were all silhouetted in the calm, smooth water of the river's placid flow as the yacht passed by. The station's club house was reputed

North Fambridge yacht station with the spritsail barge *Beric* sitting alongside in 2006.

to have started life as field hospital during the Crimea debacle, a dubious period of British history from 1853 to 1856 when we tried, with others, to exert our influence on the area! The hut sat on stilts at the top of the hard by an old barge quay; the wharf had remained in use too. Between the quay and hut, a floating walkway connected to a berthing pontoon out in the main stream allowed craft to remain afloat and have shore access. From the rails of the 'station', voices had drifted across the quiet of the river; a comment, '... pretty little thing ...' reached the skipper's ear.'

He said nothing, but smiled: the boat did look lovely, dressed in her fresh coat of cream paint and done too just a few weeks earlier.

'It's a pretty spot,' the mate said, mimicking the loafers ashore – perhaps she'd heard too!

By then though, the skipper was looking beyond. He'd spotted an old wooden bungalow that sat on the edge of the saltings, beyond the old quay. 'It's used by bird-watchers' the skipper said as he wafted a hand nonchalantly across the water.

She had glanced that way, briefly, then said, 'There's nobody else moving.' She paused, 'It was quiet on the Blackwater, but not like this – it's dead – such a lovely day too!'

The skipper had winced a little: the mate was in charge though ... she seemed to be enjoying 'surfing' round the sides of moored craft, passing far closer than he himself normally did. He grinned, but kept a weather eye on proceedings!

'What's up there?' the mate suddenly asked.

'That's Stow Creek – well, what's left of it – been dammed off! A marina uses a hole though.' There were some marshes left up stream which had helped to keep the creek clear of silt but dredging was needed. Along the edges here, the skipper had seen fresh, raw damage along the marshes. The edges were crumbling and fresh falls scattered the mud flats. 'Some, undoubtedly, caused by the wash from fast vessels,' he thought.

'Look,' the mate said, 'there's a heron on the edge of the mud over there.' She paused, 'It's so graceful ...'

'Breakfast!' said the skipper.

Leaving that all astern, the mate handed the helm to the skipper: Woman's Hour had come onto the air (on BBC Radio 4) and the mate was deeply engrossed with a serial she'd been listening to that week. She was so transfixed that it wasn't until the skipper said 'This'll do' that she realised that they weren't in the river anymore, but up a creek!

He'd crept into Clementsgreen Creek. There'd been no change of course: the river bent to the south. He'd slowly felt his way in, keeping clear of the mud line. High above the mud, the marshes trailed sea purslane along their edges. Farmland had closed in on the boat too: the sounds of animals and tractors could be heard. The marshes oozed with a rich saline scent. It tickled at his nostrils. They were strong and heady. He could taste it too. The mate had even looked up, but was so engrossed in listening to an abridged version of *Villette* (written by Charlotte Bronte) that they could have been anywhere ...

'Where are we,' she asked quickly as he disappeared forward, letting the jib run down. The mainsail rattled down as the boat slid gently and quietly to a halt in the shallows. The skipper turned, grinned, and said, 'Clementsgreen Creek,' and let the anchor go. He watched as the incoming tide slowly turned the boat, leaving a shadow of disturbed silt until she tugged, almost imperceptibly, at her cable. She'd brought up. The skipper continued to watch as the incoming current started to flow past the stem, spreading little ripples as if they were underway. The boat was at rest. Tidying the jib, he let more chain rattle overboard before taking the mainsail ties from a bemused-looking mate.

'What are we doing here?' she asked, a little impatiently. Looking up at him she

... taking the mainsail ties from a bemused-looking mate. 'What are we doing here?' she asked ... (Drawn by Gwendoline D. Ardley)

added, 'I thought we were going up past Hullbridge.'

'We are,' he said, 'after here ... there's an old hulk I want to look at.' The hulk was on the chart but wasn't in the skipper's book of barge remains.

'Ah, you didn't say!'

'I only remembered while quietly thinking as we crept up with the tide ... you were listening to *Villette*!'

'I missed some ...' she said, screwing up her face, but, knowing it was to be repeated, added, 'Coffee?'

An answer wasn't needed ... but he nodded, saying, 'Sorry!'

As the tide slowly rose, a tantalising glimpse of the other world that lay so close by was seen – several cottages came into view almost buried beyond the sea wall further up the creek in a bank of trees. Finally, the rotting remains of a vessel beyond an outcrop of marsh were seen too. Apart from numerous dog-walking adults, the land had been devoid of life. Then, all of a sudden, a tractor just below the sea wall hove into sight. It cradled numerous small people, happily chattering and laughing mixed with a few wails of anguish from some smaller beings, cradled in the arms of harassed mothers. The 'cors' and 'look' words rang briefly across the creek, until the land train had disappeared.

'Blimey, that's Marsh Farm,' the mate exclaimed, 'I know where we are now!'

'Good,' the skipper said, grinning broadly and draining his coffee. Putting his mug down, he pulled the dinghy quickly alongside, 'I'll be back shortly. You happy?' not waiting for an answer: he still had his life jacket on.

The skipper sailed up towards where the houses had appeared earlier. Here, the creek opened out at right angles and ran up to a dead end – another dam. The creek had once run a half a mile inland, but had gradually been closed off. For a short period of time, a brick and tile works was operated here, with barges coming and going from a wharf. It was said that records showed that a wharf had existed in the creek from around 1519. The creek would have run deep across marshland to the firmer edge of the Crouch Valley hills.

Before the dam, lying on a mud bank against the wall, were the still largely intact remains of an old, wooden lighter. 'Not many of those left,' the skipper said softly: it was a relic from the past. 'This was a small one though.' It looked as if it had been used as a houseboat but not for some years. Looking up, the skipper had seen that there were a few bystanders on the grass-covered wall; they'd stopped to stare at the skipper's antics as he'd circled around, tacking and gybing. He'd seen them point his way and converse – probably wondering. He'd grinned!

Returning to the yacht, the mate said, 'Right, what's next?'

'Oops,' he thought, then grinning, he said, sheepishly, 'back on schedule …' The mate had looked at him … It was one of 'those' looks. Departing, they sailed up past Hullbridge, anchoring off Fen Creek. The skipper wanted to take the dinghy into this little waterway. He'd walked with the mate along its freshwater course several times. Its source lay inland near South Hannigfield and a reservoir.

The mate was happy this time – to let him go! Departing from the side of the yacht, the mate said, 'be careful …'

He had a tranquil sail deep inland until he saw that the tide had turned. 'Damn,'

The waterside town of South Woodham Ferrers from Fenn Creek. The creek eventually becomes a freshwater stream running from the hills around East Hanningfield.

he said, 'left it too late.' The boat was out in the river swinging to her anchor with an unknown bottom close by. Tacking back out, he met a fleet of dinghies from a sailing club, finishing a race. There was a club up the creek. It proved quite exciting for a while, manoeuvring his little lug-sail dinghy to keep out of their way. 'Maybe one day I'll come back ...' he'd thought as he approached the creek's entrance.

After a casual lunch, they sailed back down river to moor along the Fambridge shore – the night's anchorage.

During the afternoon, they'd gone for a walk ashore. It was swelteringly hot. Finding a place in the marina close by that sold ices, they'd not resisted. Passing a pub, the mate had indicated her acquiescence to a beer, but the skipper hadn't wanted one ...

Later, back aboard, on the cooler river, the mate said, 'The place is devoid of stores,' then concluded, '... not much use really!'

The skipper had raised an eyebrow – they knew that!

The evening was wonderfully quiet. They rowed gently ashore to wander up to the bright lights of the pleasing and friendly hostelry that resides beside the waterside and enjoyed a couple of jars – the more delicious for abstaining earlier. The mate had griped though: the cider available had returned to a national variety – after several weeks of decent local brews!

The skipper was reminded about a tale he'd heard. The pub here had had an official lock-in – some twenty-five years earlier. A drugs heist was in operation – the forces of the law were closing the noose around their prey. The area was 'shut down' and movement home by evening drinkers was stopped! ... What tongue lashing took place that night? '... likely story ... sleep on the couch ...' most likely! Several tonnes of drugs carried on a yacht from Lebanon had sailed into the river.

The next morning, they'd planned to sail up to Battlesbridge, a place often visited by car, but the skipper wanted a top up with water. 'Should have done it yesterday,' he thought, but then both had had hair washes that morning!

The mate said, 'There's a shop in Hullbridge – I can get a loaf and some meat ...'

'We'll borrow a buoy – saw some off the hard yesterday,' said the skipper as if to confirm the decision, adding, 'and I'll get two cans of water too.'

They had a brisk sail up towards Brandy Hole, passing the mass of flooded land that was now a huge area of marshland, supporting many birds. The area had had a chequered ding-dong history, with man doing his utmost to keep the land from the sea, but alas, the sea won, reclaiming it for the river! It was now a wonderful intertidal habitat good for birds and good for fish.

Clearing Brandy Hole, the trees of higher ground coming up towards Hullbridge blanketed the breeze, but the skipper persevered, swopping tacks with a large dinghy. Finally, the skipper started the engine, handed over to the mate, and went forward to stow the sails; the mate swung the boat round into the early flood tide and they were soon fastened to a buoy right off the hard.

Without delay, they both hopped into the dinghy, clutching a shopping bag and the water cans. Leaving the mate to wander into the village, the skipper had scouted around for a tap. The clubhouse and gates were locked. Wandering into the open doors of the waterside public house, the skipper bumped into a man. He asked, in his best voice, if it were possible to have some water ... 'Certainly,' the gentleman said, momentarily leaving his job of clearing up debris from the previous evening's jollities.

Arriving back at the hard, the skipper had a natter with a waterfront loafer, well, he was a yachtsman – his boat was being lifted later for some work – he'd lost his rudder!

The mate arrived shortly afterwards and they departed. The tide was coming in

Hullbridge Hard with an old wharf beyond. A medieval bridge once crossed the river here.

and it was time to go. Passing the waterfront of Hullbridge was interesting. Many of the houses being sailed by had their own moorings – 'we should have lived here,' the skipper said, grinning.

'You serious?' the mate enquired.

'No, not really!' he replied, emphatically: the Crouch wasn't one of the skipper's favourite rivers. The last couple of days, though, had been excellent. Poking up into little holes and finding things. The river itself was largely devoid of anything – its banks were cleansed, edged only by its high sea walls, topped by swishing grasses waving in the breeze. That had a beauty – sure.

Leaving Hullbridge behind, they noticed that the banks had crept closer to them. The river had narrowed appreciably. Although the mud was still showing, the skipper felt his way, under their large jib, giving bends a wide berth or otherwise. Every now and then, patches of shingle adorned the banks on both side of the river, natural beds. It was one of these that caused the establishment of Hullbridge – the lowest fordable point on the river.

Away to the north and south, for that matter, the rolling hills had closed in towards the river too; every now and then, a natural riverbank was passed. Land grasses sweeping over the tidal mud. It was idyllic sailing in hot weather: the sun beat down almost mercilessly.

'Did you put sunblock on,' the mate asked, proffering the bottle.

'No, but I will now,' he said, as he held the tiller against his thigh, pushing it, gently, as needed.

Looking north and pointing too, the skipper said, 'The vineyard we visited earlier this year is beyond those hills,' adding, 'Purleigh.'

'You remember, the man at Purleigh said that another vineyard had been planted down towards Burnham.'

'Climate change ...' said the skipper, grinning, adding, 'It's probably the one I heard about on the hills above Althorne.' Later in the year, the skipper heard that it probably was – the first wine-making crop was being picked! There were other vineyards locally too.

Interestingly, Purleigh spawned the first President of the United States of America. A John Washington, son of the local vicar, who went to the fledgling British possession, was the great-grandfather of George Washington!

Then, looking up from putting his coffee mug down on the cabin top, they saw their target. 'Look, there's the mill!' the skipper exclaimed as it appeared from above a swishing bank of brown-topped reeds that moved elegantly in the light breeze.

Rounding another shallow bend, they passed a retired Dutch motor barge being used as a home. She sat high above, on a bank, surrounded by the lush fronds of more reeds. The river had by then narrowed to a little over their boat's length ... reeds saturated the edges; the mud flats had disappeared. This was a place that was neither land nor sea. Plants able to live in both worlds colonised the banks. On the final run in towards a looming bridge, the mate ran the sail down and rigged two forward mooring lines. Swinging the boat into a bank of marsh in the middle of the creek, just down from a bridge pier, the skipper turned the boat and edged alongside a house barge.

A chap came past, rowing a dinghy. He called out, 'Stay as long as you like.'

'That was nice,' the mate said, thinking, 'He rowed past us earlier, a little downstream.'

Feeling itchy to be ashore, the mate collected her bag and said, 'Come on ... the boat

Early on the tide, the mate points the way up to Battlesbridge. The roof of the granary can be seen beyond the house barge.

will be alright.' The skipper had been fiddling with the lines. 'Tide's not here forever – let's go for lunch. I want to walk around the mill ... the furniture places and knick-knack shops afterwards too ...'

So they went!

Leaving the place they'd had lunch, the mate said, 'Did you see how the person you ordered from looked you up and down ... and then I had to go and ask where our order was ... I know your shirt's a bit scruffy.'

'I meant to change it,' he said. The shirt had seen better days; frayed at the edges ... the mate hated it! Its days were numbered. Later that year, the skipper relegated the item to the 'working on the hard box' – clothing for antifouling and such!

'We were tidy ... bit weather-beaten ... but clean ...' she paused, and said no more: her thoughts were unthinkable!

'I'd noticed people seemed to be in their best ... never mind,' the skipper said, grinning, and then laughing. 'Anyway, we sailed here!' They were crossing a little stream and the skipper said, 'this used to be tidal – creek came round the back of the pub ...'

Sometime later, leaving in a flat calm, the skipper said, 'There used to be another mill here ... on the south bank.'

'What happened to it?' the mate asked.

'Oh,' he said, 'it burnt down – in the 1930s – happened to many old mills – neglect and old, dry wood – it was replaced though, then pulled down in the 1980s. The bread flour we used to get was milled here ...'

'What's that building then?' the mate asked, pointing back to where they'd been moored.

'That was the Granary – but it was a steam-powered mill before that. It replaced the tide mill, which was demolished – it stopped working around 1902.'

'Oh!' She looked confused.

The skipper looked across the river, pointing at a garden centre, 'The mills were closed around 1980,' he said, adding, 'Since then, the waterway has steadily silted up – no commercial traffic.'

The skipper's eyes then alighted on the sad-looking and rotting hull of an old spritsail barge, the *British Empire*. The hull, the skipper knew from looking at her on a visit by road, was full of dry rot. The barge's sisters and successors would have carried some of the grains needed by the mills. The *British Empire* was re-rigged during the late 1970s. She'd come here as an attraction – a death sentence. She rapidly deteriorated and was finally placed up on the bank out of the way. A trust was formed some years earlier with an outlandish pipe dream to rebuild her. The skipper had said to the mate, at the time, '... there are far more worthy projects ...'

As they left the barge behind, the skipper murmured, 'Don't you remember seeing her up Foundry Reach (she was berthed in the Walton Backwaters) years ago – we saw her sailing off Clacton too – it was her swansong.'

They were then moving down a stretch of water the skipper had seen in a picture on a wall inside the Barge public house. It dated from at least a hundred years before. Spritsail barges then sat at the mill berths and down stream day-sailing yachts, sails limp in a light breeze, were along the river's bank. The occupants sported the sailing clothing of the day – soft peaked caps, blazers and white ducks. The river was wide and free of silt and reeds. The skipper had smiled wryly at it.

Later, when approaching Hullbridge, a breeze was felt. 'I'll set the sails,' the skipper called '– just keep her steady will you?' Not expecting an answer, he went forward. Shortly after, the sails hoisted, the skipper said, 'We'll just about get a fetch through here,' as the sheets were tightened in, leaving the mate on the helm.

Later, the eastwards passage required short and long tacks and the skipper had

The old granary now houses an antiques centre. This was once a steam mill and replaced the tide mill, upstream, when it closed.

Retired 'Dutch' barges in use as houseboats line the old wharves. Beyond, the spritsail barge *British Empire* rests in her last berth, rotting slowly away.

taken a trick. They bustled through the moorings off Fambridge, with a medley of cockpit devotees watching, commenting and pointing. The boat was clipping along nicely with the ebb under her too.

Passing close by the wharf the mate said, 'Did you see those old cottages – I looked at them yesterday – they seemed to be almost floating!' The cottages, old Essex clapboard types that had taken up the land's minor undulation, sat behind a protective wall dressed with colourful flowers. 'Pretty,' she added.

Below Fambridge, they saw a boat up on a patch of marshes that sat in an indent in the otherwise straight run of the sea wall. The occupants had waved. Several other yachts had just passed by too, without pausing. 'We'll luff up, off the edge,' the skipper said, '... and find out if they're alright.'

'It's the couple we spoke to the other day ... they're new to sailing,' the mate quipped, 'we talked about dinghies – they'd admired ours while launching their rather flimsy beach-like thing ...'

The skipper had spilled the breeze from the sails, keeping the boat just jogging against the tide. The mate had called, 'Everything okay?' Other than the fact that they were hard aground!

The call came back, 'We're okay ... our depth sounder said eight metres!' then, 'We've a dinghy – boat's settled upright ...' It was the lady who had spoken; her voice was a little tremulous. She added, 'We've food on board ...'

'Sit back, enjoy the sunshine and have a quiet dinner,' the skipper called. Then, with a wave, he tightened the sheets and continued tacking eastwards.

'What were they doing that close in?' the mate asked.

The skipper had merely shrugged his shoulders, thinking, 'we did some silly things too in our early years' ... and remembering just one or two ... he chose silence.

Off Bridgemarsh Island, the skipper sailed in towards the marsh edge. He wanted

The chimney breast of a farm house on Bridgemarsh Island stands as a lonely sentinel to Man's past endeavours.

The remains of Lion Wharf, Canewdon, where once cargoes came and went. The shed was used for the oyster industry. Old pits can be found close by.

to take a closer look at the red-brick remnants of a farmhouse built on 'new inned' land around 1850. Brickworks followed, and a shop including a small school served the bustling community. A tramline carried bricks across to a wharf – there were up to five on the island at one time. However, it all came to an end in 1928, like the many River Medway marsh islands, finally succumbing to the sea, during that era of high flooding tides.

The afternoon was getting on as they tacked down past Canewdon, high up on its hill overlooking the river, reputedly the site of King Canute's attempt to make the tide turn back. He'd failed, of course! But, it was on those hills and at the battle of Ashingdon that Canute defeated the army of Edmund in 1016, cementing Danish hold on their half of England. Following the battle, the Daenningaes tribe arrived and settled the peninsula between the Crouch and Blackwater; from that, Dengie, the modern name of the area, came about.

Passing the entrance to Lion Creek, an inlet into a patch of marshes that originally went round into Paglesham Creek round the back of Wallasea Island, the skipper said, 'We've walked that entire bit up and down here.'

'Yes, I remember' said the mate, grimacing, for it hadn't been one of their better routes.

'Do you remember I found what I thought were the remains of an old wharf – Lion Wharf. It served Canewdon. The *May Flower* went in there with muck. Oysters were the last industry up there – remember the hut?'

'Yes. We stumbled on another wharf up Paglesham creek – it was a while ago.' They'd been walking around Paglesham.

'Yes, the creeks round here went a long way inland until quite recently ...' pausing, he grinned, '... I don't wonder. I know ... feel ...' he murmured passionately, tapping his chest, '... the sea will have it all back!'

The timber wharf at Wallasea followed and then their night's mooring bore in sight. With the wind by then on their beam, the skipper doused the mainsail and they continued under jib, but closing on a mooring, the skipper had quickly asked the mate to run up the engine as he dumped the jib, fetching onto the buoy under power. The mate had muttered mutinously about her skipper …

Sitting with a mug of tea, the skipper had looked across at Wallasea Island. He'd visited the area by road the previous spring to look at the new flooded areas. A further project was in the pipeline. Spoil from construction of a cross-London railway was to be used to build up the low land of the island's interior, prior to flooding, and the creation of a massive new marshland environment, with creeks running into the Roach. The island had been walled since around the 1400s, thus the land was exceedingly low in comparison to the real world and just opening it up would initially produce nothing more than a muddy waste. The skipper applauded this.

Local sailors and the yacht clubs had been raising concerns, feeling that an increased water flow might change their river. Also, they were unhappy that a jetty needed to pump the spoil ashore was to be built a little way down river, never mind the additional shipping.

'They're spoilt here,' the skipper had said, sometime previously. 'We're used to ships on the Thames and Medway.' He'd added too, 'A bit of a marshland border will improve that river!'

The next day, they motored gently into the town's marina for a night's stay. Laundry, showers … a wander around the town … and later a meal ashore was on the agenda. They were berthed before late risers were about!

Burnham-on-Crouch was a delightful town and the skipper and mate had a gay time ambling around and enjoying its old-world gentility. They were particularly struck by the slowness of life: cars stopped if they stood still at the side of the road

Burnham's clock tower and quaint high street.

– crossing was then inevitable with such courtesy!

Along the High Street, they saw the old clock tower. It was once the entrance to an old school originally founded in 1785. The skipper stopped to take a look. Later, he found that the school had been improved after the Education Act of 1871. The tower was added in 1877. It was endowed by a philanthropic oysterman, Labian Sweeting, being built in his memory. The school remained in use until 1973. It moved to new modern buildings. The old school rooms had since been converted to flats.

'That's the base of the ship weather vane we can see from the boat,' the skipper called out as he caught back up with the mate.

Across the street was a building that had 'International Store' below the eves. The store, the skipper saw, had another use though. The skipper had thought of a ship chandler's and foreign goods. Like many places, buildings often changed use – but inscribed names were left to tease!

'It's all old,' the skipper said, 'but still in use.' Passing an old-fashioned iron monger, he added, 'Bit like Maldon – almost self-contained.'

The mate said, 'The church is higher up the town though … and there's an old steam railway museum too – I took the boy there years ago.' She smiled. The skipper had remained silent, so she added, '… recently a building dubbed "Strawhenge" was found somewhere close by.'

'Yes, I heard that too,' the skipper said, thinking as they wandered towards a waterfront nook for their lunch, 'the church was built back there because this was all marshland,' but said, 'The Burnham Week regatta dates back to 1893 – about the time the Corinthian came up from the Medway.' The club had moved from the Medway, vacating land needed for new port works in that river's entrance. The railway had arrived in town in 1889 giving the connection to London that they'd also enjoyed on the Isle of Grain on the Medway. The Royal Corinthian at Burnham was part of the same named club based at Cowes on the Isle of Wight.

The skipper continued, 'My dad sailed his barge through a fleet of boats one year … was in the early 1960s. Sailing in from the Whitaker …' Grinning, he added, 'He'd as much right to be on the river!'

The mate nodded: he'd not finished.

'You remember Ted Heath – probably one of our more social-minded Prime Ministers of recent times – but much derided? He was a yachtsman based on the river. And there was Peter de Savary who ran an America's Cup team from here.'

'Oh yes, he was the man that wanted to build that village and marina complex up Hole Haven Creek,' the mate said.

'Yes,' the skipper said, 'a far-sighted man – what a difference that would have made to the western end of Canvey Island!'

'Here we are,' the mate said, reaching a side passage and a rise up from the street, 'we can sit out on the front …'

'The Burnham Yacht Club came first,' the skipper said, 'it later became Royal and the Royal Corinthian followed. Their place was built in 1931.'

'Yes, and it's an Art Deco building,' the mate added quickly. The building was designed by Joseph Emberton, a modernist architect of the era, and constructed with concrete. Disliking fussiness, the mate had always commented on the clean lines of such buildings, whenever seen. The headquarters of the British Broadcasting Corporation was, perhaps, one of the finer and better-known examples. It was a Myer-designed building completed in 1932.

Reaching the waterfront, the mate ushered the skipper through the hostelry's door. After ordering they adjourned outside, sitting on a veranda above the water. It was pleasant too, after a morning of boat cleaning, washing machines and their walk. Finishing his sandwiches first, the skipper was about to interrupt the mate,

The remains of King's yacht yard in the marshes opposite Burnham.

but looking up from *The Times*, she'd spoken first, 'This marshland peninsula and our own, pointing south across the Crouch, were a stronghold of the Peculiar People.' The skipper nodded: his family had had a dissenting background. 'They were fundamentalists really, Evangelical.'

'Weren't they known as the Quivering People,' the skipper asked, shaking his upper body ...

'Yes, they began during the Victorian era – died out now though – they've merged with another Evangelical church. There's one of their old chapels in Daws Heath, close to our home.' She paused. Fatal!

The skipper said, 'I took a look at some of those old yacht wrecks earlier this year,' changing the subject quickly and pointing across the river to Wallasea Island, 'couldn't get to the barge remains though – they're on islands now ever since the changes over there.' He added, 'I'd been to the barges a year earlier, before the walls came down.'

'Oh yes ...'

'I wandered around the old shipyard too. It was used during the Second World War – bit like the one on Osea Island,' he said. 'The slipway is all covered in marsh. Some stilts of a building remain too. The wharf has crumbled though. In the mud close by, I saw some remains ... probably a barge ... mounds big enough.' He paused to sip his beer, 'the yard built small coastal minesweepers, patrol craft and such. But it was first put up to build yachts – big yachts – King's yard.'

The mate looked at him, as if wanting to say something.

'There's some old oyster pits too. One still has a sluice in place,' the skipper said.

The mate had wanted to ask, 'Where was that?' but hadn't, saying instead, 'Come on,' nudging him, 'drink up. I'm having a nap this afternoon ... we're out on the town later ...' Her eyes had twinkled ... noticeably!

Remnants of a once-prosperous industry. Oyster pits gradually return to marsh to the east of King's old yard.

The skipper grinned in return as his Adnams had slipped quickly down.

The next day, after a prompt start and a short walk up into the town for stores, they'd departed the marina by mid-morning. A run up to Rochford, which sat up the River Roach, was the day's target. 'Afterwards a quiet night in Yolkesfleet Creek will do admirably,' the skipper had said earlier when looking at the chart with the mate. He'd added, '... some quiet and solitude ... and to enjoy those succulent chops.'

Clearing the marina's entrance channel, they had to manoeuvre around a large yacht that had come up into the wind to set sail ... it caused a commotion with another close behind it. The skipper had said to the mate, who was at the helm, 'they're blocking the channel – go across the shallows, as you clear, I'll shoot the main up ... then the jib.' Leaving the commotion behind, their sails were soon set and drawing nicely.

'Did you hear those shouts ...' the mate called softly as the skipper tidied the halyard ends, '... it wasn't at us though.'

He grinned and nodded, 'I think they were cross,' referring to one of the larger boats.

The skipper left the helm to the mate, having hogged it two days previously. He spent his time pointing things out, breaking the mate's concentration and offering unneeded and unheeded advice! Their mood was light. They'd enjoyed a good evening at a very pleasant restaurant, The Contented Sole.

Soon after entering the Roach, the skipper noticed that the tide flow wasn't as severe as the Crouch. This was a different river though. It was edged with a greater width of marsh; below, the skipper knew, but then unseen, were gently sloping mud banks, 'Instead of those steep ones of the other river,' he'd muttered. From the marshes could be smelt the deeply saline scents.

Looking at it too, the mate had said, 'This is more like home,' as she'd breathed deeply.

A glorious sail was enjoyed with a quartering breeze, up past Paglesham Hard and beyond. Passing a creek known locally as the Violet, the tall threadlike spire of the church at Little Wakering and its sister's stubbier tower at Great Wakering were seen standing proudly above the landscape, as was that in Barling. Little Wakering church is reputed to have been built by John de Wakering, one-time Bishop of Norwich in the eleventh century. In Essex, Barling, during Tudor times, was second only to Leigh–on–Sea in importance as a provider of ships and as a port. That might seem unreal now, but the Roach and its creeks were wider and deeper. It was before the age of mass salt marsh inning, and waterborne transportation was infinitely easier than using treacherous, poorly made roads.

All three villages sat at the eastern end of the spine of high ground that gradually fell away from Hadleigh eastwards, past Westcliff and Southend along the banks of the Thames. Beyond, above the trees surrounding the village of Barling, in a slight haze, the tall, grey-looking flats and offices around Southend were in sight too. The land seemed to be asleep. Nothing moved. Yet there were clouds of dust, here and there. It billowed up, moving as if windblown. They were the passages of combine harvesters, hidden deep below the sea walls, in the bowels of the lowland.

'There's another sail behind us,' the mate said.

The skipper had looked astern and smiled, 'There are people like us!'

Passing an inlet into a wide expanse of marsh, the skipper thought he'd seen the remnants of an old barge wharf. It was still marked on charts – but in reality it had been consumed. It would have been used by the farms around Barling. The skipper had started dreaming of loaded, russet-sailed spritsail barges, deeply laden with bricks, or piled high with hay and straw, outward bound. Others, stinking of decaying horse dung, waiting to reach the wharves, swung to their anchors. He was away ... remembering ... seeing ...

A boat came out from behind the marsh, sculled by a gnarled old man, wearing a tattered guernsey and a cloth hat. With him were two old fishermen, puffing at clay pipes and similarly attired.

'She's the one ...' the sculler called to the other men, approaching the side of a barge, deeply laden and stinking: she'd waited here in the early summer sun for several days for the tides to make. Her bowsprit was hoisted up, harbour fashion.

'Yup she is ...' one of the old fishermen had said.

'Ol' Parker's *May Flower*,' the other said, adding, 'pretty thing – gettin' on though.' She was then just over forty.

'She's lowdin 'ay after this lot's ou' of 'er,' his mate had said.

'Here we are,' the sculler said, looking across at the barge's skipper as he stepped aboard. The skiff was soon tied off at the barge's transom.

The men, hufflers, were aboard to help get the old barge up into Little Wakering creek, by sail, sweep and pole – probably the kedge too, by the time they'd finished. Hufflers were usually retired waterside folk able to give a helping hand for some payment.

The old barge was quickly getting underway: her regular crew of two had had the anchor up and down and the topsail sheeted out. Her mains'l was at her sprit, the foot sheeted to the main horse, bawley fashion, and the mizzen slatted to and fro.

'Break 'er out,' the skipper's shout drifted downwind as the rhythmic clink clank of the barge's windlass pawls rang out across the water, as the two old fishermen wound away.

The mate had set to work hoisting the topsail; the skipper had ambled forward to

Hufflers aboard a spritsail barge (the *May Flower* when owned by Greens of Maldon). Hufflers assisted barge crews in getting their vessels up long, narrow waterways, often doubling as pilots.

help swig up the last foot. As the anchor was broken out, the foresail, held aback on its bowline, forced the barge round and she bore away across the channel. At the skipper's call of 'le' go', the foresail slapped across to the leeside. Then the mainsail, dropped from its brails by the mate, was sheeted in by the skipper and the other huffler aft ...

'Ready about ...'

An onlooker on the sea wall enjoyed the sight of the barge's sails, accentuated by the summer sun, radiating a russet glow as they filled, driving her forward; they saw the helm respond to the gurgling flow of water passing by her deeply immersed rudder, bubbling at her transom. Then they continued to stare as the sails alternately appeared russet and dark as they slatted in that slow, undulating way during the tack ... then grow darker as the barge reached back towards Paglesham and make her turn into the creek running southwards ...

'What are we tacking for?' the mate asked, looking at her skipper and adding, 'you alright ... ?'

'Err, what's that?' the skipper said, shaking his head!

'The water's narrowed,' the mate said, dragging her skipper back into the here and now, still looking at him again, quizzically.

It had too, but the skipper said nothing; he just grinned.

Some way up a narrowing channel, marked by withies, they dropped anchor over the mud flats to sit and relax over lunch. Sitting watching people go by on their craft, they received many curious looks.

'We're causing some consternation,' the mate said, adding, 'That other boat anchored up too –'

'Doing the same as us,' the skipper added, continuing with his repast.

By the time lunch had been cleared, with the tide then further advanced, they departed under power, pottering up towards the Broomhills, by Stambridge Mill. The waterway there had become deeply marshy and the skipper turned the boat about off a yard, marsh grasses passing close alongside as he did so. That marsh growth had all happened in a very short space of time too: the mill had only closed down within the last five years. The site was to be developed – at some time.

The skipper and mate had not been to these parts before, other than on foot. It was, for the skipper, an enjoyable experience. Both were surprised at the extent of yacht moorings though. It was a bustle of activity with many powered craft coming and going. The mate wasn't enamoured. She was by then looking forward to places south of this river!

Rochford was an ancient market town and was the centre of a large, mainly rural council stretching the full length of the Crouch, above the two Thameside areas of Southend and Castle Point (Hadleigh, South Benfleet and Canvey Island). The town's name was derived from old English for Ford of the Hunting Dogs. The Roach was originally known as Walfleet (creek of the foreigners). The skipper, learning of this, imagined marauding hoards of people from across the North Sea and/or invading fishermen from outside the area …

Clearing the head of the river, the sails were set and they'd initially been able to reach away down river. Passing the dammed-off creek of Barton Hall, the wind direction meant some tacks were needed. It was grand sailing in flat water.

Coming back past Paglesham (they were on a close reach, and relaxing after being on the jib), the mate said, 'I wonder if that old ship investigated by the Time Team (a

The reputed site of Darwin's *Beagle*, somewhere amongst the saltings and old oyster pits near Paglesham Hard.

television archaeological programme) was Darwin's *Beagle*?'

'Well,' the skipper interjected, 'it's never been proven – though it seemed likely,' adding, 'A book has been written about the ship – it was mentioned on BBC Radio Essex some while ago.'

'The 1851 Census places her here, I've heard,' the skipper said. The craft, Watch Vessel Number 7, was used by the coast revenue service. It housed operatives and their families. The old ship, reputed to have been the *Beagle*, was initially moored in the river but age eventually caused her to be put in the marshes. The remains, if they are of the ship, lie deep below the present marsh level to the north-east of the hard. The skipper and mate had paid the area a visit during a walk they'd done together.

He said, referring to their walk past that spot, 'The dominant scene was one of decay. There are old rusting hulks ... the remnants of an oyster industry and loads of other rubbish littering the marshes.' And thinking too, but remaining quiet, 'should all be cleaned up!'

'There are oyster beds marked on the chart,' the mate said. 'Look, there's some withies over on that bank.' The skipper had seen other warning signs on the river wall earlier.

Thinking of a book, the skipper said, 'It's reputed an Ardley – one was registered close by, in Prittlewell – worked with an oysterman on this river around 1850. There's a mention of "... with his man Ardley he has been raiding my beds ..." one son was complaining to his mother – the lady of the manor, or such, about his brother's antics on the river!' He grimaced, for he'd lost the chance to obtain the book some time earlier – and hadn't seen it since. The two rivers and its creeks were once a very important oyster fishery. Disease and pollution had done their best to rid the river of the molluscs, but recently, a fresh impetus had begun in the industry.

Closing the entrance to Yolkesfleet Creek, the skipper and mate had discussed the approach and position desired – while looking at their chart. 'I'll swing back and forth

Seals popped up and watched, noses twitching ... (Drawn by Gwendoline D. Ardley)

across the channel to gauge the best water,' he'd said. Sailing in, the jib was stowed. After finding their spot, they'd rounded up and as the anchor had splashed overboard, digging in soon after, the mate had had the mainsail down.

'Tea?' she called, passing up the sail ties.

'Ooh, yes!' the skipper said, grinning broadly and adding, 'Please.'

During the afternoon, the mate had dozed ... while the skipper had done a watercolour sketch of the world around them. Seals, which had been seen around the boat soon after anchoring, were by then colonising the mud flats just ahead of two other craft. The seals numbered over two dozen, the mate had counted later. It was a sight to behold. From beyond the high walls of Potton Island and Foulness Island, the two pieces of land they sat between, the sounds of farm machinery could be heard, incessantly travelling back and forth gathering the cereal harvest. It had been a good year, by all accounts, in these eastern quarters.

In the evening, before the sun had gone, the skipper had gone off for a gentle sail up and down the waterway. He was joined by two other little sailing tenders, all enjoying the tranquilising effect it had. Seals popped up and watched, noses twitching, as the dinghies had silently cut the water in the dying breeze. As the sun hit the horizon, casting a shadow from the sea wall tinged with orange, the skipper had been the last to turn for home and his waiting mate. One seal, a young pup, had followed the dinghy for a short while, waggling its head back and forth, twitching its nose. What the doglike eyes, deep and dark, saw, the skipper couldn't fathom!

Later, talking over their coffee, it was decided that their passage to the Medway would be the day after the next. The forecast had looked favourable. On the morrow, a planned passage round Potton and Rushey Islands passing Havengore Bridge would be made.

Whimbrel sailing through Potton swing bridge.

'We'll have to pass through Potton Bridge – by the way, it's a swing bridge,' the mate said excitedly, adding after a pause, 'Shame we can't go out the back door,' indicating the Havengore Bridge.

'Tide's wrong for that,' the skipper said, emphatically. He wouldn't have minded though: it was on his agenda for another time.

'Afterwards,' the skipper said, 'we'll anchor above the old quay off Foulness Island.' Then he added, 'It's close to the Crouch and our way out – things look good.' A moderate north or north-easterly had been forecasted for that time. 'I bet it isn't,' the skipper had chortled, upon hearing the weatherman's words for the period. He was right!

But, that evening in Yolkesfleet, it was something else. Idyllic would be too simple. A bright orange moon had appeared after the sun had gone. Its beam, a rod of light, struck across the smooth surface of the creek. It lit up and shimmered on the wetness of the mud banks surrounding them. The tide was still ebbing and seals could be heard snorting in their search for a late supper … an occasional fluttering or chatter was heard along the tideline – curlews or oystercatchers or a heron, perhaps?

'Idyllic …' the skipper said, trailing off.

'Yes,' the mate said quietly, in almost a whisper, as close by along the mud edge a plaintiff cry rang out.

The skipper, whispering, added, '… curlew's restless – a fox perhaps?' remembering another stretch of marsh where they'd enjoyed a similar reverie … down on the Swale.

9

They Dawdled ... in the Path of Others

A voyage up London River was something they'd never made. It was into the unknown. A plan was hatched. Its inception was during one of the short days of winter, on a visit to London, which was, incidentally, the mate's birthday ...

After delving into the delights of Fortnum & Mason's for some little delights, delicacies even, as a treat for their Christmas festivities and a browse through a bookshop or two, where they were never known to leave empty handed, they'd enjoyed a picnic lunch. The lunch was savoured in the tranquil gardens of a city-centre church. The gardens had been laid out for city people to use, to sit and seek a little peace and solitude too, if desired. It was a delightful spot: quiet contemplation was a natural consequence.

The day was cold, but it sparkled too and the sun shone down upon streets teeming, busy with people. In the garden, the mate appreciated the quiet and the warmth that came from the sun too: although she liked the cold of winter, she was, it must be said, severely wrapped up against the chill. The skipper rarely felt the cold – even when out on the water, where his own contemplations often occurred. And in that garden, it would've been easy, the skipper thought, to drift into a reverie ...

The skipper hadn't mentioned sailing all day: it was his mate's day out. With the dry, cold, sparkling weather they'd been enjoying, the skipper had thought, guiltily, how pleasant it would be to sail out of their creek at the eastern end of Canvey Island. Involuntarily, he'd sighed lightly. The mate had looked at him discreetly and smiled. She'd smiled because she rarely missed much ... She'd said nothing and only a gentle squeeze of the skipper's hand, in mutual recognition, betrayed her thoughts. With the light northerly, the skipper mused, they'd have been able to turn with the tide up the narrow waterway that led between the island with its marshes teeming with wildlife and the sea-walled shore. Beyond that wall, protecting the low grazing land, the Downs of Hadleigh rose up steeply beyond. The slopes were dappled, he knew, with faded greens of tired grass, and differing hues of wood and scrub: it was a favourite place.

Much later, after watching a delightful play, a matinée starring one of Britain's late-twentieth-century television stars from *The Good Life*, they'd come to rest at a little watering hole along the Strand. The mate had said, 'You know, we should bring the boat up to London next summer and use it as a base for a few days or so.' She studied the skipper's face for signs of any thoughts on the matter. His look was blank as he took a long pull at his glass of ale.

The mate, not having any intention of dropping the subject, said with a little firmness, 'We could book to see a play at the Globe,' knowing the skipper always enjoyed live theatre, and too, it was the best place truly to appreciate a Shakespeare play.

The skipper looked towards the mate and smiled: earlier when the mate had paused, as if waiting, he'd been thinking. A plan had sailed around his mind. He'd then looked knowingly into her eyes and said, 'Yes, I know. I've been thinking ...' pausing, '... actually ... when we come up in the spring, we could walk along the South Bank and drop into the Globe to book up.'

The mate's surprise was a picture.

'We can get information about Saint Katharine Dock before crossing Tower Bridge,' the skipper added quickly, as if to reinforce the point.

'... or off the internet ...' the mate added quickly, thinking of both.

So it was agreed.

On a later visit to London in the spring, all was duly accomplished. The boat would have to be up river, or somewhere else, in easy reach of London. The mate knew that the skipper was not likely to give up using the boat in the middle of the summer, so in a way, she'd had him lashed, firmly, over a barrel ...

Later that year, after a pleasant cruise down from Suffolk, in slow fulfilling stages, wending their way in and out of their favourite places en route, they'd fetched up in Stangate Creek, on the day before their planned voyage up the Thames.

During the day before, on the tide, they'd sailed up the three shallow, muddy creeks that led to Lower Halstow, Twinney and Callows, a wharf beyond Shoregate Dock: all were entwined with the skipper's youth. It was a funny day: hot with blazing sunshine, it ended with the most spectacular thunderstorm they ever remembered seeing. The colours were not unlike those in the angry and spectacular scene as depicted by Turner during the early 1800s, in his vivid painting *The Storm*, subtitled *Shipwreck*. In their storm, it started eerily quiet. The creek's surface was absolutely flat. Then, gradually, it had been pitted with a myriad of tiny volcanic craters. Each raindrop audibly plopped and they were at first well spaced, but gained rapidly in intensity, multiplying, until the surface was a deep mist. Their sky, unlike Turner's storm, had been somewhat darker, and more foreboding, especially with the encroaching night. Thunder had soon crackled in awesome, resonant explosions. Lightning lit the clouds in multifarious colours darting to earth. They'd been motoring out from Lower Halstow from visiting the skipper's mother to anchor clear of a mussel bar at the foot of Stangate, near Slaughterhouse Point.

In the morning, there was a gentle breeze, generally from the south-east, with hazy sunshine. The forecast was good too, which was a bit of a revelation!

They departed some hours before low water: the skipper wanted to sail against the sluggish ebb of a neap tide in the lower reaches of the Thames, aiming to be approaching Gravesend by the turn of the tide. In the event, they were somewhere along the Mucking Flats. It was a gorgeous start, in grand fashion too, sailing away from the anchorage.

Later, after a short period of fitful light airs, when going up the Nore Channel, the skipper had started the engine. The mate had stood agog, wondering if her skipper had turned over a new leaf or had become unhinged: he only burnt diesel as an absolute necessity! The mate, though, was not about to voice any opinion on the matter, for the Nore was an anchorage and base for the British fleet during the Bonaparte wars with France. She hadn't wanted to suffer the fate of the mutinous sailors (who'd only wanted a fair wage from the misers at the Admiralty)!

The Nore Mutiny of 1797 followed that of the Spithead Mutiny on 15 April of that year, when some concessions were made by the Admiralty addressing grievances over poor pay and bad food. Admiralty pay for their sailors was a quarter of that paid to seamen in the mercantile marine and it had not been increased since the reign of Charles II. Sailors' families were living near to destitution. The men – mostly pressed – would, on the whole, have had honest occupations ashore beforehand. At the Nore during that May, the fleet, under the command of Admiral Duncan, lay at anchor awaiting orders. On the morning of the twentieth, seamen aboard these mighty British

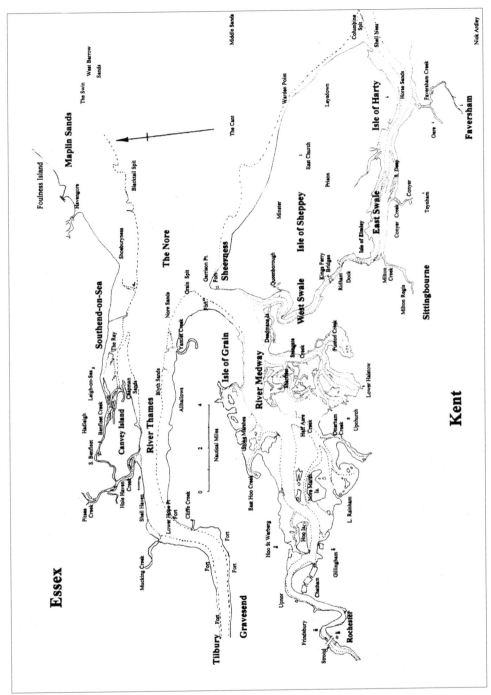

Chartlet of the Lower Thames, Medway and Swale.

ships mutinied. Brave deeds perhaps, but with the country at war, right or not, the leaders paid the ultimate sacrifice. The Admiralty did eventually bring about changes, so the loss of life for principles of human decency and fairness was not entirely in vain. The mate wasn't of that calibre!

By the time the low-lying smudge of Canvey Island drew abeam, a breeze had filled in from a north-north-westerly quarter; the engine was quickly silenced and *Whimbrel* picked up her skirts with a welcome rustle under the forefoot.

Canvey Island was gradually overhauled in bright sunshine. The island's name was thought to be derived from the Island of Canna's people. Canna was an Anglo-Saxon local bigwig. Over the years, post-1066, this was gradually corrupted to become Canvey Island (Canna's Island Island!).

Along the eastern end of Canvey Island, a lighthouse manned by keepers had sat for years. The lighthouse was needed to warn ships away from what was then a dreaded and treacherous sandbank: the Chapman Sands. Its reputation must have been severe, as it can be seen marked on maps going back to at least the fifteenth century. The last structure, a little 'Heath Robinson' in looks, was built on angled piles. It had the appearance of a 1960s space capsule, or an early military bomb, sat atop a set of spider's legs. The lower section contained a house in which the men lived. The light was arranged above. The light has been made famous by Joseph Conrad in his novel *Heart of Darkness*, a story that runs from the Thames, through the rambles of Conrad's character 'Marlow', to the Congo, deep in the heart of Africa. The lighthouse was removed in 1957. It had replaced an earlier lightship in 1851, so had served seafarers well for over a century, now a standard, mundane channel buoy sits on the edge of the shallows with the addition of a bell that peeled in a series of dull, unrhythmic clangs as it bobbed to the wash of ships or the short, sharp seas that build in this area in rougher weather.

They'd been sailing along the southern side of the river close to the shallows of the Blyth Sands. That, with another bank coming up on the northern shore, added to the treacherous nature of the channel. The channel had in the past gained a mysterious

The 'Heath Robinson'-looking Chapman Sand lighthouse in 1955, as remembered by the artist. (Drawn by Gwendoline D. Ardley)

reputation amongst the maritime fraternity: it looked so wide but yet ...

Conrad also described the approach to London while sailing on the Thames estuary. In *Heart of Darkness*, his thoughts mirrored those of the skipper's as he, too, sailed in the path of others. In *The Mirrors of the Sea*, another of Conrad's books, he wrote, '[It] is not beautiful ...' and, 'It has no noble features, no romantic grandeur of aspect, no smiling geniality; but it is wide open, spacious, inviting, hospitable at first glance, with a strange air of mysteriousness which lingers about it to this day.' Yes, even on the day the skipper and his mate sailed by. And that mysteriousness would continue until Armageddon ...

The skipper commented to the mate, 'Don't suppose smuggling is as rife now as it was in Conrad's day ...' the mate was not interested! He'd tried another tack, 'Look,' pausing to ensure he'd gained the mate's attention, 'that's the Scars Elbow buoy over there – funny name. I've seen it marked on an old sixteenth-century map. To me, it looked more phallic than an elbow, it does stick out rather ... even today,' as he thrust the chart under her nose. He added, 'The bank might be something to do with the tidal forces as they pass the entrance to Hole Haven Creek close by. The deep water channel is very narrow in these lower reaches.' He paused, adding quickly, 'Of course, you knew that.'

The mate, thinking, had cast her eyes across the wide expanse of what looked like navigable water, then as if to reinforce what the skipper had said, she pointed to a number of seals popping up and obviously sitting waiting for the tide to ebb further. They'd soon be stretching out in that luxurious fashion they relish, to bask and soak up the warmth of the sun. She scrutinised the chart and ran her fingers over its surface, as if feeling the expanse of the shallows with its drying patches out in the middle of nowhere.

'The edge of those Blyth Sands is almost a sheer drop,' the mate said. 'Look at these contours,' pushing the chart towards the skipper; 'we must be right along the edge.'

Then, pausing, as if a sixth-sense alarm was sounding, 'Are we too close in?' she said quickly.

The skipper was looking across the water at the seals, but the colour of the water around them caused a rapid thought. He'd automatically, instinctively, sheered the boat out. The sounder echoed his gut feeling too. They'd almost strayed into shallow water: the centre plate had raked the sandy bottom before the water deepened. The skipper had shivered: going aground up some little mud creek, whilst poking about was one thing; it was another to go aground on hard sand on the edge of a major ship channel. As if to drive home that point, several ships were seen coming up river, in a line, astern of them. On its way down was another ship. The wash from these modern vessels was, more often than not, quite severe. The skipper had shuddered, again. 'Not a good place to go aground!'

The skipper was reminded of an old family friend, the last sailing coaster mate, author and journalist, who'd sailed past here one day, some years beforehand, and grounded on the sands. He'd said, in *On and Offshore*, 'It was no good, she was hard ashore atop the Blyth Sand. Resignedly I shipped her legs to keep her upright, and philosophically prepared myself for six or more hours marooned on a sandbank with the red roof of the Lobster Smack, so near, yet so far, across the other side of the shipping lanes.' Being so near, yet so far from the pub would have been that skipper's greatest problem – 'he'd agree, if asked!' the skipper thought.

The skipper's mind went back to the years of the Second World War: although it was before his time, he'd read, in various books, about an anti-submarine boom that was constructed across the river in the vicinity of the Scars Elbow. It ran across to the Kent shore with a removable section to allow passage of vessels. The boom particularly annoyed the sailormen who manned the humble spritsail barges: they often lost their tide because of it.

The opening at the western end of Canvey Island was soon behind them. They were sailing as if in a funnel, the sides were rapidly narrowing. Hole Haven, the opening passed by, and its creeks, led inland where its channel split, as if a two-pronged fork. One prong, East Haven, ran eastwards round Canvey Island and the other went up to the villages of Pitsea and Vange, parts of Basildon. The creek was deeper and carried much greater volumes of water in past times, but marsh reclamation had reduced the haven to little more than a 'mud hole', barely able to keep a few inshore fishing vessels afloat. The haven had appeared in a number of literary volumes. The writers generally mentioned the old coastguard cottages and the famous public house that now peeped, imperceptibly, above the sea wall. In the past, these buildings had stood proudly above the wall, displaying their intent.

The public house, the Lobster Smack, had peered over the top of the island's sea wall for centuries. The wall now virtually obliterates the famous view from the water: it was raised, around 1980, following the building of the Thames Barrier. 'Dickens,' the skipper felt, 'would still recognise it.' Dickens placed it in his *Great Expectations*. The Lobster Smack started life around 1500 and had had various names, such as, The Sluice House and The World's End. The haven was a favoured watering hole for watermen, sailormen and fishermen. Now it was little visited.

A 1980s 'Thatcherite Entrepreneur' Peter de Savary had grand plans to build a marina village with a school, medical centre and shops on land just inside Hole Haven. Unenlightened, vociferous opposing forces stopped it. It would have been a grand use for a brown-field site that still sat scarred by dismantled industry. Part of the site had though, surprisingly, become a haven for a number of endangered invertebrates and was now protected.

The literary genius, one-time politician, political thinker and sailor Hilaire Belloc sailed these waters in his yacht, *Jersey*, during the 1930s. The yacht assumed, strangely, the name of the island to which it had belonged as a pilot cutter, and was thus registered as *Jersey*. At the imminent encroachment of hostilities in 1939, the *Jersey* was laid up in Hole Haven Creek. She rested in a mud hole, becoming little more than a hulk. After the conflict, a couple of demobbed Royal Air Force men came along, purchased her and dug her out. Where the yacht went and what happened to her was a mystery; but for them, the poor old *Jersey*'s bones would still be there, her bones protruding from an island of marsh, as had happened to many other vessels, now long forgotten.

Opening up a sharp ninety-degree turn in the river's course, at the end of the long lower sea reach of the Thames and leaving the line of tanker jetties of Coryton and the redundant empty berths of Shell Haven behind them, they'd moved to the northern edge of the river. It positioned them correctly to pass port to port, as required by the seamanship rule of the road.

Along the northern side of the river, the skipper, had pointed across the water and said gruffly, 'Look, over there, there's another load of London's rubbish being unloaded. That stuff has been coming here for decades – well, probably a hundred years,' he paused. 'The marshes round the corner, back there,' the skipper added, pointing astern, 'up Pitsea Creek – off Hole Haven really – were filled in too. The rubbish was originally carried in spritsail barges. They were replaced by strings of lighters towed by tugs.' Scratching his head, he'd said, fervently, 'Down from London, daily!' He'd then grinned broadly, 'There's little room left now': he was pleased! Changes in London's rubbish management were afoot.

Like similar areas in Kent miles from any real habitation, the area had also been used for munitions works. One was sited up Pitsea Creek, at the lower end of what was now a country park. Some remnants still existed. Concrete barges, used for transportation of oil and water; huge concrete pontoons, known as Phoenix units,

Mucking Reach with a fleet of spritsail barges and Shell oil terminal in background, 1930s. (Artist unknown – author's collection)

were built up these creeks too. The Phoenix units were towed across to the Normandy beaches and sunk to construct the Second World War D-Day landing Mulberry Harbour. One of the units never made it out of the Thames and still rested, with a broken back, on the sands off Shoeburyness lower down the estuary. Concrete barges could still be seen all round the East Anglian and Kent coasts, and other places, in use as mooring barges or sunk as breakwaters.

The country park was named after Wat Tyler. In *Companions into Essex*, Thompkins said that Wat Tyler, a leader of the Peasants' Revolt of 1381, hailed from Essex; however, he was actually understood to have come from Kent. Well, in *The Peasants' Revolt* by Webber, he was variously said to have been born in Maidstone, Dartford and even Colchester (hence the varying theories). At the time of the revolt, Wat Tyler was known to have been living and working near Maidstone (as a roof-tiling and odd-job man). Webber said, '... he had been a soldier and had seen plenty of overseas service. At one time he may have been employed by Richard Lyons, a London merchant. Now he was more or less a landless adventurer doing odd jobs such as tiling for a living with perhaps a little thieving on the side.' He ultimately led the men of Kent to London. After a meeting with the leaders of the Essex revolt at Blackheath, Tyler became the mouthpiece of the revolt in general in the South East. Later, after the mob's meeting with the King at Mile End, Wat Tyler met his death at Smithfield, effectively ending the revolt. Essentially, it took another two to three hundred years of the growth of the small trader to eventually break the medieval shackles that bound the common man. One could argue that it wasn't until the 1920s and the vote for all that the Peasants' Revolt really succeeded, the skipper believed!

Essex, too, had its own heroes of that time. One was a Thomas Baker a native of Fobbing, a village across Vange Creek – close to the park – perhaps the municipal personages who choose names failed to do their homework! There were in actual fact many, now nameless, leaders from all over England. Two others came from Corringham and Stanford-le-Hope, but at least one of those leaders had a memorial for their collective brave deeds, for which most paid the ultimate price.

At the time of the revolt, Fobbing (or Phobinge) was surrounded by marshes: the village stands on a bluff of land. The village had access to the Thames either from the dammed-off Manor Fleet which ran through the Coryton oil terminal, or from Pitsea Creek where there is a dammed entrance to a lost stretch of water close by a mud horse, called Fobbing Horse. The place was a haven for fishing folk and traders. Here too, with all the others built in conjunction with London's barrier at Woolwich, sat another of man's modern dams to stop the tide. Both of the creeks would have met the needs of the villagers. What a pity that they don't today – but that's another story: it was all down to oil and rubbish! The area's biggest reception centre for London's rubbish was now near the dammed entrance to Mucking Creek – also once freely navigable – and soon to be opened up as a salt marsh environment in lieu of a new container terminal.

A fleet of spritsail barges were operated from Mucking, the skipper told the mate. The barges were used in the ballast trade, on the whole. The company had later run motor barges carrying sands and shingles extracted from the river right under where they were passing. It was understood extraction was stopped due to undermining of the river walls. Sand was also dug between tides, by hand, from banks off Leigh-on-Sea, east of their own home moorings.

'Look,' the mate said, 'have you seen the tug ...' pointing ahead, '... some lighters too?' She'd grinned wickedly, 'Probably full of YOUR rubbish!'

Earlier, as they bore away up past Mucking, in Lower Hope Reach, the skipper had noticed that the north-north-westerly breeze had strengthened a little. He'd thought, unconsciously, 'the ebb's about done too,' glancing at the logbook.

The mate saw him and had smiled to herself – saying nothing, but thinking, 'His thoughts are on his timings ...' She hadn't sailed here before, but the skipper had: some years previously, he'd sailed up to Gravesend on a breezy, late-September day – purely for therapy! He'd been here as a child on his spritsail barge childhood home, she knew.

On their port side, the skipper saw another of his pet hates, the structure of a huge, ugly jetty where gravel and sands dredged from the sea were landed, or had been. It was built on a bluff of land on the site of Cliffe Fort. The fort, when built, was surrounded by water and boggy marsh flooded on the tide. The area was now a freshwater nature reserve. But, returning to sea dredging. It was a proven fact that sea dredging had caused a rapid increase in coastal erosion. To circumvent this, dredgers now work much further offshore, but, a hole dug will automatically fill up – in time. From where does the infill come? The shore of course – 'It must do,' the skipper had muttered ... The mate had looked at him – the question wasn't for her. It was in his head!

'Look,' said the skipper, he liked that word: it always grabbed attention, 'That creek entrance – behind the jetty. It once ran deeply through the marshes towards Cliffe. Dickens used the area in his novel *Great Expectations*.'

'And *David Copperfield* too, I don't doubt ...' the mate added. The skipper grinned: he remembered the mate hadn't a penchant for Dickens – in general.

'Look, you can see Cooling Church up there on the Kentish hills. The village looks across too to Stanford-le-Hope and Fobbing on our Essex side. All were used as watch-towers to look down Sea Reach.'

The mate smiled benignly – continuing to look ahead.

'Stanford-le-Hope was once connected to the Thames by a creek too. Conrad lived there, before moving to Kent, when writing during the late 1890s.'

The mate had then opened her lips, as if to start saying something – nothing emanated, there was just a smile. And that look – well-known to the skipper ...

The skipper rambled on about Joseph Conrad's friend, G. F. W. Hope, a retired merchant marine officer, who'd lived close by too. Hope had had a yacht, an old yawl, the *Nellie*, in which the two of them often sailed upon the estuary. The skipper had enjoyed many of Conrad's books and thought him an outstanding writer of sea stories. (He was considered, by many literary experts, the master of the sea tale.)

While that discussion raged, the speed of their little yacht had risen appreciably. Breaking his gaze of the receding ballast wharf, and the Kent hills, the skipper looked up into Higham Creek. It was dry as they passed; a creek nonetheless, but a dammed one too. The shoreline was littered with debris, mostly of jagged rusting steel from goodness knows what. From whence it had all come, the skipper could only wonder – channel clearances from the 1939-45 war?

Alongside a disused and derelict wharf sat an old wooden sailing vessel. She was the *Hans Egede*, a Baltic auxiliary schooner hulked during the 1970s. The skipper had mused over her history: later he'd found she'd had a chequered past – catching fire – being laid up – being abandoned – then reaching her final resting place. To the west of the creek and the more tangled wreckage, the more familiar ribs, stem and sternposts of another vessel appeared. Her rotting, broken hull rested out on the wide open mud flats and looked, to the skipper, distinctly like those of an old, decaying spritsail barge or a similar sized vessel.

Approaching a turn to starboard, into Gravesend Reach, they saw another sail. It was the first for some time: some craft had shot past earlier, strung out in a long line, going down stream, the discharge from London's marinas of earlier that morning. The skipper had said something about, 'their non-use of sails with a decent beam breeze ... probably left late ... missed the ebb ... so have had to fight the young flood.' The yacht was passing Shornemead and it rapidly drew level with them across the other side of the fairway.

The *May Flower* on the Thames in 1963 – in calmer conditions. (Courtesy of G. D. Ardley)

A little later, looking behind them, the mate saw that 'their yacht' had turned and was then coming up astern. 'It'll take some time to do so,' she thought and nudged the skipper. He took a surreptitious look.

For a while, the boat passed from their minds: they were passing Coalhouse Point and its fort, which at the time was being maintained by a group of enthusiasts. The village of East Tilbury sat beyond the sea wall too. The skipper, though, had little interest in the fort, except it dredged up a memory – way back to his childhood, in fact.

When sailing on his old sailing home, the spritsail barge *May Flower*, during a heavy-weather race in 1962, the weather chine had regularly lifted out of the water for long periods of time. They, his siblings and himself, were allowed to sit on the deck aft of the leeboard and lean over the rail to watch. (He shuddered at the thought!) They'd called back to their Father, at the wheel, when the chine lifted: it was an indication that the barge was sailing at her maximum and would take little more. A crewman was standing by, at the tops'l halyard! Things that had never moved tumbled about down below – creating havoc for his mother!

The skipper looked skywards, as if for inspiration, 'You know,' he said, 'in 1963, the river here seemed filled with a mass of sailing barges. We were always in the rear of the staysail fleet and the crack racers owned by the barge companies came surging towards us with foaming bow waves, flying a cloud of sail. It was spectacular. They were majestic barges.'

The mate saw the picture, from the expression on his face.

'Champion class barges they were called – fitted with enormously outsized rigs. Their sails dwarfed ours and those of the other barges.' He stopped, as if overawed, then continued, 'The Thames was represented by an old barge firm belonging to the Everard family. They kept three working barges in sail, specifically for playing with, but they'd still had at least one barge, the *Cambria*, operating under sail and a few auxiliary barges too, carrying cargoes.'

The mate knew of the *Cambria*, but said nothing. She'd been told about F. T. Everard, a firm then based at Greenhithe. They'd operated quite a fleet of motor coasters and tugs – all gone now – in an amalgamation with James Fisher & Sons Plc and the once-familiar funnel and 'bob' had disappeared into the history books.

'The *Cambria* was then under command of Bob Roberts – he sailed the Everard number three, *Dreadnought*, in the annual races,' the skipper added.

'London & Rochester – they became Crescent Shipping – based on the Medway, they still had one barge kept for racing. She was the *Sirdar*.'

'Didn't you write about her?' the mate asked, referring to a previous book.

The skipper had nodded, murmuring, '... what a waste ...' then looking at the mate, 'They weren't really working barges,' he said reflectively: none of those barges had, by the end of the 1950s, carried a cargo for a considerable period of time. The *Sara*, it was said, hadn't since the late 1930s, having been purchased by F. T. Everard for her racing prowess. 'The *Veronica* carried her last cargo in 1947.' She'd been involved in a collision on the Thames. Laid up, she languished on the riverbank as a partly floating derelict for some five years. Amazingly, she was hauled up the slip and rebuilt for racing: the boys on the Medway were winning too often! Thinking of that barge, the skipper said, 'Within fifteen years she was full of dry rot ...' grinning, he added, 'from poor-quality timber – probably.'

'I remember the pictures,' the mate said, smiling, '... but ... what about the other one.'

'The *Dreadnought* – Everard's had purchased her during the 1950s. Initially to ensure they won in the last staysail class. Her cargoes? – I understand they were few indeed. Then the class was boosted by yacht barges and she was re-rigged with a cast

Above: The *Veronica* on the Thames in 1963. Her spars went into the *Edith May* in 1964. (From an original print by Leslie G. Arnold, courtesy of Keith and Marian Patten)

Right: The *Dreadnought* viewed from the *May Flower* preparing for the 1962 Medway barge match. After being broken up, her spars went into the *Will* formally the *Will Everard*. (Courtesy of G. D. Ardley)

off from the *Sara*, when the *Sara* was 'yachtified' even further.' He paused.

The mate interjected, before the skipper could start again, 'No, what about the Medway barge.'

'The *Sirdar*'s last cargo was around 1954. She was done up some more and given a fresh layer of outer planking, nice and smooth!'

'Oh!' she said, a little surprised.

As the skipper had surmised in a book about his childhood, *The May Flower: A Barging Childhood*, those 'trading' barges were yachts. Indeed they were! In 1963, the match, the last of the trading era matches, the committee allowed a privately owned yacht barge, rigged with a bowsprit, to sail with the champion class. She was the *Venta*. She'd been around, as a yacht barge, as long as the *May Flower*. The poor old girl finished her days along the bank of the River Medway at Cuxton and was filled over during land reclamation. Staysail-rigged yacht barges had been brought into the fold by 1959.

Near the fort, the mate had been looking at a strange structure. It looked like a water tower – a box on stilts perhaps. It sat on the north bank. Later, they'd found that the tower had been part of the country's radar early-warning system, developed during the Second World War up the coast at Bawdsey in Suffolk. The tower had also been used, it was said, for coastguard operations.

But, back to the forts: a yacht, as relatively slow as they were, can travel far in moments of fancy and distracted concentration. They'd earlier passed the remains of another on the Kent bank. It sat in the bight of the river at Shornemead on the edge of Higham marshes. The Tilbury forts and those on the Kentish shore once formed part of the British Realm's protection. This river was an important conduit of world trade. The Port of London, collectively, but largely Tilbury, remained the largest port for general trades. The place had been important for centuries. Tilbury was even mentioned by Bede, the Northumbrian monk. Strugnell wrote, 'Saint Cedd, of Lindisfarne, built a church here (at Tilaburh – Tila's Fort) in the seventh century.'

About the forts, Fautley and Garon have said that the fort at East Tilbury (Coalhouse Fort) was in a useless state at the time of the Dutch raids of 1667. Afterwards, the fort at Tilbury (further up river) was reconstructed, but Coalhouse Fort had to wait until the Napoleonic Wars and the invasion fears that pervaded to prompt action towards the end of the 1799. By the 1850s, both Coalhouse and those across the water at Shornemead and Cliffe, on the Kent shore, were being enlarged. The development of ironclad warships led to a new appraisal of coastal defences. In 1859, the forts were rebuilt again. Colonel, later General, Charles Gordon directed the latter stages in 1865. They were completed in 1874 and did nothing for nearly seventy years! The forts, though, saw service during the Second World War – as anti-aircraft batteries – a hundred years on and against our previous ally too.

Tilbury Fort is a huge star-shaped affair with a moat, dating from 1672. It was erected on the site of a blockhouse built during the reign of Henry VIII. The fort was continuously occupied by the military until 1950. When they departed, the site was taken over by English Heritage.

They were by then sailing along Gravesend Reach – enjoyable it was too. Here, the yacht chasing them caught up as they passed the old passenger terminal at Tilbury, where so many had departed to far-flung (Empire) countries across the seas, and others, too, (from the old Empire) came to start a new life during the 1950s. Looking at the terminal and ignoring the yacht, the skipper said, with a certain level of sarcasm, 'Could do with a coat of paint.' It was still in use and not a pretty sight. 'Look, it's peeling. What a delight for passengers!'

However, the other yacht had, it seemed, wanted to come in close. The skipper, glancing across at his mate, sighed and eased the sheets a little, to let the boat slow.

As the yacht had closed with them, one of the crew had hollered, 'Beautiful boat you've got there.' As they came right up on the port quarter, 'Where do you come from? What is she?'

The skipper delivered the answers, tactfully!

'Enjoy your sail ...' reached across the water as the yacht had pulled away, '... she's so pretty,' drifted across the increasing distance. The skipper was greatly embarrassed: he'd blushed! The mate had beamed!

Sailing at a fair clip past Gravesend, the skipper gazed at the waterfront across the rippling Thames flood. It had glistened in the early-afternoon sunshine. It was a pretty picture, yet it had something missing. It was bereft of a traditional maritime look. At home, they'd a print of the waterside town, dating from the latter end of the nineteenth century – a collection of shrimp boats and a miscellany of river craft crowded the anchorage. 'Off Gilingham,' thought the skipper, 'there's a line of traditional craft ... they add so much ...' There were a few yacht moorings giving a semblance of a nautical air. Added to those there were some dilapidated old coasters strung out between dented buoys, streaked with reddish stains of rusting metal. 'At least the clock tower on the front hasn't changed.' The skipper turned away.

The next reach turned towards a more north-westerly direction, it meant that they'd had to come harder onto the wind: it was less favourable. The sheets were hauled in and the boat settled comfortably, but it had soon become apparent that they would need to tack. 'Nothing for it, but to get on with it,' said the skipper, as a broad grin spread across his face: it was the type of sailing he relished! The boat heeled and shouldered the murky Thames waters aside, her clinker planking scrunching through wash waves created by the bustle of greater activity in the river that had become apparent.

That short reach, Northfleet Hope, soon became a dead beat, but the flood tide running strongly in their favour gave them generous lift in the right direction. The skipper's phone had rung an urgent tune during that beat. Leaving the mate to beat to windward, the skipper had gone below to try and hear what was what. It had been the skipper's publisher: a local radio station was asking for him to join an afternoon show to talk about his childhood afloat ...

Regaining the deck, the mate had asked who it was. 'Oh ... publisher's publicity girl

Tilbury from Gravesend waterside, 1930s. (Artist unknown – author's collection)

– she was concerned at all the noise – "said we were tacking up the Thames." She'd gasped!' He'd grinned, then, 'I said, "My wife's in charge!"' as he'd squeezed her arm ...

The mate had relished the sailing: the sun sparkled and danced across the water. It added to the romance of the exciting, unknown territory ahead. She kept up a running commentary of questions to the skipper, as well as dipping into the pilot book and gleaning information from the chart. The land was by then being passed by rather quickly.

Though they'd no intention of resorting to the engine, it was run briefly near the entrance to Tilbury Docks: listening to their radio, tuned to river control, a ship was on the move, outward bound. The entrance to Tilbury Docks sat along what was known as the Black Shelf. Here, the river was steep to the Essex shore. It had made river access to the docks, when constructed, simpler in terms of dredging requirements – a natural entrance. With the run of the tide being hard onto the bank, it's a dangerous place and many ferry accidents had occurred here down the ages: above the shelf, in the Grays bight, a ferry once ran. Samuel Pepys, it was said, landed here whilst on business during his tenure at the Admiralty, carrying out some official function or other.

Their friendly yacht, they saw, had gone into moor at Grays off the yacht club. The mate mentioned Grays as a place they could use to stop over – 'another time perhaps,' she said, browsing their copy of *East Coast Rivers*, a superb sailing companion and pilot book. The book had a history itself: it was edited by Janet Harber, with help from her sister. (Both are Jack Coote's daughters. Jack was the originator of the pilot book, first published in 1956.) The skipper reminded the mate that boats from their own club had often used those moorings, on up river passages.

Along the Grays shore, until recent times, were a mass of cement works harvesting huge quantities of chalk from the only chalk hills in Essex, just inland. The huge Lakeside shopping complex resides in the worked-out quarries. The seams were really part of the Kent Downs. Those cement works had infected the area and most of North Kent bordering the edge of the Thames. Their departure brought many blessings, from beneficial air quality to a greatly improved aspect to the town. Hilaire Belloc, historian, Edwardian politician, biographer, man of literature, sailor and more, a sceptic of socialism and hater of capitalism who believed passionately in fair distribution, reckoned that Grays was, 'a very pleasant place.' That was in the days of its dirt and filth. Would he be more impressed now? Probably! Another writer who had nothing but praise for Grays was Frank Cowper. He described it 'as a capital place to lie off'. And so, it seems, it has remained.

Close by the yacht club sat the Gull Lightship, a wooden vessel dating back to around 1860. Her number was 38 on the Trinity House ancient list. Her mast had been removed recently by the local authority, it having become a hazard. Her hull was reputed to be in a bad way, but the authority said that it wished to preserve it. It does not bode well, unfortunately, for the fortunes of history.

A sharp, turbulent point, Broadness, was suddenly reached, where the water seemed to boil and froth. Wavelets jostled and tumbled over each other, endeavouring, it had seemed, to rip one another apart as they tore up river on the fast-flowing flood. Although it was very deep, silt had swirled up from the bottom. It whirled in a soup of many brownish shades. 'Another tack was needed,' the skipper had thought, but not said: the mate, at the helm, was doing a sterling job. Tacking was not her forte or favourite pastime! 'Well done!' the skipper piped, as the river's flow gave them a helpful lift neatly round the headland. Rebound wavelets slapped against the hull in a tattoo of clinker scrunches, as if in salute.

The next reach, Clements, was taken from point to point. Opposite that next point, which was aptly named as Stone Ness, was the little town of Greenhithe. Once a bustling hive of maritime industry where spritsail barges, ketches, and a host of early motor-driven coasters had been based, it was now empty. The world of shipping and commerce had gone. Here, telex messages would arrive from distant places. Now it was a simple nothing place. It, sadly, looked the part – new – austere – lacking in any personality. 'It has no life ...' the skipper retorted, pointing.

On the next long reach (which was so named) up to another turn at Crayford Ness, they'd sailed long and short tacks, continuing to make excellent progress. The riverbanks around the Queen Elizabeth II Bridge, taking London's outer arterial motorway high above them across the Thames, were filled with commercial wharves, ships and activity.

'We clear?' the mate had called cheekily.

It was a weird feeling sailing between the two tall pillars; the skipper had looked up, way up past the masthead. 'Well clear!' he called back, with a huge grin.

'Ha Ha!' they both chirped.

Still tacking in long and short boards and just before they'd reached that next looming point of land, Crayford Ness, the skipper had noticed an entrance to a muddy marsh-fringed creek. Crayford Ness, like Stone Ness, had helped to shape the mighty Thames. They were stone deposits. The opening that the skipper had noticed, and nearly missed, was Dartford Creek. The creek once wended its way past Dartford and onwards inland to Crayford. The creek was the salty end of the River Darent. The river was a renowned inland beauty. It had though, some years ago, all but dried up in its upper reaches, as a result of our insatiable appetite for water: its source was deep below the downs in the chalk aquifers. Its source spring had been reduced to a mere trickle.

The abundant marshes that once fringed the creek, allowing a balance between silting and an economical channel, had long since been walled off. The Victorians, those people of purpose and 'can do attitude' had built a lock. The creek had continued to support, until quite recently, motor barge traffic. The lock was now disused and a flood defence gate hung above the languid surface near its meeting with the Thames. It was dead. Its dam, like so many along this river, helped to cause, especially when closed off early, abnormally high levels during spring tides in the river's lower regions.

Leaving the entrance to Dartford Creek behind them, the skipper sighed deeply: he'd for years been particularly unimpressed by these dams. Too much of the once-huge expanse of nature's river and coastal flood control, a natural phenomenon, of marshland, salt grazing and deep gutways had been enclosed. The coastal fringe over the millennia had shuttled back and forth, freely, as sea heights changed, but for a few hundred years, man had interfered. Man's greed had made our present predicament with global warming's sea-level rise worse. Even as far back as the early 1700s, land reclamation around navigable tidal waters and its resultant effect, was accepted by enlightened individuals, but ignored by the majority and land greedy. 'What's changed?' the skipper thought.

Having cleared a northwards leg, up Erith Reach, the next few reaches were pretty mundane. The wind was on their starboard beam, an easy reach, allowing time to enjoy the views, have quiet contemplation and watch the changing shape of the river. Passing Rainham, on the Essex shore, the skipper had finally remarked, 'There used to be a ferry from here across to the Kentish shore.'

'There were probably lots – tea?' said the mate, deflecting his comments and had disappeared below to boil a kettle. 'Cake?' she called.

The skipper merely nodded.

It surprised them both how much of the river frontage was still green. The skipper mused on these things while drinking his tea. Since leaving the Medway, earlier that morning, they'd seen only patches of salt marsh, little bits, here and there: the sea wall tended to front the river, directly onto mud flats. Along past Erith though, around the yacht club, an expanse of the marsh still existed. This was the last piece seen. Land was deemed too valuable to be left in its raw, wilderness state for the use of wildlife only. This had always seemed such a shame, a crime almost, the skipper had long considered. But, even at Grays, heavy machinery were seen at work on the fringes of the little town, busy covering what had looked like marsh with material to raise its height.

The marshes along the outer London reaches, now enclosed, once swept back inland and acted as a massive tide-surge buffer. The marshes bounding the Thames' Essex and Kent coasts had been inundated some four times between 1898 and 1953. After major coastal floods in the early 1920s, large areas of grazing land and marsh islands, within the River Medway, had been abandoned – a sensible thing to do. Yet in most areas since, the answer had been to progressively raise the heights of the sea walls, forcing the tidal waters ever higher. Stealing from the title of Jane Austen's famous novel, *Sense and Sensibility* – these were attributes not in evidence. 'A controlled retreat is but the only sensible option …' the skipper muttered, adding, 'where it can be done – of course!'

Topping his mug up with tea, he pointed to the Rainham shore, 'The frontage here was reckoned to be the pleasantest spot on the Essex side of the river! I found a passage about it in *Companions into Essex*,' said the skipper. 'The dump we seemed to have taken ages to pass was mentioned even then too. Did you see the trucks and spreading machines crawling about it? Like ants they were!'

She nodded.

'It was considered high even in the 1930s.'

'I'll top the pot up …' The mate said, picking up the teapot.

Later, passing the gated entrance to Barking Creek, with its elevated dam high above, as if a guillotine, the skipper said, 'That creek had something to do with the Gun Powder plot!' According to Defoe, the plot was said to have been hatched in a house in Barking – says Thompkins. The creek entrance was then a haven for fishermen too. Catches were sent by water directly up to Billingsgate Market. 'Nothing much here now,' chirped the skipper.

Clearing Margaret Ness, they reported into the barrier control by radio and were told, 'Don't call until you've the barrier in sight.' The skipper pulled a face! He'd made a note of 'when to call' on their chart. 'Oh well,' he thought and went back below where he'd been preparing their dinner – the mate was helming.

A little later, at a prompt from the mate, the skipper had popped his head out of the hatch to look at the approaching barrier, 'It looks …' he said, '… as if it were a wild thing.' Grinning, he added, 'A wild thing from outer space; perhaps one, or more, of a fanciful species dreamed up by science-fiction experts.'

'The sea tanks!' the mate exclaimed. 'Yes! They're John Wyndham's weird and wonderful, all-powerful jellyfish in *The Kraken Awakes*.'

The skipper had nodded: Wyndham's book was a classic – a fascinating story of intelligent life from outer space. The life could only live in the ocean depths. The sea creatures melted ice caps and floods devastated the world: the greater part of the world's population lived at a level of no more than 100 feet above its current level. It was a tale they both adored.

'It was Wyndham's warning!' the skipper said, grinning.

The skipper took the helm then and the engine was run – as required … and left ticking over: Greenwich yacht club rapidly approached. There, a mooring was soon picked up from amongst a row of vacant buoys, under the shadow of the Millennium

Approaching the moorings of the Greenwich yacht club. The towers of Docklands and the futuristic Millennium Dome (O$_2$ Arena) loom.

Dome. It had been a ten-hour passage. 'Pretty good,' the skipper thought – glancing at the mate – both feeling tired, 'mostly sailed too!' he said aloud.

Relaxing, a beer was enjoyed as the sun had set. It seemed to set early over London's tall buildings, casting long shadows edged with the fiery colours and reflections from many a mirrored wall. Those shadows and light shafts danced in the wash of river traffic. The traffic, fast ferries, had been felt as soon as they'd moored; they passed incessantly to and fro, rocking the boat severely. Their supper was soon on the cockpit table – a superb Bolognese. It had been slowly cooked during the last legs of their passage. It was sumptuous, especially washed down with a glass, or two, of red wine amongst the twinkling lights of the city, as the day passed away into the evening ... romantic? Yes, it certainly was!

Afterwards, sipping their coffee, the bright, twinkling lights had taken over the night. It was a clear night, but few stars were seen: London, at night, lived in its own blurred, hazy white hemisphere of reflected light that blotted out the natural world beyond – a modern blight. The passage had tired them, so, with that knowing look, they'd not sat up to enjoy a nightcap, but answered their bunk's call.

Their arrival at Saint Katharine Dock was on a bright and sunny August day. The last part of the passage was a short, yet thrilling sail from the shadow of the dome, where the river was dominated by the tall buildings on the Isle of Dogs. It was a fairly leisurely start: the lock times allowed this. Departing in faint, fluky conditions: the breeze was bent and wasted by the high-rise buildings, creating short gusts, calms, and back eddies completely at random – it was a little frustrating for the skipper, who'd been at the helm, but the flood tide helped enormously. The mate wouldn't have bothered to try! Later, after rounding the Isle of Dogs, the breeze, actually crisp in nature, lost its earlier complications, and came obliquely down a long reach that ran northwards ahead of them.

Passing along Greenwich Reach, they'd both stared in awe at the breath-taking beauty, the sheer splendour, the majesty even, of the buildings that made up the old Royal Naval College. They'd seen them from the land many times, but passing the twin, domed buildings that framed the Queen's House, from the water they'd simply marvelled at the sight. The Queen's House, a work of art, looked no different to the view depicted in a famous painting of the Thames by Canaletto, painted during the rich days of Britain's fledgling empire back in the mid-1700s. That impact of the building's perfection could only truly be acknowledged from the river. Even the modernity of housing fringed with green trees beyond was not out of place: Greenwich Park, that oasis of magnificent, ancient hunting woodland, thinned out, now provided for the general population, rather than monarchs.

Passing Deptford, something caught the mate's attention: many years beforehand, she'd spent several years at a college here. The waterfront had changed beyond recognition. Old buildings had been demolished to make way for new blocks of flats. What remained of the historic place? Who would know, or care, for that matter, about the ancient dockyard that once stood here? It had built and furnished the nation's navy during tumultuous times throughout Europe. The little ancient church, the mate saw, was still there. She said, 'On the gateposts of the churchyard are stone or metal skulls. They signify that the ground has been used as a burial ground,' she paused, 'but it was a bit more than that – morbid even. It's a mass burial, or charnel ground, from the Great Plague.' She continued, 'Samuel Pepys worked at the victualling yard at the Royal Dockyard. His diaries record him having to account for goods during the early 1660s when in the employ of the navy.'

The skipper thought, 'He must have risen quickly – I bet he stepped on a few toes on his way to be the Secretary!' but said nothing.

'Later he set about organising the King's Navy. The system is still largely in being today,' the mate added.

The old naval college at Greenwich frames the Queen's House beyond.

'You know,' said the skipper: the mate appeared to have finished, 'along that bank over there,' pointing at the shore of the Isle of Dogs, 'ships, military or otherwise, slipped into these murky Thames waters. Isambard Kingdom Brunel's huge iron giant the *Great Eastern* was built on that spot – amazing, isn't it?'

'When was that?' said the mate.

'Not absolutely sure,' said the skipper, adding, 'I think it was late 1850s – she was used to lay a telegraph cable across the Atlantic later in her life.' The ship was actually built in 1858 and was revolutionary for her time. A section of the slipway, rediscovered during redevelopment works, could still be seen, if one took the time to explore ashore.

'There's another shipyard – the Thames Ironworks – opposite Blackwall Point by Bow Creek. It built and maintained ships up to around 1987. Its successor was just a graving dock by then. I visited when at (Poplar) college in 1972.' He added, 'Was almost opposite where we were moored last night.' The yard had built HMS *Warrior* in 1860 and their last large naval ship was HMS *Thunderer* in 1911. The yard built over 140 ships between 1840 and 1911.

On the long tack up from Greenwich towards Limehouse, hundreds of river passengers had looked agog at the little yacht, as it wended back and forth between the hard Thames riverbanks. The fast-moving craft had, generally, passed cleanly round the yacht's stern – leaving her dancing and curtseying in wash waves, criss-crossing the waterway.

Passing the Prospect of Whitby, still the quintessence of its type, the skipper caught a glimpse of their destination. No further time for gazing about looking at this or that: the sails had to be stowed. During that exercise, the skipper had to cling on tightly to a swaying boom as another high-speed multi-hulled ferry zipped silently close by. The driving force of these craft were water thrusters, they caused immense displacement and swell, which threw the little yacht about like a little top. After stowing the sails, the skipper quickly got the warps and fenders ready. Even before he had finished, the mate was saying, 'I'll just circle until you're ready ...' After a short wait, they'd locked into Saint Katharine Dock.

The dock, London's newest, when built in the 1820s, and best protected, had displaced a hospital of the same name. It was, unfortunately, almost too small for the rapid growth in the size of ships by the time it was completed. Cargoes such as spices and ivory were imported into the new, heavily protected dock system. The high, protective walls, or parts of them, can still be seen. The skipper had been into this dock when a babe. His parents had sailed their barge up the Thames in 1955, berthing here for a few months. The two visits were over fifty years apart.

The stay in London was well used. An evening at the Globe, pre-booked earlier in the year, was quite superb. Visits were made to various galleries and, of course, to what the skipper called 'our town house' at the top of the Mall. Thoughtfully, the tenant was conveniently away for the summer! The mate had wanted to make a visit to the Museum of Childhood at Bethnal Green, a place she'd visited many years before. It had since been given a fresh look. It was a pure delight – even for the skipper, with exclamations of 'look at those cars ... those tin toys ...' They'd walked via Brick Lane, sampling with interest and delight its interesting ethnic diversity. On another day, they trekked, in searing heat, to Camden Lock, a superb dive of the exotic and bizarre, then on to Highgate Cemetery by bus.

The visit to the cemetery at Highgate was interesting and thought-provoking. Walking round the winding paths, they'd seen poignant reminders of why their country was at the time deeply involved in a conflict many thousands of miles away in Iraq. A war to render it possible, it was hoped, for others to enjoy the freedoms that they themselves, often selfishly, enjoyed: in one little corner were the recent graves of

Locking into St Katharine Dock.

some of that country's brave men. From the dates, it was clear that they'd gone against the dictator that had, until ousted, been in charge. It saddened them deeply.

The skipper had said, 'Who knows what trauma followed them to their deaths. Many were not old, by any means ... they rest in this green, verdant oasis, so full of life – listen to those birds – they're singing to those poor men – to their souls.'

The mate hadn't added anything – she'd grimaced, her lips moved imperceptibly, and then nodded, as if in agreement.

They left the cemetery deep in thought. It was a wild place, deeply choked with trees of every description, obviously self-seeded. Nature was fighting for control. Later, over a drink, they'd both thought the place was an advert for what would happen to this world of ours if man should suddenly leave.

One other superb find, when passing Canada House, was an exhibition about the War Graves Commission. It was simply awesome – they walked round – looking – in silence – remembering.

A Sunday came round. They'd attended the ancient church of All Hallows by the Tower, close by the Norman fortress. It was interesting: after the service, they were allowed below, down in the crypt, where Roman road surfaces and pavements were seen. The church was, in the past, the resting place of those unfortunate enough to lose their heads close by! More recently, it had been the spiritual home of the mercantile marine, and a memorial for the thousands killed during the last century's two main conflicts sat just across the road.

'A fitting place,' the mate said, 'for two sailors to wander into.'

Hanging, suspended on long wires between the arches of cold, grey stone, were some ship models. A reminder of a maritime past, largely forgotten or marginalised by people today, even though Britain remained a maritime nation. To the surprise of the skipper, there was a model of an Everard spritsail barge; it gladdened his heart to see a part of the river's heritage there.

The gardens of the memorial to the men of the Mercantile Marine who perished in the two major conflicts of the twentieth century.

During their stay in London, the skipper and mate were, it must be admitted, very lazy and ate ashore most evenings, finding many interesting places around the marina to service their needs. Many pubs were visited too: beer needed to be sampled ... it was hot in the city! It was a little frivolous? Yes! But tucked up in that marina, they were as if at home ...

Departure was delayed for two days due to high winds. Finally the boat was readied: the wind had moderated greatly. It was a joy to be on the move. By late afternoon, they had locked out and the sails were soon set up and pulling sweetly – they'd not been covered for so long since the end of June and 'enjoyed the stretch', the skipper had thought as he'd surveyed the rig to make sure, in his own mind, that all was well.

'Now – let's wend our way to Faversham,' said the skipper, feeling buoyant. There was a club 'meet' planned.

A spanking sail down to Erith, of some three hours duration, was their reward. They chased a much larger cutter too. Sometimes catching up with her and then falling behind in an almost predictable yoyo fashion. The cutter had eventually pulled away, a reach or two, before Erith Rands, reaching cleaner air earlier. 'So it should have done too,' the skipper had said to the mate, who had smiled broadly: she too had enjoyed the race!

Reaching the barrier, the skipper had started the engine, but as the boat was on a run, hadn't engaged it ... The mate, lifting her eyes away from the fast-moving shore, said, pausing as the barrier's shadows cut across the cockpit, 'Shall I stop the engine? I don't know why you bothered to start it ...' She gave him a long, quizzical look too: it had been one of those looks, a look known only to people that have been together for eons.

A little earlier, the skipper had annoyed the mate by interfering with her sailing ... For a while, she'd been silent: it had been foolish and unnecessary. He'd realised that as he'd uttered the words and needed to make amends. The skipper had grinned ... returning her conciliatory look and nodding his affirmation about the engine. Then he'd smiled casually saying, 'It was just in case ... it was – honestly' – giving her a hug too! He was relieved, too, to be back in her good books: both, fortunately, had neither taken offence for long nor held a grudge. Life was too short for trivial insensitivities. The skipper was sorry though, and his look conveyed the heartfelt message.

The mate had then talked about the shoreline she'd been quietly gazing at, so intently. 'You know, the waterfront along here is so dead.'

'Built on a marsh – Thamesmead, I think it's called,' said the skipper cheerfully and with interest – giving the mate encouragement.

'Yes,' she said. 'It seems to have been the same for miles. What were the planners thinking of?'

They were, at the time, sailing down Gallions Reach and passing the old entrance to the Royal Docks, now devoid of the ships that had come from every corner of the globe. Interestingly, the area had once been part of the County of Kent; why, the skipper had not been able to find out.

Margaret Ness soon appeared and there followed another point, called Cross Ness, opposite Dagenham. During that time, the skipper made a pot of tea, for himself, and some coffee for the mate. They relaxed, sipping their drinks – the helm easy on the hand as the wind and tide took them effortlessly, in twists and turns, eastwards.

'The river is full of names that have legends attached to them,' said the skipper.

'Would take a book itself ...' the mate said trailing away.

After a period of quiet, the mate had continued with her comments of earlier, 'Last week, on the way up, I noticed' she paused, 'but was tired then and didn't get my head round it. All those flats we passed earlier are inward-looking. There is no life on the riverbank, no cafés or anything similar.'

The skipper nodded.

'I mean, there's no encouragement for people to come out and enjoy this wonderful waterway that flows past them. It's a shame.'

'Planners can be so sterile – inward-looking – like those flats!' the skipper replied: up river, opposite the haven they'd been hibernating in for a week, were a long line of old warehouses converted to flats, and other newer buildings – what set them apart were the cafés and wide walkways beside the river – It was alive.

'It's sad,' the mate said finally.

Erith, the planned stopping place for the night, was not, by then, far away: they were passing round Jenningtree Point, a strange name. Looking at the chart, the skipper thought, 'The bluff of land has the comely shape of a naturally supported breast ...' he often had those thoughts ... like the soft Suffolk hills further up the coast ... that also reminded the skipper of womanly delights. Showing the mate, she'd not been amused!

Turning out of their bunk the next morning, they departed from Erith just as dawn had broken. It was grey. The sun shone the previous evening from amongst fluffy clouds, sparkling and dappling the ripples of the fast ebb; it had been blotted out. It was not for the first time that season. The trusty diesel was used to get clear of the mooring they'd borrowed the previous evening. The sails were soon set. A silence pervaded as they slipped silently away from the muddy marsh-fringed bight, sipping hot coffee to ward off a chill that crept up from the river.

The skipper had cast a long look at the remains of a poor old spritsail barge, the *Lady Mary*, which sat like a beached and broken whale on the mud flats close to the marsh edge. Its stem stood forlorn, bereft of planking. Amidships, the old lady had a relatively intact look. The old girl's stern quarters, apart from her sternpost, were wasted down towards the mud line, the skipper presumed, for he could not see below the oily-looking surface as it flowed round the splintered wood. Weed hung from her, the skipper saw through his binoculars, dripping incessantly from its recent soaking by the tide, now well on the ebb. The barge, the skipper knew, had been used by the yacht club as a store for a number of years. Finally, she'd been abandoned. The skipper thought, silently, '... on the mud she rots slowly, so slowly, in this lonely place.'

Beyond the hulk, next to a concrete hard, sat the floating clubhouse of the yacht club – it was a converted ferry. Those bulwarks of solidity soon merged into the backdrop of the river's edge and quickly receded astern as the fair wind with the mighty ebb, ably carried the yacht seawards.

Continuing to muse, the skipper was reminded of an old bargeman, the last of the sailormen, who'd operated the last of those colourful workhorses of this corner of the country, a spritsail barge in trade. The sailorman had sailed out of Erith in his youth too in smaller boats. The old boy was known to have been a down-to-earth bargeman; he didn't like 'yotties' as a whole, but trained more than one to be his mate during the last decades in sail trading, generally coming back to Erith to find a willing lad. His last, though, had come from the skipper's home waters.

The previous evening, the twinkling lights on the upper deck saloon had beckoned the skipper, but not the mate: she was aching for some solitude amongst the marshes. There in the rand, they'd been as close to the marshes as they could get on this river. The call of a curlew had welcomed them. It is a harsh cry and once known was never forgotten. It was a delight – missed in London. Around the skyline, light interference was still great, but above was less so and the mate had enjoyed sitting out under the stars, looking for a while ...

A little later that morning, sailing serenely down Lower Hope, approaching Cliffe Creek, the mate had gone below to produce bacon sandwiches. As the aroma of grilling bacon drifted up from the galley, the skipper had gazed towards that creek. It was an indent in the sea wall only but had a little gutway with a small area of marsh beyond, unlike the majority of the creeks that flowed into the Thames. Most were mere outfalls through the sea wall – some had been mentioned by the skipper. Here though, the marshes were extensive inland and had been designated a wildlife reserve. The last true creek was the Yantlet, further down Sea Reach. It once ran through to the River Medway, when the Isle of Grain had been a true island. The Yantlet, after its promising shingle entrance, was now a muddy marsh-filled gut, dammed off a short distance in. For some, it remained a favourite little puddle to anchor in for a quiet night and beach barbeque.

The sea proper could be smelt. The skipper breathed deeply the salinity. It felt like they were home. The sea smell mingled with that of cooking bacon. It had reached that stage when the fat and rind had begun to sizzle and crisp up. It made the skipper's wait for those sandwiches almost unbearable.

His wait hadn't been for long. When passed out by the mate, they'd been enjoyed with gusto, washed down with the inevitable mug of coffee, while tramping down Sea Reach. The sun came out too – it had crept out from beneath the early cloud layer and shone under a huge open sky lightening the huge panorama of Sea Reach. That vista spread in all directions, as if painted in mellow shades on a vast canvas that stretched to infinity – a glorious sight indeed.

To the north of them, passed a week earlier, but not commented upon, was Shell Haven with its long stretch of eerie, empty, jetties. They were once busy with tankers, bringing crude oil into a Shell Oil Company Refinery. The refinery was dismantled during the late 1990s and a container terminal was planned for the site. Shell (Royal Dutch Shell – an Anglo-Dutch company), an oil conglomerate, had no connection with the name, Shell Haven, or Shield Haven as it was formally known. Thompkins had said, 'Pepys mentions that the "Dutch Fleete" was at Shield Haven (Shell Haven) on July 24th 1667.' They'd previously '... battered down the tower at East Tilbury' and that 'Fobbing Tower (the church) was shot at and hit'.

Interestingly, a few years later, we, Britain, had a Dutch Prince on the throne as our King: Prince William of Orange (clever bloke) married a Stuart Princess, the Princess Mary, and was ultimately, by invitation of Parliament, the heir to the British throne. True to the times though, they were known as William and Mary and not vice versa!

Passing the West Nore Sand, the skipper had gazed across the river towards their club, the Island Yacht Club, which sat at the eastern end of Canvey Island. Grinning, he'd said to no one in particular, for, some seasons ago, he'd often been one of the merry band too, 'The compound boys will be into their second pot of tea by now!' Those boys, mostly retired men, worked around the club, doing good works, odd jobs and dreaming of others. It kept them busy and non-seafaring wives were happy to have their men contented (and out of the way) in their retirement – 'but use your boats too,' the skipper had exhorted – many times. As he'd got older, the skipper had found numerous similar gatherings around the foreshore – every creek and mud hole had them.

The skipper was reminded of another of his sailing heroes, Erskine Childers. He'd passed this very place some one hundred years earlier, in a half-decked sailing boat, of between eighteen and nineteen feet. The voyage had been his first single-handed foray into the estuary. Remember, reader, that the river then was a much busier and more congested waterway by far, especially in numbers, than it is now – sailing craft of all types, lighters (in the upper reaches) often drifting freely on the tide, launches, small fishing craft, coasters, tugs and sea-going cargo and passenger carriers, filled the fairway. Steam was the main mode of propulsion and acrid smoke blurred the horizon. As often as not, if another fire had been lit, for instance, in an old scotch boiler, on a vessel in the immediate vicinity, visibility would have been reduced to that experienced in a fog. It was a fascinating era and the skipper often wished that he'd lived just a few years earlier – to experience it for what it was: the spritsail barge had dominated the river.

In *A Thirst for the Sea: The Sailing Adventures of Erskine Childers* (Erskine Childers was a politician, writer, historian, Irish [and British] patriot), Hugh and Robin Popham relate how Childers had described the difficulty in preparing his breakfast of tea and boiled eggs during an early morning sail down river on his yacht *Marguerite*, and for Erskine, the time had gone on too. Childers said in a journal, 'It was my first essay at a single-handed cruise, and from Greenhithe, to Hole Haven and thence almost to the Nore there had been nothing to mar the exultant sense of freedom and power. A west wind and a sluicing ebb had whirled me down Sea Reach in company with a whole fleet of Thames barges ... The sun was setting in a sombre haze, the estuary broadening into vast and dim proportions ...' The skipper and mate's passage that morning had been only marginally longer than Childers' own voyage. Fittingly, the aspect, and the weather too, had seemed little different – one hundred years later.

A fleet of spritsail barges were now only witnessed on this river during the annual barge races from Gravesend to Sea Reach and back; a passage match to Pin Mill; and during a match off Southend. The skipper himself remembered vividly barge sailing during his childhood and the spectacle of a fleet of red ochre sails, though always seemingly black when in shadow, was something that he'd carried with him through life. That morning, perhaps, a mere half dozen large ships had passed by, ugly container and car carriers on the whole. Other than those, the river had been empty, but there'd been a solitary sail in the distance ahead of them all morning. That feeling, though, of seeing the grand canvas that Sea Reach presents, empty or otherwise, had not changed since the moment our great writers had written too. It was a satisfying thought – gratifying – timeless.

The solitary sail, a bright whiteness picked out by the sun against the ever-changing colours of the river ahead, was the same yacht seen the previous evening, they'd thought. Later, cutting across the shallows of the Grain Sands, they'd gained upon her appreciably and, with eased sheets, passed her. Slashing through the last of the ebb in the entrance to the Medway off Sheerness, both had kicked up a flurry of spray that sparkled in the sunshine. The skipper had watched, and smiled too, as the other yacht had had to slip under their stern, heading hard on the wind, 'pinching', the skipper thought, on her way up river. Two people, a man and his wife, well on in years, sailing their pride of many seasons, had lifted their arms, their hands moved, as if in a royal salute.

By late morning, after an enjoyable passage, they'd picked their spot and were soon moored immediately downstream of the floating pontoon at the waterside town of Queenborough. Sitting back in the cockpit after they'd cleared up and stowed sails, harbour fashion, the skipper commented, 'That was an excellent sail – engine was barely used!'

'In fact,' as he'd perused the boats log, 'we used the engine for barely thirty minutes – no more than a mile or so – all the way from Saint Katharine Dock.' He grinned broadly: use of fuel was almost abhorrent! 'Brilliant! Be one to savour.'

They'd supposedly been meeting a brigade of club yachts for a visit to Faversham. None had appeared though. The skipper had laughed. A bitter-sweet laugh: he'd not been entirely surprised.

The mate exclaimed, 'Typical!' Then she added with a little sarcasm, 'I've shopped for all those extra-tasty goodies to share too.'

They'd not go to waste ...

The next day, a Saturday, broke with bright sunshine. That morning, the forecast for the next couple of days was a bit mixed, but some bright spells had been confidently pronounced. Although the forecast indicated that some overnight rain was expected, the winds were no more than moderate – for them, the important criteria.

Sitting in the cockpit after they'd breakfasted, the skipper said, 'You know that old map I told you about, showing the areas of habitation on the Isle of Sheppey?' He paused.

The mate released a drawn out, 'Yes ...'

'Sheppey was so named because it was an island full of sheep!' He grinned, then laughed, loudly.

'Still is,' quipped the mate – hastily! 'Go on ...'

'Queenborough, interestingly, was the largest and most prominent place, with its castle and creek lined with buildings going eastwards into the island. It used to be Qumbough – though there have been various spellings.' He paused, briefly, 'Sheerness had a fort and an anchorage only – it wasn't a place at all – only a Ness.'

By mid-morning they departed, with a single reef in the mains'l, 'as a precaution only,' the skipper had said. A fast beat round to the bridge had kept things lively! On the way, monitoring the bridge communications channel on their radio, they knew that an opening was imminent. It was missed by mere minutes – their engine would not have got them there any quicker. The bridge-keeper was most discourteous – not for the first time that season. They were snared. The wait grew and grew. 'Four trains an hour with big gaps,' retorted the skipper. He growled as the anchor was finally let go above the new bridge, barely in view of the navigation-control traffic lights. Another boat called up. 'Did you hear that?' said the mate. He had, their wait was going beyond the hour!

A new bridge had been opened the year previously. It took the island's (major) traffic high above the waterway. It should have made the passage for vessels through the Swale easier. But, according to records in the skipper's logbook, where he'd for years religiously recorded timings, the passage was taking longer – 'funny old world,' he was heard to mutter, as the mate popped below to boil a kettle.

Motoring down past Ridham Dock, the mate expressed surprise at the number of small ships berthed in the harbour – there were four of them. It often surprised the skipper too. Rounding a bend in the channel, the skipper gave the dock a satisfied last look as it passed out of sight. His brother had spent time on a Bowater's ship bringing rolls of news print in from Newfoundland – that was years before ... With the breeze on the nose, they'd continued to motor down to the Lilies by Milton Creek. 'We must go up there,' the skipper said, pointing to the waterway.

'What's up it?' the mate asked.

'Nothing much,' he said, tongue in cheek. There's lots actually – history and beauty.

The tide had been on the flood for nearly two hours at that point, and with a fair wind and time on their hands, the mainsail only was set. Their boat had picked up her skirts as she'd swept between piles off the ferry hard at Elmley, leaving a wash that gurgled and frothed as it crossed the shallow mud flats. Astern, the dinghy was up on the plane, its painter stretched out taut. 'It's Grand,' he called to the mate, who was below preparing lunch.

In the bright sunshine, it was a glorious sail through the banks of the Fowley Channel. A family of seals were observed sunning themselves, luxuriating in the

Bustling through the Swale on the first of the flood.

knowledge that the fresh food was, effortlessly, coming their way as the tide filled the rills around them. It was exhilarating stuff.

Munching on a sandwich and holding the tiller between his buttocks, the skipper had said, 'That old map I told you about,' the mate nodded, '... didn't show Elmley Ferry – I'm sure one must have existed though.' He looked astern, wryly adding, 'perhaps it wasn't as important then as it later became.' Looking thoughtful, he then said, 'There was another ...' stopping to munch more of his tuna sandwich, '... it was from a point on the mainland somewhere near the entrance to the South Deep.'

The mate had wanted to say 'Don't talk while eating ...' but hadn't.

The ferry had gone across to the eastern end of Elmley Island, at the entrance to Windmill Creek and the old creek round the back of Harty. Windmill Creek was now a marsh-choked wilderness and the other round Harty was dammed off eons ago.

'Neither the Isle of Harty nor Elmley are true islands,' the skipper needlessly said.

The mate nodded, smiled and continued to quietly enjoy her sandwich and watch the panorama.

Sailing fast past the very spot, more or less, where the ferry known as Red Ferry had been, their wash slapped the cardinal buoy marking the long, treacherous end of Fowley Spit. It curtsied, as if in agreement to all it may have heard. The buoy marked the entrance into the South Deep. The skipper hadn't finished though. 'Of course, Fowley was a much larger island then too and a long time ago it was all marshland inland from it too.'

The mate could remember two smaller marsh hillocks at Fowley's western end: the island had wasted greatly in the past two decades, and too, the skipper talking to her about the changes that had taken place in the area. The old creeks running inland towards Teynham and Conyer too: man had reshaped the topography immensely.

The mate had, throughout the skipper's warbling, remained quiet. She'd had her own thoughts of the barrenness of their surroundings. The area had such an emptiness. Yet, it was suffused with history. She closed her book, which had sat on her lap, her finger poised on a page for some time, and said, 'It's so difficult to imagine any level of human activity here.' Looking at the skipper, she added, 'The counties of Essex, Suffolk and Kent were some of the most populated for centuries, running towards the beginning of the industrial age.' Pausing and looking around the vast open scape, she said, 'I suppose the ferry points indicated a need.'

'Yes,' the skipper said.

'The land wasn't enclosed ...' then she paused as if in thought, '... well, not to the extent it has been and there would have been far more open, wild marshland.'

'Well ... yes ... it would have been difficult to move around.' The skipper added – in agreement.

Of Stinket Ness, the site of two old explosives wharves, a spritsail barge, the lovely-looking *Greta*, a local barge, passed, westbound. She'd had her topsail and foresail set with her mains'l lowered to the sprit: there was more than a decent breeze blowing. A gracious wave curled away from her bluff bow, leaving a frothy wake. As it drew level, a number of people aboard hailed the skipper – in name – waving – with repeated calls.

The mate turned to the skipper and said, 'They must know about your *May Flower* book – I remember, you described our clinker yacht in it too. Ha! You've been recognised!' she exclaimed, laughing raucously, in a most unladylike manner ...

The skipper grimaced and uttered, 'Bloody Hell!' He'd felt a little embarrassed too; colour rose across his face, noticeably, the mate saw, even under his tan of many weeks cruising.

Faversham spit had then rapidly approached. They turned sweetly round the cardinal buoy, still sailing, of course, and on the approach to Oare Creek, the mains'l was stowed as the trusty diesel was started. On the way up the creek, a big yacht, flying a French ensign had, for some inexplicable reason, cut well inside the run of channel buoys marking the fairway … they were hard on the mud. They were fortunate: they got off the next day, it was heard up at Iron Wharf the following day. They'd been there for several days!

Moving up the creek, closer to where land met the sea, the usual saline scents came drifting off the marshes and mingled with soft, summery wafts from the land, beyond the low wall. It was heavenly. Along one reach, out of sight behind the sea wall, a combine harvester was heard whining and roaring. Chaff flew up in a cloud and billowed above them. It had fallen, like snow, in a fluttering shower, peppering the decks with tiny pieces of shattered stalk. Underfoot, the droppings were like powdered chalk. It would need to be washed off!

On the final approach, the tall wedding-cake spire of the abbey church and thin lines of spritsail barge spars were seen against a backdrop of fluffy clouds and a blue sky. That last reach was something they'd both grown to love – it was timeless – yes … and enchanting. Some enjoy the solitude of the deep oceans for their sailing, but for the skipper and his mate, this creek and others like it, nothing could compare.

It had been a lovely passage. The sunshine had sparkled on the water, reflecting the blueness of the sky, tinged with darker, moving patches from those typical, scattered, cauliflower, white clouds seen in summer. And with the colours of the landscape it had combined too to add to the pleasure – an indulgence even as thoroughly satisfying as pure English honey.

'I loved it …' the mate said!

It was well into the afternoon, so no sooner than they'd been tied up, the kettle had sung its welcome song: tea. The skipper had purred: a pot of tea and a hunk of cake were soon laid out on the cockpit table in front of him. While drinking his tea, he eyed the creek and the direction of the soft, warm air that gently tweaked at the burgee. The heavier breeze of earlier was on the wane.

'Thanks for the tea …' he said as he got up.

'Going for a sail … ?' the mate asked, needlessly.

The skipper had only nodded. It was not long before the dinghy was rigged, then, as the mate settled back against a cushion with her book, he slipped away, to tack lazily on the last of the flood up the creek, to gaze upon the ever-changing waterfront. It was one of those little moments to reflect on and to remember with such sweet pleasure … something to hold onto, perhaps, for the time when the skipper would have to hang up his sailing shoes: he was not immortal!

Later, he wandered round the boatyard, where an eclectic array of craft always sat, some more like wild gardens than boats: creepers and brambles had invaded, others, proud little ships, were being lovingly readied for the water again. It was a grand place to explore, full of fascination and interest.

Later, as the sun began to set, some tasty bits and pieces were dug from the locker and a drink or two enjoyed: they were firmly tied up – in port – definitely not out at sea or on passage. (New drink and helming laws were in the pipe line … a legal minefield: on a small vessel, a family-run vessel perhaps, the who's in charge … on watch, conundrum rises to the fore. What do the legislators really know? On most, if not all small craft, the sailor is both sensible and sane and did not need the hand of big brother to tell him, or her, that they shouldn't drink and put to sea: it was dangerous enough out there as it was – how many yachts had sailed onto a beach with the crew as pissed as farts? Few, indeed, worth counting! The new laws were designed to use a sledgehammer to crack a nut: the trouble lay, on the whole, with beach and holiday trippers.)

After a shower, the skipper and mate had ambled ashore for an excellent supper at the Anchor public house, just up from Standard Quay. The food and beer at that establishment had, as they'd come to expect, been simply superb.

Sunday broke fine and sunny. After a late start, the skipper and mate had walked up into town for breakfast. Initially, the plan had been to sit outside, but the blackest patch of cloud that they'd seen all summer had crept up. It seemed to stop over the centre of Faversham. Yes – it dumped its load. Breakfast was adjourned and enjoyed inside instead. It hadn't lasted and soon drifted away.

A lazy middle part of the day was spent looking around. A visit was made to the Fleur de Lis Centre, a heritage building and local tourist office housing a museum and a bookshop with many local-interest books on offer. It was 'a must do' for any visitor and the skipper browsed deeply. The old gunpowder mill was considered, '... there's always another time,' the mate had intimated, '... we've visited once before.' That had been a while ago.

Around lunchtime, well maybe a little later, they'd walked round to Brent's. It was a quaint area of seafarers' cottages of the Victorian two-up two-down variety. Slowly though, over recent years, it had gained an up-market yuppie feel. It sat opposite the brewery towards the top end of the creek, by the Pent Bridge. A public house, frequented in the past, had become a tavern ... of sorts, selling Euro fizz and meals advertised on brightly coloured menu cards that dazzled in their new glossiness with pretty-looking delicacies – that, in reality, never seemed to match ... Chucking the menu down, the skipper snorted, 'It's never like that ... on a plate!' as he quaffed his pint. They scarpered after a single drink to quench their thirst and await the end of a little shower.

On the way back, the skipper had paused on the old Pent Bridge and gazed over

At Faversham, amongst a veritable mountain of timbers and a verdant jungle, an old-timer awaits her fate.

the silted tide pool. '... small coasters could stay afloat behind the ruined lock gates,' he thought, saying, 'Shame the water isn't used by the river conservancy to flush the creek now ...' Sadly, that had stopped some years ago. 'Our fore fathers knew a thing or too ...' the skipper muttered, thinking of silt ...

'Come on ...' the mate said impatiently!

The afternoon had almost been balmy. The forecast for the morrow, during the evening, spoke of cyclonic winds of moderate to fresh. Appointments loomed at home, so homewards it was decided they would go. 'We should jump now ...' the mate said.

The skipper acquiesced, and in the event, the next day, a pleasant, moderate north-westerly blew – not enough to give cause for concern. But, they knew, wind was due.

It was with a bubbly spirit that they set off that evening. The mate had found a natty little restaurant down a quiet narrow lane that led through a maze of apartments converted from old mills and maltings buildings. There, an excellent but lighter meal than the previous evening was enjoyed before wending homewards for an early night.

Waking at a premature hour, the skipper found, upon looking outside, that indeed a pleasant north-north-westerly was blowing, but, off to the east, the new day was coming up looking very grey indeed! 'We'll need our oilies,' the skipper called below: it was damp, though not really raining. Later, after a little drizzle, it had progressively improved. The cloud above them thinned and broke and typical sunny spells surrounded them, and the Swale. Their jackets were soon discarded, but their trousers were left on: for it felt uncommonly chilly on the water – akin to an autumn day.

Looking down Faversham Creek from the marsh-fringed Brent shore. Beyond, on both sides, salt marsh has established itself beside once-busy quays now crowded with waterfront dwellings.

Motoring away, both had cast surreptitious looks astern: Faversham was lit up from the eastern horizon. The rising dawn against the darkened backdrop of the western sky had illuminated it. It looked atmospheric – beautiful.

'Do you think we'll be back this year?' the mate said in a hushed tone.

The skipper nodded: he was sure they'd try.

The tide was a sluggish neap, right near the bottom of the tidal cycle. The mud flats were just covered and the rills were becoming water-filled. The boat's gentle wash produced a line of ripples that radiated out from the stem. They lapped the base of the marshes and gurgled in the gullies. Wildlife was on the move too. A couple of egrets had kept on lifting off, alighting further on. Their behaviour was repeated until some instinct in them, perhaps, had said, 'Let's go behind!' On a run of sea wall, above a wide swathe of grazing marsh where sheep usually fed, the ground was empty except for a group of pewits. The marsh, usually full of colour here, from summer-flowering sea purslane, sea lavender and thrift, had a darkened, subdued look. It was caused by the gloom above them.

On the approach to the Shipwrights Arms near the juncture with Oare Creek, the sails were set and soon pulling. Off Harty, where the ebb had set in hard, the engine was left running and they'd motor sailed westwards to escape the rush of the outbound tide. Passing the Fowley Spit buoy, the engine was silenced and they'd set to, tacking through the narrowing and increasingly shallow stretch of the East Swale channel. When near the last red buoy, the skipper was able to work a fetch through to Elmley. Once, the plate had scraped the bottom. It sent a tingling feeling through the skipper at the helm. The mate had glanced enquiringly.

Approaching Elmley, the mate had gone below. Bacon had soon begun to sizzle and the aromas from cooking had wafted from the open hatch where they'd lingered. Those flavours had rolled around the skipper's taste buds and awoke in him a feeling of impatient, frenzied hunger – only sated by the appearance on deck of his plate ... 'Ah – Yes – That's what sailing, the open air, and early starts are all about,' he said, thanking his mate, profusely.

For the sheer hell of it, in the decent breeze, they'd tacked up to the bridge – the West Swale ebb now with them. Their wait that time was only half an hour – the skipper sailed back and forth while enjoying a coffee, while the mate washed up from breakfast.

Clearing the bridge, they'd continued to tack northwards. Upon rounding Long Point, a spit of land that one almost circled, they'd fairly scooted towards Queenborough.

The skipper said, grinning, 'Do you remember the glue works ... they were to the south of the town's creek?'

The mate had – it had been her first Swale pleasure – and had nearly put her off! The wind direction would have allowed them to enjoy that factory's flavours, but it had long been dismantled. For the skipper, those memories ... well, they'd gone back to his childhood. On that site now, a marina complex had recently been proposed, with housing and shops.

'Marina's long been needed,' the mate had said, when they'd seen a plan. 'It's the facilities ... I'd be interested in,' she'd added.

The skipper had let loose a long, 'Hmmm ... !'

The quaint waterside town was soon far behind them.

Out off Sheerness, the boat was in its element and the skipper and mate had revelled in it. The wind was more northerly out in the open and they close-reached across to the northern shore. The young flood helped: it gave them a useful lift to the west as it gathered strength in its body. Tacking as they closed the shallows near to the Phoenix wreck, a concrete caisson built in 1944 for the Mulberry harbour that had sunk after breaking its towline, splitting open on the edge of the sands.

There, the skipper had rambled about what he'd seen marked on another old map. He said, 'To the east of here, there were two tongues of sand that licked westward, close by was a patch marked as "See (sea) Timbers" – they'll still be here. The area's known as the West Knock,' he grinned, adding, 'To the south is an area marked as the Middle Ground; it's a name still used on present-day charts. Here look,' pointing down at their chart. 'The timbers are remnants of an ancient petrified forest. They're probably covered by the shifting sands beneath these swirling, silt-laden estuary waters we're sailing through.' There he'd paused, for breath and to tack, and then he'd added, 'There's another area of "sea timbers" more commonly known about in our area. We passed them last week, along the north bank of the Thames, way up river, near to Rainham marshes.'

'Oh yes,' the mate murmured softly.

'Stone Age axe-heads and artefacts from the Bronze Age were discovered ashore there, as well as pottery from the Roman era. It shows that the coastline was delineated by a different sea level. Some similar finds have recently been found around Mucking Creek too.'

The marshland around Mucking Creek's entrance was being prepared for reversion to salt marsh as compensation for the port building that was taking place close by.

Getting back to their immediate area, they talked about Southend Pier. It sat across the wind- and tide-ruffled water, ahead of them. 'That pier has had more than its fair share of excitement too. It's had fires, as you know, as well as coasters and barges tramping into it.'

The mate had stopped him, and said, 'I sent you a paper cutting of a coaster tangled up, some years ago – you were at sea then ...'

He'd grinned at that! 'One of the coasters I was referring to was that old concrete ship abandoned at Hoo. She's used as a jetty – the old *Violette* – caused quite a lot of damage to the pier, according to a picture I've seen!'

The mate nodded.

'I've told you about her and her sister the *Molliette*, both were concrete auxiliary sailing coasters built by Pollock's shipyard in Faversham during the First World Conflict.'

'Yes!' she said sharply: the skipper had left her sailing back and forth while he'd gone off in the dinghy to photograph a little bit of the *Molliette* that had poked enticingly above the surface of a particularly low tide over the Mersea Flats some weeks beforehand. It had been a quiet, well, fairly quiet, grey sort of day. The skipper, too, had remembered: his memories were of the strange swirls and undercurrents that stirred the languid surface around the wreckage, much of it not far below the bottom of his dinghy, and he'd kept his distance.

'That one over at Hoo surely deserves preservation as much as the good old *Cutty Sark* does.' The skipper had said this to the mate before and hadn't expected comment: there wasn't any!

Along the northern shore, they had a glorious reach into the Ray Channel where the fresh flood churned the sands, like a 'weak coffee' around the conical buoy that sat marking its entrance. The tide was then running well; it gave an appreciable lift, sending them racing on their way. They were on the home straight – it felt like it too: the skipper had left these waters many weeks earlier and it felt as if he'd returned from a deep-sea voyage, harking back to when he'd been a professional aboard a ship: the feeling, he felt, was the same upon reaching the British coast again ... Older seafarers knew that feeling and over indulgence as 'the channels'.

Sailing up to the entrance to Smallgains Creek an hour or so after low water, the mate had beamed with pleasure: a thoroughly enjoyable weekend, and most of all, a scintillating sail had punctuated their summer holiday cruising.

What more could any sailor ask for ... except, 'Can we go again ... ?'

Grinning widely, the skipper mouthed an answer to his mate's unasked question '... soon ...'

10

Reflections from around Milton Creek

The skipper, always the optimist, had chortled on more than one occasion during 'that summer': he'd met a prodigious number of disgruntled sailors – often where men tend to meet … after a few jugs of frothy ale – complaining about the weather …

The skipper was fortunate enough to enjoy free time during the summer and had always made the most of whatever else came his way. August, even September too, for that matter, were often fine. 'But …' the skipper often reflected, '… umpteen sailors fail to make the most of what is dished up.' However, instead of unleashing a tirade at the mate, who was apt to say, 'I've heard you before …', the skipper kept his thoughts bottled, and his head below the gunnel.

That summer had been one of too many days with high, grey cloud cover. Those clouds, though, had, at times, lulled them into a false sense of security: they'd been burnt on several occasions – the safety officer, the enduring mate, hadn't insisted on smothering them both with sunblock … With the cloud, stronger winds had dogged them too, necessitating a reef in the mainsail on too many occasions.

Their summer, though, had included visits to many regular ports of call, places they'd not been to and others they'd not poked the boat's bow into for years. It must be said, 'they'd made the most of it.' It had been late August: a long weekend with suitable tides beckoned. 'Faversham,' they chorused together! Its pull was like that – magnetic.

Their short visit over, the morning of their departure was, as it happened, on just another of those coldish grey days. Both had felt that it hadn't been such a bubbly interlude, but that wouldn't hurt their long attachment, love really, for the quaint and pretty creek-side town. 'The spirit had been willing,' as was oft said …

The previous evening, walking ashore, they'd been saddened at the mass of housing built on a meadow close by Standard Quay. A campaign to stop the development had failed. A high fence blotted any view creekwards. It was all barely above high-tide level. 'They'll have the waterfront here too,' the skipper had sarcastically remarked as they walked past a barge yard.

At Standard Quay, the skipper had had a long look at the *Cambria*, the last spritsail barge to trade under sail. She'd won a lottery grant and was being rebuilt. Fresh new frames were completed. 'Almost ready for her new planking,' the skipper said, grinning; 'they know what they're about.' The barge, it's said, is to be used for educational purposes. Some local schools were already aboard. 'The *Cambria* is going to represent Kent at the 2012 Olympic Games too,' the skipper had added.

'That's inspired,' the mate said.

'Yes, she'll make an attractive and picturesque tableau. I can see her topsail, emblazoned with the Kent Horse,' the skipper further remarked.

'Don't suppose our county would've thought of that,' the mate said decisively, firmly putting the subject to rest.

'It would've been apt: Essex is the spritsail barge county now …' the skipper had thought, but kept it to himself.

Queenborough had been their planned destination, as they'd left with an hour of flood to run. The breeze, that morning, a south-westerly, allowed a sailing departure. It had to be done. After singling up and setting the jib, the skipper waited for his moment, while the breeze ruffling the creek's surface flicked at the sheets.

Glancing shoreward, the mate had noticed a gaggle of bystanders – quayside loafers – looking smugly their way. 'We're being watched,' she said, very quietly.

Not looking, the skipper called softly 'Cast off.' The tide eased the bow out; as always, without any qualms, their boat responded in the manner expected. It came from a long association between the three of them, which had then run for twenty-five years.

They were away on a run as the breeze kicked out the jib as it pulled.

A little later, a walker stopped and stared as they sailed slowly down the creek. The mains'l was set as they turned into Blueman's Reach, past a couple of cottages, 'Black Houses', which sat on high ground on the edge of the Nagden Marshes. The wind was then on their beam, but it had soon come harder on the bow and they creamed along with a curling wash that danced towards the marshes, gurgling into the rivulets along the edges.

It was mesmerising to sail near the top of the tide, with the water lapping just below marsh edge, the open gullies and rivulets full and reflecting … The scents too, from the previous tide's inundation, were heady and strong. The air was full of saline freshness. Sheep, as was common along that creek, meandered across open areas grazing, cropping the green, salty grass to a carpet texture. In the rougher marshland, wilderness summer plants still blazed colour. Both had stared in awe and wonder.

Later, below the inn that sat by Oare Creek, a brief spell of engine was needed to round a wide bend: it had an expanse of mud on its inner side. An attempt at tacking, it must be said, was attempted … but was a struggle against the tide. The boat had caressed the mud twice – the skipper grinned, inwardly – the mate passed one of those looks – 'a third time, near the top of the tide might be foolish,' the skipper had reflected. 'I'm not that much of a purist? Am I?' he said to the mate, asking for the engine to be started!

Her look had said it all: no words were passed! On a more recent sail out of Faversham, they achieved the passage by wind alone.

Rounding the marsh edge, immediately under the sea wall, in some two metres of water, the skipper brought the boat hard on the wind. A group of astonished bird-watchers had gazed agog, probably wondering what the heck the little yacht was up to – were the crew mad? An inbound yachtsman had gesticulated, 'this way!' The mate, smiling, had lifted her hand in a nonchalant wave, thinking, there's ample water.' They'd cleared Faversham Creek.

Sailing hard on the wind off the old ferry inside a line of moorings, they'd reached westwards along the marshy shore of the East Swale, keeping out of the early ebb. It was a shore that, eerily, had entombed within its bosom a veritable fleet of spritsail barges, abandoned way back in the last century (talked about in *Salt Marsh & Mud: A Year's Sailing on the Thames Estuary*). The reach took them well past a buoy; a red can, with a large '2' emblazoned upon it. The top of the buoy had been dressed, white, with guano. Here, the Fowley channel was still wide and deep, but it narrowed quickly, from then on, to a shallow gully at low water.

The skipper had then tacked the boat westwards – the mate did the business with the jib, and sterling work it was too: the breeze was strong enough and good progress was being made. The tacks became shorter and shorter as the channel narrowed. By a later buoy, with an '8' on its side, the skipper noticed, as it reeled in the flow, that the tide had set hard against them, making it difficult to maintain their short tacks. The shallow edges of the channel had searched for the centre plate, scuffling through mud and shell as they turned. The mate had had several long looks at the skipper ... as if to say, 'how long are we going to keep this up?'

Then, amazingly, the skipper shook his head, murmuring, 'We've done well. Let's anchor off the Lilies for the night. It'll be quiet with no wind over tide bouncing us about either ...' Adding, 'Queenborough will be hectic.'

The mate had looked quizzically at her skipper, though initially taken aback at his unprovoked ceasing of the silly tacking lark; she'd had the engine running in a jiffy. Then, looking back at the skipper, she murmured, 'Where's that? ... Remind me,' not understanding his intentions – they usually discussed such things!

'It's under the southern side of Elmley, you know, just past the old ferry crossing, by those marshy islands – the Lilies.'

'Oh yes ...' her voice trailed off: an explanation still hadn't materialised.

'I want to potter up into Milton Creek – tomorrow.'

'Ah – ! So that's it,' she'd grinned, 'OK!' Appeased – but shaking her head in wonder.

They hadn't been up Milton Creek for a number of years. The last being when their son was a little boy of nine or ten ... So with the engine running sweetly, the sails were soon stowed.

Reaching the Lilies, a marsh liberally covered with sea purslane with shallow patches of cord grass between that loiter ominously, ready for the unknowing or foolhardy in the entrance to Milton Creek, they'd circled to find their spot. The anchor had soon splashed overboard south of a cardinal buoy known as the Lilies. It was considered by the skipper to be just perfect for the fairly strong south-westerly that was building. A deep table of mud flats spread out from the southern side of Elmley Island – so why it hadn't been given a name like 'Elmley Ledge' was a mystery!

Soon after anchoring, the weather had started to pick up, it no longer threatened rain, but it was windier. Thick blackish clouds of earlier had broken and fluffy grey, white cumulus, probably, filled a largely blue sky, giving a generous percentage of gorgeous sunshine. They'd both settled down to their respective books. The mate below, in the comfort of the cabin, and the skipper propped up on a cushion or two: he liked to look about.

It looked an empty place. Well, not completely empty: on the western side of the Swale shore, below the entrance to Milton Creek was a jetty, where ships still come and go. There's the old ferry hard; back east a ways, the wrecks out on the mud, and over to the north under marshes fringing Elmley were the remnants of another old vessel too. To the north, across the island, some way inland and partially hidden in a bank of trees, the skipper could see a lonely collection of farm buildings known as Kingshill.

The skipper's mind was abuzz again. Sometimes ... he just wished that it wouldn't, but it just seemed to, on too many occasions, just drift ...

In a booklet, *The Three Sheppey Islands in the 19th and 20th Centuries*, by John A. Rymill, the skipper had found a potted history about the islands of Sheppey. It'd made compelling reading.

The skipper knew that Elmley had had a cement works, the Turkey Cement Works, round on its western shore; about this Rymill said, 'The cement works was started in 1860 by William Levett & Co. By this time Portland cement was discovered and replaced sand and lime for building work. The industry flourished at Elmley until around 1902 when the works closed.'

The works weren't demolished for many years – usually only when the buildings started to become unsafe! During the cement making years, the population of Elmley peaked at around 200 souls, after which it dropped rapidly to about forty. The island supported a school too; it lasted for forty years from 1885. A church was built, in 1853, to look after the needs of what was then a fairly large community. About the church, Rymill says that it was demolished during the 1960s, and only one farm now remains on the island. The island is owned by All Saints College, Oxford, who, according to Rymill, have had the privilege since the benefice was granted by Henry VI.

Booklets about a locality 'can often be found in newsagents and other such shops,' the skipper often said. He'd always browsed: information was a fantastic thing. The reader, of course, was free to do the same!

Putting his book down, an urge to intrude upon his mate was resisted. 'Besides, she can read about it herself,' he thought. With that, he'd pulled the dinghy alongside, donned his life jacket and called out in the direction of the hatchway, 'I'm off ... for a sail.'

The skipper sailed eastwards, where he gazed across to the old wooden minesweeper. She lay on the mud flats, mud had oozed over her deck through a shattered bulwark, as if battered and lolled to port, on a heavy, leaden and oily sea swell. She was a piece of flotsam from the last century, from a time when the country had needed hundreds of such minesweepers to fight magnetic mines strewn around the ports of Britain. Those days were long gone and Europe had had, in the main, a sustained peace never before known. Man had been liberated – those ships had helped. None have been preserved as a reminder of the brave deeds undertaken out amongst the sands and silt of numerous British estuaries.

The minesweeper hadn't just been abandoned: she'd had a purpose. On the foreshore on the mainland side of the ferry hard, to the south, sat the remnants of other hulls drawn up onto the beach. They'd been brought into this quiet corner for reclamation. But then, it hadn't been a quiet corner: all around, industry abounded. The creek to the west was still busy. Furnaces had roared. Smoke, dust and other fumes had belched forth continuously, from cement, brick and paper-works. It had gone on for over two centuries. It would now have been considered a blot on the landscape.

The unwanted wooden minesweepers and many other types of craft were dismantled for their wood and precious metals. At the time, during the late 1940s and 1950s, those materials were in desperate demand. A number of rotting bottoms lay against another sea wall, to the east of Otterham Creek, off the Medway. A number, too, had been laid up in the creek that was the skipper's childhood home and has been talked about in a story of his childhood.

Up on the mud flats, under the growing islands of marsh at the foot of Milton Creek, sat other oddments: rusting boiler drums, stems of small craft and other things. They were barnacle-encrusted and trailed dangling fronds of that black popable weed, whose name sailors could never recall. Watching, briefly, as the breeze had swished those fronds back and forth in a hypnotic way ... he remembered ... the weed that is – it's wrack. Wrack gives fun to many at play on holiday beaches. It too provided nutrients when used as fertiliser, as it still is, around various parts of the British Isles.

Terns plopped all around the dinghy. Looking at the water, the skipper saw that there wasn't any tidal flow. It was slack water in that little pool: here the tide split. It ran from Elmley towards the east and to the west. (The split travels east/west of here depending upon the point in the tide cycle.) The water, the skipper saw, was alive with small fry. 'Terns know more than us,' the skipper had chuckled!

'It's a wonderful feeding ground,' the skipper murmured, but his thoughts waded back to an industrialised time, the latter part, he remembered.

The water was clean, dark and deep. The skipper pictured the cloudy effluent that had, for decades, been swilled from a paper-works on the west bank of Milton Creek. The effluent had flowed from huge open pipes in a continuous gurgling gush. A

Decades after her masters had finished with her, the brave old ship lolls as if on an oily, post-storm sea in her long, lingering death.

deathly flow it was too: the Swale, east and west for some distance, had been a rotten, stinking, dead pool. Sailors tended to avoid the area, or certainly, hadn't dallied. It had had a bad name.

All of that had changed. The effluent no longer contained the washings from paper making: everything has to be removed. And just so! The environment, after time, picked itself up. It rejuvenated itself. Healthy plant life inhabited the intertidal mud flats and salt marsh proliferated – though cord grass grows anywhere! The waters of the Swale are now alive with sea creatures. The skipper and the mate often saw seals along to the east of Elmley Island and could remember clearly when they'd started to reappear. It had been one of nature's wonders – one of man's successes too. Darwin would have approved!

The skipper sailed his tender up into Milton Creek, but ran out of water. Turning about, he ran down past the jetty, known as Grovehurst, waving to a number of relaxing foreign seafarers who'd been sipping a cup of something, 'probably coffee,' for it was that time, the skipper had thought. The skipper, though, hadn't been jerked into any sense of time himself by his observations: he'd continued to cruise contentedly. Cranes with grabs were dumping 'smoking' piles of material, gypsum it was, the skipper believed, onto a conveyor. The cargo was disgorged ashore, adding to a man-made mountain of the raw material that rose up close by. The 'mountain' gave the anchorage pleasing protection: its grass-covered slopes were south-west of the anchorage. The jetty, strangely, is still known as the Coal Jetty – from when coal for the paper-works was unloaded here. Shaking himself, the skipper pointed the dinghy's bow homewards along the Elmley shore.

Elmley was now a quiet, peaceful and secluded place, often marsh harriers could be seen, hovering above their prey. The natural world had gathered back the place, from its industrial past, firmly into its bosom. Glowing with satisfaction about that thought, the skipper sailed his dinghy, nonchalantly, one foot up on the gunnel, back towards the ferry pool.

Once there, he gazed across at the rotting remnants of the old *Webster*, a spritsail barge hulked under the island's marshy southern bank. The old barge had been abandoned, supposedly, the skipper was told, rigged and ready to go. She'd been old, even then, and had served her purpose. She was built as far back as 1865. Her stem and transom stood proudly: a testament to her builders. The skipper had thought of going for a scrabble over the mud – mudlarking – for a look at her – but – alas it would have to wait for another time. 'The old barge has rested over there long enough – she'll continue to do so – for a while yet ...' he said wistfully.

Then, for some inexplicable reason, the skipper had looked across at the yacht, his comfortable floating home, which he'd, by then, departed quite some time earlier. A wildly waving figure met his gaze. Hurriedly looking at his watch, the skipper gasped, 'Heck, I've been away for ...' It was much longer than he'd thought – his mate was not going to be best pleased!

Heading homewards, he ranged the dinghy alongside and apologised immediately! The mate already had their lunch waiting. It was a bashful skipper that accepted the proffered offerings and with good grace too. The mate, bless her, had grinned, saying, 'When will you grow up ...' Chastisement? No, she'd ruffled his hair – just as an adult would a child!

On the next morning, after a tranquil night with much less wind, a quiet breakfast was enjoyed. Then, some two hours after low water, the skipper 'hauled their anchor' and with their trusty diesel rumbling gently beneath the cockpit floor, they pottered up Milton Creek. The good water had been marked by withies, dangling red and green floats, running more or less centrally between the mud and marsh of a nicely dished creek; its course was easily seen early on the flood. The markers, they found, ran up to a wharf at Murston, the home of the Sittingbourne Yacht Club.

At first, the creek had appeared empty ... yet, by peering closely at the marsh edges, the skipper saw the remains of an extensive wharf, close to a factory, inland, behind the huge hill. Within a swath marsh lay sunken spritsail barges, their stems and mast cases poking above the cord grass and sea purslane. It had felt eerie. It sent a series of shivers down the skipper's spine: the souls of those vessels affected him. He'd closed his eyes too, briefly, his imagination conjuring up those old sailormen gliding out from the wharves, then alive and vibrant, loaded down with cement or bricks, while other barges crept in loaded down to their scuppers, with, probably, another load of rubbish from the London metropolis.

A paper-mill had arrived at the top of Milton Creek, in Sittingbourne, during the seventeenth century. Another was built, much later, at Kemsley, across the marsh and fields to the west of the skipper's eerie wharf. Victorian entrepreneurs built huge factories all the way up the creek producing bricks and cement, eating up local mud and clay from the Swale. Kentish fields provided brick earth too. Many fields were now lower than the surrounding roads – the result of extraction – usually planted with orchards – hops too.

One local industrialist, George Burley, manufactured cement. His product was known as the Dolphin Brand, and later, before the industry's demise, Bournecrete (from Sittingbourne). Before the demise of trading sail, chalk and all other needs were shipped in from the Thames chalk pits around Erith and Grays, or from the Medway pits above Rochester; after, the lorry serviced the industry's declining requirements. Burley built a shipyard to build a fleet of spritsail barges. He and other builders such as Smeed Dean built over 500 vessels by the end, around 1920. Kent was truly the centre of barge building. After the demise of Bounecrete, the barge yard and buildings, at the top of the creek, came under the care of the Dolphin Barge Museum. The museum operated for about forty years, but the buildings though, the skipper had heard, had been burnt down in mysterious circumstances.

A disused brickfields wharf just above The Lillies still has a robust look about it. In a sea of cord grass, the windlass bitts and frame tops of the *Gladstone*, built in 1867, indicate her continued presence.

While the mate had helmed, the skipper danced and pranced around the cabin top, camera in hand, taking photographs, gazing at the often barely visible remnants of all that industry. The mate's voice heard, but often unheeded, had pleaded for the skipper to stop blocking her line of sight: he wouldn't have stood for it!

Beyond the mud and marsh-fringed edges, with its abundant birdlife, one wharf passed, on the west bank of the creek, had looked as if it had only recently ceased use. It had had the look of immediate readiness – 'what a crying shame,' the skipper muttered: the industry has, in the main, turned inwards, away from the water, ignoring the transportation possibilities that had served so well. The wharf was fenced off.

The birdlife was spectacular, as good as that found along the shores of Stangate Creek and was far more abundant than the skipper and mate had witnessed in such places as the Ore, Deben and the Orwell, the picturesque and lauded Suffolk rivers. Dozens of egrets strutted along the water's edge; a myriad of small waders and oystercatchers skittered along the mud banks. Terns were in abundance too – they dove all around for small fry. All ignored the passage of the yacht, a slowly moving island, and continued to feed.

Progressing up the creek, in a slow and leisurely fashion, barely faster than the incoming tide, the mate negotiated the runs of the unseen creek bed with consummate skill. Around them, everything looked to be asleep. It was a time capsule … slowly rotting away … merging back with nature. That was brought home, to the skipper at least, as they'd passed a wharf front engulfed in marsh – Churchfields Wharf, the skipper later discovered. Stout posts still supported, after a fashion, a gnarled, rotted wooden wharf front covered in a slimy film of mud and weed, from which water leached and dripped. Sea purslane hung over the higher-level remnants – now an integral part of the marsh edge.

Churchfields Wharf has merged with the environment, but the impressive squat tower of Milton Regis church still looms beyond the low seawall. A park and nature reserve is planned for this area.

Up a side shoot, from the creek front, the remnants of the wharf ran into the marshes – a long-abandoned dock. Beneath a mound of purslane, tinged with yellow summer flowers, the bow planks of a vessel appeared. It was a spritsail barge. She was entombed in her last berth, in that lonely dock, 'When did you come here?' the skipper gently mouthed. He knew not the answer to his unspoken thought. The skipper recognised her rudder head, mast case, stem – they alone let the world know of her existence. The skipper, murmuring, had caught his breath in a sudden rush of sadness, 'Wouldn't it have been better, a more honourable end, for the old lady to have been broken up?' But, it had provided a bed for all that marsh.

Across the marsh, from the wharf, and a low sea wall, amongst a stand of trees, was the squat tower of Milton Regis church. In that village would have lived many of the army of brick, cement and wharf workers who'd have known the creek intimately, a mere two generations ago. Milton had once been a prosperous place and it had a large number of fine timber-frame houses along its high street, as well as an ancient timber court hall and gaol – a small museum. In any other part of the country, it would be a honey pot; here, it lived.

Murston on the opposite bank was its twin. Both villages were once industrious and prosperous places. Both have been sucked into the greater conurbation of their sister, Sittingbourne, a mile further inland, from Churchfields Wharf. Modern industrial estates now sit on many of the old workings, giving continued employment, but their raw materials and finished goods travel by road.

At Murston Wharf was the headquarters of the Sittingbourne Yacht Club. The club had had a floating pontoon installed. Passing it so early on the tide, it sat up on the mud above the tideline. The wharf could be reached, the skipper had pointed out to the mate, by road. Here too was an old public house, the Brickmakers Arms, now a private dwelling. It sat up on high ground, its garden a dash of colour where it tumbled over an embankment towards the creek. The mate had looked briefly, but had quickly got back to her job, commenting, 'Yes, alright, yes, it's beautiful … but I'm busy … if you hadn't noticed!'

The yacht club's fenced facilities were spacious and sound, it seemed. Above the wharf was a wide, concrete slipway, the remnant of a barge and coaster repair yard, the skipper presumed. 'It's in excellent condition,' he thought. The slip ran across the mud and into the water. 'What a facility,' he spoke loudly, pointing as he did so, thinking too of the fine facilities found at his own club, the Island Yacht club, and others along his home shoreline.

It was a lack of access to the shore, the skipper thought, which had been the reason why the countless vessels, plying the Swale, ignored this creek's existence and possibilities. A place to moor and get ashore was all that was needed. But would it happen? Would the yacht club be allowed to develop such a facility? At the time, the skipper had thought not: news had reached him that summer of a threat. A bridge!

Earlier that summer, the skipper had investigated those reports about a bridge. He'd found that the Kent County Council, in their infinite wisdom, desired to build a low-level bridge across the waterway, just above the creek's entrance. 'It will kill, at a stroke, any possibility of navigating the waterway other than in a rowing boat!' the skipper had said. 'What would be wrong with a sliding bridge,' he'd ranted at his mate, 'or a moderately high-level bridge even?' Our country had an abiding desire, it seemed at times to the skipper, to block off the natural highways of our tidal waters. 'It wouldn't be allowed in Holland!' he'd almost screamed, while seated at his computer screen. 'Poppycock. Fie!'

'On land,' the skipper had later raved, in a gentle way: it hadn't been the mate's fault, 'A new road at least puts a footpath beneath it or over the top of it – rendering the footpath as passable as before. Yet, they don't care, when simple sailors are concerned …'

'Why? Why? Why?' He'd kept on saying.

'Yes, yes, yes! Calm Down, Calm down. There's nothing you can do!' were the mate's mollifying words, as he'd continued to splutter, huff and puff.

'Oh yes there is – I'll write about it!' So he'd done so. The stupidity of our modern-day planners would be forever anchored into the mud and murk of boating lore around his sailing grounds. He felt for the small, but active yacht club that had for years sought a suitable foothold on the edge of the Swale. It made him angry: he'd muttered, 'why – football clubs get what they want, but of course, "money talks" doesn't it!'

However, back to the creek … Nearing the headwaters, the boat had briefly touched on some shingle, by an outfall. Fortunately, the flooding tide had not swept the boat round and pinioned her across the creek: moments later, the boat's long keel scraped over, leaving a disturbed cloud, behind them, into which a flurry of terns dove.

Along here, the local Swale Borough Council were planning to set up a country park bordering the creek. 'It's a grand use for the creek side without doubt,' but 'don't hold your breath,' the skipper had muttered when he'd read about this. 'There'll be no thought to visitors from the water.'

The authority in his home locality, too, provided little or no access to the saline waters that surrounded its patch: the majority of access points were either at yacht and boating clubs or boatyards. Higher up the County of Essex, and into Suffolk too, it was very different. The skipper had often wished that a more enlightened approach to visitors was taken by creek, river and coastal authorities. Many ancient points of access to the water had become disused – but why couldn't new, more user-friendly points be instituted? The skipper would shout, indignantly, 'Go to Burnham … Go to

The *Nellie Parker*, once a proud vessel sailing under the Parker's 'hand and heart' bob from Bradwell in Essex. The barge was originally a sister in the same fleet as the skipper's boyhood sailing home, *May Flower*.

Brightlingsea … Go to West Mersea … Go to Pin Mill …' at the mate: she, bless her, was his only audience!

The skipper, at a call from the mate, realised that the width of the creek had narrowed considerably. They were near the creek's head. The boat's bottom was feeling the creek bed too, though no scraping sounds were heard, so the skipper had continued to leave the mate to it, 'going off into his own world' again!

On the eastern bank is the sad sight of the spritsail barge *Nellie Parker*. She'd been built in 1899 for, and was owned by, the Parker family of Bradwell, Essex. She sat forlornly in a patch of cord grass, sea asters and purslane. It was obvious to the skipper that, until recent times, it had been within the creek proper, the muddy edge of the creek. Her hull was shattered and broken from age and the ravages of a hard trading life. Her bow had fallen. Her name, though, picked out in golden yellow in a faded blue on her crumbling transom, is clear to see.

Motoring slowly onwards, the skipper saw to port a fork that led up to the Dolphin Yard, the museum. Part of the land on which it sat had been reclaimed by a developer. An ancient log pond had been filled in. The way up to the yard is now over the top of a set of barge blocks, for the creek bed had gone too. Its usefulness has been ruined. Deeds such as these should be rectified: the status quo returned. But it never was.

Up at the head of the dock is an old spritsail barge, the *Celtic*. Her spars bereft. The *Celtic*, a big steel barge of 120nrt, was built in Holland in 1903, one of a class of twelve large coasters built there. All were towed back to the East Coast for fitting and rigging out. The fate of the barge looked delicate. The fate of the museum too remained in the balance.

This is what inconsiderate developers do. Near the top of the creek, a once-thriving museum and barge yard have been destroyed.

To the astonishment of the skipper, and the mate in particular, they'd been able to continue. They bore away, following the creek bed to starboard, but soon it narrowed, considerably, as it ran up towards Crown Quay Reach, right into the heart of Sittingbourne. There, they knew, there'd be no place to land.

The mate spotted a piece of debris in the creek bed. 'What's that?' she said quickly, pointing beyond the boat's prow.

The skipper then remembered something or other. It had been mentioned on the website of the yacht club, a copy of which he'd read up on earlier. 'Okay, you nose the bow into the mud. I'll set the jib – the wind will take us away.'

Setting the jib as the boat nosed into the soft, glutinous mud of the creek bank, the skipper watched as the boat's stern had been swept round, then, as the breeze had flicked at the jib, he'd called out, 'Sheet it in,' and they were away, slowly heading back the way they'd come. The infernal engine, useful as it was, with its low reverberations, was silenced – Wonderful – Bliss. The skipper then took over (the mate wanting a rest – the skipper wanted to sail!).

'You know,' the skipper said, 'the creek's channel, the mud banks and marsh are amazingly clear of debris.' This was largely the result of clear-up sessions carried out by volunteers from the local yacht club. General rubbish, in fact, they noticed, 'was at a lower level than in their own creek …' it was a credit to the area.

It was a delightful sail back out. The mate, relieved from her post, made some coffee and also had time to look about her and take in some of the panorama that her skipper had been warbling about.

A light railway ran, during the summer months, from Sittingbourne to Kemsley. Kemsley was just inland from Ridham Dock. The railway had originally been built after silting in Milton Creek reached dire proportions, along with the docks, in 1913. Raw materials needed by the paper-mill at Sittingbourne could then be shipped in, directly, by sea-going vessels and the finished products exported the same way, negating the need for transhipment by barge. Previously, the factory was served by a horse-hauled tramway from the head of Milton Creek, then, later, by 1903, by a steam locomotive service. The expansion at Kemsley had required an extension to the railway. By the time the mill in Sittingbourne was sold and closed down, the railway was the longest and last industrial narrow gauge working in Britain.

The skipper had thought, 'Wouldn't it be nice if the railway was part of the country park ... maybe it will,' but he'd not voiced his thoughts. Much later, he'd discovered, the railway had been living under a cloud ... the owners of the land having served an eviction order. 'It could be the end,' he'd thought. (The outcome is yet unknown.)

Approaching the last reach before the open water of the Swale, the mainsail was set. A spritsail barge was spotted coming up the Swale from the east. The barge, the *Greta*, had a charter party aboard. They met, not physically, of course, by the junction of the waterways. Her astonished gaggle of passengers stood gawking at the little yacht as she shot out of Milton Creek: she'd a bone between her teeth. The skipper grinned. The mate waved, as was the custom.

While leaving the creek, the skipper had gazed across at Sheppey as the sun, from shafts of light, between high, scudding clouds, shone and twinkled on the windows of Eastchurch Prison. It had jolted memories: he had been there! Not as an inmate, it must be added! He'd been a Server at his village church not so far away, in Upchurch, a historic village overlooking the River Medway and fed by Stangate and Otterham creeks. There he and a pal had often drunk beer on Saturday night and done penance on Sundays! They'd gone to the prison for a service.

The prison was opened in 1950, for lower-category felons. It has, of course, not always been a prison. That, the skipper knew. Later, he learnt that the village, even,

A spritsail barge ... coming up the Swale from the east. (Drawn by Gwendoline D. Ardley)

had dated to before 1066 and had had quite an illustrious past. Lords of the manor served the crown well and were suitably rewarded – as was the way.

But, closer to our own time, before the First World War, an aerodrome was built at Eastchurch. It was there that Sir Winston Churchill learnt to fly. Short Brothers, too, established an aircraft factory, and from 1916 until 1948, the Royal Air Force occupied the aerodrome.

For flight aficionados, the Isle of Sheppey has had a strong connection to early flight. Away to the east, along the beach at Shellness, Rymill says, '... Leysdown was the birthplace of British Aviation. The first pilot's licence was issued from Muswell Manor ... Shell Beach at Leysdown made aviation history in 1909 when J. T. C. Brabazon, later Lord Brabazon, piloted a British-designed and British-built aeroplane, succeeding in accomplishing a circular flight of one mile at an altitude of 30 feet.' The Wright Brothers visited here too and it must have seemed a desolate place, even for them.

'It's strange,' the skipper always felt, 'the marshland which pervades, either side of the Swale, looks so innocuous, so empty, yet it has had such a busy, enterprising, and an industrious past.' That was especially so in our more recent, well-recorded times. 'What ...' he mouthed '... has not been recorded?' And, 'Who could tell?'

They followed in the barge's wake, up towards the bridge. The mate, who'd been listening to her skipper's rambles for the past two hours, said, 'I don't suppose any of that lot' (pointing to the charter party) 'know of the history within the creek we've just explored.'

'Or around and about us,' the skipper said, tongue in cheek!

'No, I doubt it,' he said quietly. 'They'll be much the same as those I met on the *Repertor,* a few seasons ago. Now that was weird – strangely frightening in many ways.' The mate looked at him.

'Surely you remember, we were in Stangate – I'd gone off for a sail in the dinghy after supper.'

'Oh yes – leaving me with the dishes.'

'None of them knew about the brickfields or that barges had worked, and been built even, hereabouts.' (The Lower Halstow areas.) He stopped. Then, looking reflective, he continued, 'The barge, her sisters and what has been, seemed of little consequence.' He grinned, 'I found that extremely sad. Here too is a creek that remains full of historical interest. Maybe I'm wrong. Maybe I get too passionate ...'

'... Passionate ... ?' The mate had grinned. Then, smiling, she said, 'but really ... there's nothing here ...' She'd not seen a lot!

'Nothing ...' the skipper had snorted, indignantly, 'it's all around you!'

'Perhaps they're only interested in sailing,' the mate added coyly.

They'd both laughed. The mate hugged her skipper, saying, '... More coffee?' Adding, 'I think you need it!'

(A footnote to the story should be added: later, during that autumn, the skipper learnt that a bridge is to be built across Milton Creek. Sadly, soon, it won't be possible to sail up an ancient waterway that has been open to seafarers since time immemorial. That, as a historical matter, is a sad prospect indeed. In 2009, they sailed up the creek again, to Crown Quay, deep into Sittingbourne. While turning, under sail, the chugging of a forklift in a riverside yard stopped as several workmen came to a fence. They waved and cheered! The skipper called, 'You'll not see sailing yachts up here again ...')

11

Mince Pies and Christmas Cheer

The skipper and mate experienced, over a recent Christmas and New Year holiday period, one of the longest settled spells of weather witnessed for many a year in their locality. Yes, it was cold, but the breezes had been gentle and mainly off the land. It was ideal weather to be out on the boat, to sail on protected waters, and relish it. Well, the skipper had. The mate too had enjoyed more than she usually was able to do.

That winter, down at the skipper's club, a myriad of craft were left afloat, ready for immediate use, but apart from two or three, or there about, the remainder hadn't moved, other than up and down, with the regular coming and going of the twice-daily tides that washed through the moorings. It was sad.

The skipper, a sensitive soul at heart, as was his mate, was greatly saddened by the sight of all those lonely craft devoid of the comforting weight of their human owners, using them, enjoying them, loving them even: boats had souls too, the skipper believed: 'It's only when their sails are hauled aloft or the engine is set throbbing that a boat truly comes alive,' he always said to the mate, often adding, 'The soul has to be nurtured: a boat needs to be used!'

With his mate, the skipper had had a gorgeous sail on the morning of Christmas Eve. It was short, for they'd been enrolled to help out at a funeral breakfast at their church. The skipper had acquiesced but at the time he'd been a bit miffed: although the old boy hadn't been a sailor, he would have understood, the skipper believed.

That morning, the weather was sublime. Just enough of a northerly had wafted across their creek for them to ghost slowly out against a sluggish incoming neap tide. Apart from a certain level of cold, but a dry cold, it was akin to a glorious summer's day. The sky was an amazing blue, clear and bright. The sky coloured the water gloriously; its hue was a delight. The sun shone down and the many reflections around the creek's entrance dappled and glinted alternately in the gentle ripples left by their boat's passage.

Clearing the mooring trots the pair of them had gazed in awe as waders roosting on patches of marsh had taken off producing a fantastic display of their flying skills: knot, dunlin and others had swarmed around the point at the outer end of the island's marshy spit, diving in huge, dark swirls. For the skipper, the sight always conjured up an image of a troupe of ballerinas swinging, swishing and spinning to an unheard piece of music. In and out of patches of yellowing cord grass Brent geese paddled in the shallows around the marsh edges searching for weeds or other equally tasty titbits. The panorama was always a sight to relish and they never tired of it – it was what made winter sailing so evocative.

Leaving the creek behind and by then alone on the wide expanse, east of their home moorings, they'd pointed the boat's nose broad to the wind for a lazy reach across the breeze; 'a reach out and a reach back' had been the unanimous plan. Both then settled down to enjoy the occasion.

Then, joy of joys, another craft was heard. A motorboat appeared, her engine coughing and spluttering, from behind the creek's moorings. They watched as it came into view, moving sedately along. 'Good man,' the skipper had thought.

The skipper then watched briefly as its engine had been opened up. Her powerful throb changed tone and began to sing a higher-pitched tune. Passing a trot of moored fishing craft, swinging quietly to buoys, the boat's wash slapped against their sides. A hand was raised in a salute. The mate, watching too, had responded.

The exultant shout 'Yippee!' could almost be heard from its driver, hidden behind a windshield, as it had sped past. Its wash was no more than a few ripples by the time it had reached the slowly moving sailing yacht. The yacht's bow rose up gently and nodded to her powered sister, who by then was far off.

The little day power cruiser was often seen out by the skipper and he was mesmerised, briefly, by the motorboat's antics. It had rushed away, moving easily across the placid surface of the water, skimming in wild zigzags, before circling back round on itself in an endeavour to give more bounce to its passage. 'The driver's obviously enjoying himself,' the skipper said to himself, smiling, before turning away.

A little later, after a glance at the clock, the skipper had said, 'We've no time to dally – we'll need to turn shortly.'

'I'll make coffee …' the mate whispered: loud speech, even spoken softly, felt incongruous.

The skipper had nodded, saying, at his mate's enquiry, 'Yes, we've time for that.'

The kettle soon sang its welcome song. 'Here …' the mate called, proffering two steaming mugs of coffee, '… take these.' She'd followed, clambering, a little stiffly, from the cabin clutching a plate of mince pies, pre-warmed before they'd left home.

Just beyond the moorings of the Island Yacht Club, Brent geese dabbled amongst stalks of verdant cord grass at the eastern end of Canvey Island.

'Delicious,' he said, grinning like a little boy and munching away. As he'd munched, crumbs had scattered in every direction. The skipper mechanically picked a few of the larger ones up: he was always gently chastising his mate for such behaviour!

She'd seen, smiled to herself ... and said nothing.

The time had gone quickly. Wonderful though it was, they'd eventually, reluctantly, grudgingly even, turned for home.

'Okay,' the skipper said quietly, 'time to disturb the world!' At that he'd run up the engine and engaged the shaft – indicating his wishes for the sails.

The mate stowed the jib whilst the skipper dealt with the mains'l leaving the boat heading for the creek with the diesel gently purring beneath the cockpit floor – the skipper gave the tiller an occasional nudge with a toe or hand, which ever was closest, when needed. That activity with the coffee had warmed them greatly: even the skipper had started to feel the chill.

That evening, the 'weather men' asserted that the fine spell was to continue. The gods were being kind. 'That's brilliant!' the skipper exclaimed, turning towards the mate.

When New Year's Day came round, the weather was still benign in their eastern corner. The skipper and mate had hotfooted it to the creek, to be ready as their little yacht lifted. The skipper had gone on ahead and he'd rolled up the mains'l cover and dumped the jib on the foredeck before his crew was seen coming along the jetty walkway making excitedly towards the waiting yacht, reaching her just before she floated.

The mate had been waylaid by one of the waterfront's old hands. He was an agreeable soul – ever ready for a natter to discuss the world in his dry, articulate way. The skipper had laughed, 'Did you wish him all the best?' knowing the question was rhetorical: the mate had had a soft spot for the old gentleman. The dear old man has since passed to the Elysian Fields.

He said, 'Good on you – have a nice sail – I'll be thinking of you ...' The mate had smiled at him sweetly.

Setting the burgee aloft, the skipper had watched it flutter to the decent northerly that was blowing gently across the creek. It was light in nature, but heavier than on some of the other 'Christmas' sailing they'd enjoyed. (Except, that is, for Boxing Day — it had then been much heavier – the skipper had been alone though. Water had sluiced along the side decks splashing his trousers as he'd sailed hard on the wind out of a choppy creek entrance!) Briefly, the skipper had watched as the burgee flipped lazily back and forth above the sprig of Christmas tree set at the masthead. 'It'll do nicely' he said smiling, and adding, 'Happy New Year' as he patted the boat's mast!

Departing the mooring, the breeze drove them assuredly over the flood, leaving the engine to its silence after its short burst clearing the berth. Leaving the moorings behind, they'd close-reached out along the entrance channel, clipping past nodding navigation buoys and chattering Brent geese. The mate was at the helm. She'd concentrated hard, working the boat out, with barely a thigh's depth beneath their bottom.

Upon clearing the creek, the mate said, 'Here, you take over ...' and she'd gone forward to sit on the coach roof in anticipation of the expected spectacle beyond. She was not disappointed: clouds of knot were seen wheeling and swirling around the marshes, swooping down and skimming the surface. They wheeled and gyrated in seemingly impossible veers. Except for a rustle, from a gentle slapping along the clinker planking, it was gloriously quiet.

Then it happened. They were sailing past the point. A huge swirl of knot had swooped down over the masthead, around the stern and away over the water beyond the boat. The yacht's company had all jumped! It was the closeness of the swishing, of a thousand or more wings, which had caused the crescendo. Both had turned and looked at one another, in astonished silence.

The skipper had then looked as a movement had caught his eye. Across the water, a large gaggle of Brent geese had lifted off from the saltings, the flight was heading south, 'off to the North Kent marshes to feed,' he'd knowingly said.

'What a grand sight' was the softly spoken comment that crept back from the mate who was still up on the fore hatch top.

He'd called back, firmly, 'Don't get chilled!' She'd nodded, but the skipper knew she was happy there.

Out in the river, the tideway was quiet. One ship lay in the waiting anchorage, south-east of the marshes. 'I've done that a few times in the past,' the skipper thought as he raised a metaphorical glass to her crew saying quietly, 'Season's greetings ...' The mate had not heard.

Maintaining a close reach, they'd worked eastwards, towards the northern shore. The skipper was in his element, relishing the sail. 'What a Christmas present ...' he said: he'd had a wonderful time during the twelve days of the festival – moments to savour.

The boat's mate continued to sit as if glued to her perch by the mast. 'You'll get a chilly bottom ...' the skipper called, almost in a whisper, 'come on, move about ... it's very cold.' She'd nodded and shifted stiffly, got up and crept awkwardly aft.

Out on that wide expanse of water, they were alone. Well, nearly: the sail of a lonely dinghy was seen over by Southend Pier. Nearing the shore, beyond Chalkwell, the skipper had set a course to run westwards, towards Leigh-on-Sea.

Looking at the mate as she shuffled her feet, moved her legs and massaged her thighs, the skipper remembered something, 'There was once a plan to build a marina off here,' he said. 'It was during the 1930s – nothing came of it though.'

'Shame,' the mate said, adding, 'Didn't you say that your Dad designed something like that?'

Brent geese had lifted off ... heading south, '... to the North Kent marshes to feed'. (Drawn by Gwendoline D. Ardley)

'Yes, he came up with a plan to dam the ray between Two Tree Island and Canvey Island – allowing for tidal flow – locks as well, I believe,' he paused. 'Mother still has the thesis in her loft somewhere.' The thesis was part of his father's architectural training.

Passing the 'Essex', which sat under the green-covered park that clothed the hillside above, they'd gazed at winter walkers – sturdy folk braving a cold amble along the cinder path, the traditional name for the path along the front – from when cinders had been used to surface it. Passing the old minesweeper – the club ship *Wilton* – the skipper giggled, remembering his salute to the vessel when she'd first arrived. A group of men had ignored the noble deed.

'Shall I?' the skipper said.

The mate shook her head.

Passing Victoria Wharf, the mate said, 'Do you remember coming past here on Christmas morning?'

The skipper had nodded.

Back then, a gentleman was seen engaged in a spot of scenic photography. 'Must be a new camera, from a loved one, perhaps,' the skipper had said. Then he'd called out, 'Send a picture ... please.'

Cutting clearly across the open water, 'Okay' had been the quick response, 'What address?'

The mate had quickly called out, clearly and concisely, their electronic mail address – for all the world to hear!

Later, that kindly soul sent a beautiful picture. 'Bless you,' the skipper had said on his electronic reply. It had been strangely surreal: such things rarely happened.

The picturesque shore of Old Leigh. Modern cockle sheds and fishing craft line the creek before the old yard of Johnson & Jago is reached. The Belton Hill nature reserve is beyond.

Clearing the wharf, the mate had gone below to make coffee.

Stamping his feet and looking across at Old Leigh, the skipper had waved an arm at the cockle sheds along the waterfront. 'Right mess they've made of that shore,' he'd barked: he remembered the cockle men, of recent history, with their dairymaid's yoke carrying a brace of baskets that swung to and fro as they'd walked across springing gangplanks up to the boiler sheds.

'Those boats are damned ugly, aren't they?' he added.

The mate's head appeared in the hatchway to look.

'They're functional ... they're giant Hoovers really!' the skipper added looking at his cold-looking mate, seeing her shiver, involuntarily, 'You alright?'

'Yes ... I got chilly on the foredeck ... warming up now though ... here's your mug.' Her teeth were chattering.

'Mmmm! Something smells nice ...' the skipper said, '... do I smell mince pies?'

The mate had looked at him. Her look saying, 'You know there are.' Before leaving home that morning, the pies had been warmed and foil-wrapped, and she said, 'I'm just warming them a bit more under the grill.'

Emanating from the hatch was that deep, succulent, sweet bouquet that only comes from home-produced mincemeat heavily laced ... The flavours too, after the pies had been passed from the galley, shouted loudly with Christmas Cheer!

Munching a pie, the skipper remembered something about oysters. Why, who knows? Many years before, oysters had been farmed on the flats off Southend and

Emanating from the hatch was the deep, succulent, sweet bouquet that only comes from home-produced mincemeat heavily laced ... (Drawn by Gwendoline D. Ardley)

pits were dug in a triangle of marsh in the vicinity of Leigh's 'new' station. It has been said by (Hervey Benham in *Essex Gold*) that oyster farming happened by accident: a fisherman who'd apparently had too many oysters for his lunch dumped some on the mud flats. A year later, he'd been at the same spot and found a fat clutch ... that was around 1730. The fisherman realising the potential, quickly took a lease out on the foreshore and within a year had earned enough to build a house! By 1872, it had all ended, except, surprisingly, some 'layings' in Hadleigh Ray, which was farmed well into the early 1900s.

There were no signs of the Leigh pits now: they sat under the site of a boatyard. The yard, now a mud-creek marina, was formerly run by Johnson & Jago. They'd at one time been builders of fine yachts and fishing craft. The coast's famous sailor, Maurice Griffiths, had had a boat, his *Lone Gull 1*, built by them in 1938. At another yard, Seacraft and Co., boats by Griffiths, similar in design in many respects to the skipper's *Finesse 24*, were built. They were known as the Cockler class and were, probably, the *Finesse 24*'s forebear – true or not, the similarity was stark.

Meanwhile, what with coffee supping and pie munching, they soon found themselves closing the creek's entrance. The mains'l was lowered and stowed. The boat had then, more or less, worked herself up, against the weak ebb, under her jib. Her crew were in an exuberant mood. Gloriously, the sun danced off little wavelets that lapped around the moorings, flicking reflected light back at them.

Off the mooring, the mate had gone forward to run the jib down. As it had fluttered to the deck and was gathered in, the little cream yacht with her varnish work glinting in the sunlight glided into her berth in silence ... it had all been so gentle, the effort so minimal, both of the crew glowed.

Leaving the boat covered and ready for another day, they'd adjourned to their clubhouse for a congratulatory pint – well, the skipper had had one ... his kindly mate having previously agreed to drive home.

Later, walking towards their front door, the mate had stopped the skipper. Grinning and then smiling broadly, she'd hugged him and said, 'We showed them ... it was good ... I so enjoyed it.' Brushing away a single tear that glistened in the sunshine as it rolled down her cheek, she'd added, 'Happy New Year ...' and planted an affectionate peck on her skipper's lips.

'Yes, indeed!'

Bibliography and Further Reading

Ardley, Nick, *The May Flower: A Barging Childhood* (Tempus Publishing Ltd, 2007).

Ardley, Nick, *Salt Marsh & Mud: A Year's Sailing on the Thames Estuary* (Amberley Publishing PLC, 2009).

Blake, John, *Sea Charts of the British Isles: A Voyage of Discovery Around Britain & Ireland's Coastline* (Conway, 2005).

Cowper, Frank, *Sailing Tours Part I: The Coasts of Essex and Suffolk* (Ashford Press Publishing, 1985; first published 1892 by L. Upcott Gill, 170 Street, London, WC).

Coote, J., *East Coast Rivers* (Yachting Monthly, third edition, revised, 1961).

Conrad, Joseph, *Heart of Darkness and Other Tales* (Oxford University Press, revised edition, 2002).

Durham, Dick, *On and Offshore* (Ashford Press Publishing, 1989).

Durham, Dick, *The Last Sailorman* (Terence Dalton Ltd, 1989).

Faultley, Mathew, and James Garon, *The Essex Coastline – Then and Now* (Updated and second edition, Potton Publishing, 2005)

Harber, J., *East Coast Rivers* (Nautical Data Ltd, 2001)

Irving, RN, Lt-Cdr John, Rivers and Creeks of the Thames Estuary (Saturday Review, 1927).

Parkhill, Gordon, and Graham Cook, *Salvation Army Farm, A Vision Reborn* (Shield Books, 2008).

Popham, Hugh and Robin, *A Thirst for the Sea, The Sailing Adventures of Erskine Childers* (Stanford Maritime, 1979).

Priestley, J. B., *English Journey* (First published by Heinemann Ltd, 1934. Published in Penguin Books, 1977).

Rymill, John A., *The Three Sheppey Islands in the 19th and 20th Centuries* (Green Arrow Publishing, 2006).

Shrapnel, Norman, *A View of the Thames* (Collins, 1977).

Simper, Robert, *Essex Rivers and Creeks* (Creekside Publishing, 1995).

Simper, Robert, *The River Orwell and the River Stour* (Creekside Publishing, 1993).

Simper, Robert, *Woodbridge & Beyond* (Creekside Publishing, 1994).

Society for Sailing Barge Research, *The Last Berth of the Sailormen* (Society of Sailing Barge Research, 1996).

Strugnell, Kenneth Wenham, *Seagates to the Saxon Shore* (Terence Dalton, 1973).

Tripp, H. Alker, *Shoalwater and Fairway* (Conway Maritime Press, 1972; first published 1924).

Tripp, H. Alker, *Suffolk Sea-Borders* (Conway Maritime, 1972; first published 1926).

Thompkins, Herbert W., *Companions into Essex.* (Methuen & Co. Ltd, second edition, revised, 1947).

Wardale, Roger, *Nancy Blackett under sail with Arthur Ransome* (Jonathon Cape, 1991).

Webber, Ronald, *The Peasants' Revolt.* (Terence Dalton, 1980).

Weightman, Gavin, *London River, The Thames Story* (Collins & Brown Ltd, 1990).

East Coast Digest (Parrett & Neaves Ltd).

Private publication, *History of the Island Yacht Club* (Island Yacht Club, Canvey Island).

The Essex Coast ... Beyond 2000 (published by English Nature, 2000).

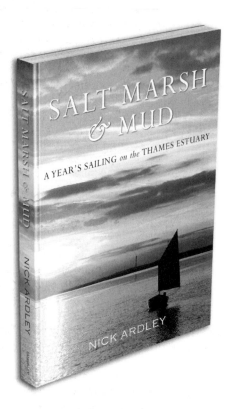